HODDER GCSE HISTORY FOR EDEXCEL

WARFARE THROUGH TIME
c.1250–present

Sarah Webb • Ed Podesta

Although every effort has been made to ensure that website addresses are correct at time of going to press, Hodder Education cannot be held responsible for the content of any website mentioned in this book. It is sometimes possible to find a relocated web page by typing in the address of the home page for a website in the URL window of your browser.

The wording and sentence structure of some written sources have been adapted and simplified to make them accessible to all pupils while faithfully preserving the sense of the original.

Hachette UK's policy is to use papers that are natural, renewable and recyclable products and made from wood grown in sustainable forests. The logging and manufacturing processes are expected to conform to the environmental regulations of the country of origin.

Orders: please contact Bookpoint Ltd, 130 Park Drive, Milton Park, Abingdon, Oxon OX14 4SE. Telephone: (44) 01235 827720. Fax: (44) 01235 400454. Email: education@bookpoint.co.uk Lines are open from 9 a.m. to 5 p.m., Monday to Saturday, with a 24-hour message answering service. You can also order through our website: www.hoddereducation.co.uk

ISBN: 978 1471861697

© Sarah Webb and Ed Podesta 2016

First published in 2016 by
Hodder Education,
An Hachette UK Company
Carmelite House
50 Victoria Embankment
London EC4Y 0DZ

www.hoddereducation.co.uk

Impression number   10 9 8 7 6 5 4 3 2

Year   2020 2019 2018

Cover photo © l Central Press/Getty Images; r Searching for the Deserter, Collins, Hugh (fl.1868–96/© Smith Art Gallery and Museum, Stirling, Scot and /Bridgeman Images
Illustrations by Barking Dog Art, Oxford Illustrators and Tony Randell
Layouts by Lorraine Inglis
Printed in India

A catalogue record for this title is available from the British Library.

CONTENTS

1 Warfare and British society – the Big Story from c.1250 to the present

This book covers 750 years of the history of warfare. That may seem daunting, but by the end of this chapter you will be able to describe – in outline – the main developments in warfare from c.1250 to the present. Once you have that outline in your mind you can start building up more detailed knowledge.

1.1 What is this thematic study about?

The theme of warfare has two strands, shown in the diagram below – the nature of warfare and the experience of warfare.

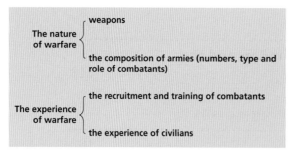

The nature of warfare
- weapons
- the composition of armies (numbers, type and role of combatants)

The experience of warfare
- the recruitment and training of combatants
- the experience of civilians

Our main purpose is to identify patterns of change and continuity in the nature and experience of warfare between c.1250 and the present. You will find out what has changed – how rapidly and by how much – and what has stayed the same. You will then explore the resons for these changes and continuities.

1.2 The importance of chronology

You will be covering a lot of history in this book – more than 750 years – and so it will be important for you to be a master of chronology. This means sequencing events in the order in which they happen, and using the correct names for periods of history.

Historians divide the past into chunks of time, or periods, to make talking about the past more manageable. You will have come across some of these period names before: the Middle Ages, the Tudor period, the Industrial Age and the Victorian era.

Have a go at the activities on the next page to see how good your mastery of chronology already is. Identifying when you are not sure about something is actually very helpful in showing what you need to work on in order to improve your understanding.

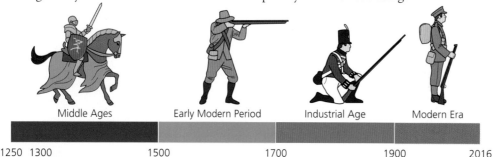

| Middle Ages | Early Modern Period | Industrial Age | Modern Era |

1250 1300   1500   1700   1900   2016

PRACTISING CHRONOLOGY

1. Is 1298 in the twelfth or thirteenth century? Can you explain why?

2. Give an example of a date in the sixteenth century.

3. Identify, using the timeline, the historical periods to which each of these dates belong:
   a) 1916   b) 1415
   c) 1645   d) 1815
   e) 1298   f) 2003

4. 'Modern times' is only a loose definition of the most recent period of history (1900 to the present) – in the future it will probably not be known in this way. Make some suggestions as to how this period might be referred to in the future. What are your reasons for your suggestions?

5. Identify the period in which you think each of the following weapons was invented:
   - nuclear weapons
   - cannons
   - muskets (a basic form of gun)
   - tanks
   - crossbows

You will find out later in this book if you were right.

The importance of getting the chronology right

Every year students get confused about chronology in the exam – it's one of the most common mistakes. It can also be a very big mistake to make. If you get the chronology wrong you can end up writing about completely the wrong things. If you are asked about developments in one period of history, but write about an entirely different period of history because you've confused the name or dates of the period, you can lose a lot of marks.

You don't want to make these mistakes, so make sure that:

- you can put the periods of history in the right sequence
- you know the approximate dates and centuries of the periods.

We will identify common mistakes that students make and make them visible so that you can see them. Then you have a better chance of avoiding those mistakes yourself.

Visible learning

Getting better at history – why we are making learning visible

As you work through this book you will come across lots of new information and sometimes you will feel puzzled, perhaps even confused. What do you do when you feel puzzled and confused? You have two choices:

Choice A

Muddle on, try to ignore or hide the problem and don't tell your teacher. You may lose confidence and stop working hard.

The result – you make mistakes in your exams and do badly.

Choice B

Think about why you're puzzled and **identify** the problem. Then admit there's something you don't understand and tell your teacher.

The result – your teacher helps you sort out the problem, your confidence increases and you do well in your exams.

Choice B is a lot smarter than Choice A. With Choice B you are taking responsibility for your own learning and your own success. It may sound strange but one crucial way to get better at history is to admit when you're confused and getting things wrong – then you can start to put things right.

One very important word in Choice B is **identify**. You cannot get better at history unless you and your teacher identify exactly what you don't know and understand. To put that another way, you have to make that problem **visible** before you can put it right.

It's okay to get things wrong. We all do. And often the things we get wrong and then correct are the things we remember best because we've had to think harder about them. Saying 'I don't understand' is the first step towards getting it right.

1.3 The Big Story of Warfare from c.1250 to the present

We are starting with the Big Story because it helps solve a key problem some students have. Many students know the details of individual events and periods but cannot 'see' the Big Story: the overall pattern of changes and continuities in warfare. This is a serious problem because you need to write about long-term changes and continuities in your exam.

To get an understanding of the Big Story let's meet four soldiers, one from each of the historical periods we will be studying in this book. Their experiences give us some understanding of the big changes and continuities in the nature of warfare. We will learn more about them later.

SUMMARISING THE BIG STORY

1. Draw a timeline like the one on page 2, leaving space below it to write some notes.
2. Read the profiles of the four individuals on pages 4–5.
   a) Add the weapons used in each period to your timeline.
   b) Add information about the composition of armies to your timeline (for example, information about the numbers, type and tactics of soldiers).
3. What seem to have been the main changes in:
   a) weapons?
   b) the composition of armies?
4. Were there any similarities between periods in terms of:
   a) weapons?
   b) the composition of armies?
5. Between which two consecutive periods do you think there were the biggest changes in the nature of warfare? Explain your choice.

SIR GILES OF TRUMPINGTON

A knight at the Battle of Falkirk in 1298

Sir Giles of Trumpington was a **knight** who probably fought with the English army at the Battle of Falkirk in Scotland in 1298. Sir Giles was a wealthy landholder from Cambridgeshire; knights were only recruited from the social elites.

In this image he is shown wearing chainmail armour and armed with a sword (knights also used lances). Knights usually rode on horseback and fought using hand-to-hand combat. The **cavalry** charge was one of the most decisive forces on the battlefield in the early Middle Ages, although by 1400 English knights preferred to fight dismounted in battle.

Knights like Sir Giles only made up a small proportion of English armies (no more than 25 per cent); the majority of troops were **infantry**. Infantry were usually **spearmen**, and **crossbowmen**. By the end of the period infantry were almost all skilled **longbow** men. The overall size of armies fluctuated since there was no permanent army (troops were assembled into armies when there was a need), but on average numbered between 9,000 and 26,000.

▲ Brass rubbing of Sir Giles of Trumpington

OLIVER CROMWELL

A cavalryman at the Battle of Naseby, 1645, in the English Civil Wars fought between supporters of King Charles I and supporters of Parliament

Oliver Cromwell was a Member of Parliament (MP) and the leader of Parliament's cavalry at the Battle of Naseby in 1645. Like all cavalrymen he was from a reasonably well-off background. The cavalry were armed with basic (and somewhat unreliable) pistols, although the sword was their main weapon.

The picture shows him wearing a plate armour breast plate which was typical for cavalrymen. They no longer wore full body armour – there was no point limiting mobility with heavy suits of armour which could be penetrated by the shots fired from the **muskets** (guns) that were used by the majority of infantrymen by this time. Fortunately for the cavalry, these muskets were only capable of one shot every two to three minutes.

The cavalry faced another threat – pike men (infantry armed with long poles topped with metal spikes) who could create a line of spikes that could halt a cavalry charge. **Artillery** (cannon) began to be used more frequently on the battlefield from the later fifteenth century, although it did not have a major impact.

There was no permanent army in England until 1660 when a small standing army was established of little over 20,000 men in its early years.

WILLIAM LAWRENCE

An infantryman at the Battle of Waterloo in 1815

William Lawrence fought as an infantryman at the Battle of Waterloo in 1815. He voluntarily enlisted in the army as a very young man, as a way to escape poverty and a cruel employer. The low pay and harsh training in the infantry meant that it was often chosen only by desperate men. The cavalry, which recruited from the wealthier social elites, was quite different.

Like all infantrymen, William Lawrence's main weapon was a musket with a bayonet attachment. An infantryman could usually fire two to three shots per minute.

Infantry made up the largest proportion, usually three quarters, of the English armies. Artillery played a big role in battles. Cavalry, armed with pistols and swords, still had an important role, but were increasingly ineffective due to the increased firepower of muskets and artillery on the battlefield. The English Army was a permanent professional force, but its size fluctuated considerably according to need. It usually numbered 100,000 men but often doubled this size in times of war.

WILLIAM TICKLE

An infantryman in the First World War at the Battle of the Somme, 1916

William Tickle was an infantryman at the Battle of the Somme in 1916 during the First World War. He voluntarily enlisted at the age of fifteen, while still underage. Thousands of civilian men volunteered to serve at the beginning of the war, although **conscription** was introduced from 1916, compelling men to serve in the army. During the First World War the British Army numbered almost 4 million at its largest.

William Tickle, like most infantrymen, would have gone into battle armed with a Lee–Enfield rifle (capable of fifteen shots a minute) with a bayonet attachment and hand grenades. He would have faced artillery shells, machine guns, rifle fire and poison gas. Tanks were also used for the first time in the First World War. Cavalry had no real role in the First World War; they were too vulnerable to modern firepower.

1.4 Identifying patterns of change in the Big Story

You have begun to build the Big Story of the nature of warfare from c.1250 to the present. You will have noticed similarities (continuities) between periods as well as changes. Some changes took place gradually over a long period of time; some were more dramatic transformations. The graph illustrates some of the main types of change.

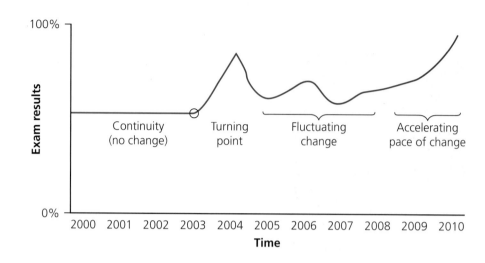

Word Walls

You are going to use the words describing types of change in the activity opposite to start to create your own Word Wall. A Word Wall is made up of words that will be particularly useful to help you do well in your history exams. These words might include:

■ technical words to do with warfare such as cavalry
■ words that explain patterns of change and continuity, and which help you explain your answers more clearly.

Some teachers put Word Walls up in their classrooms. Perhaps there is one in your classroom. But it is best not to leave all the work to your teacher. You have a much better chance of doing well in your exams if you take responsibility for your own learning and identify words you think might be important or are tricky for you and add them to your own Word Wall.

A VOCABULARY FOR CHANGE

1. Match the following definitions to the phrases on the graph that describe the type of change.
   – Gradual change
   – No change
   – A sudden, dramatic and substantial change
   – Change happening at an increasing pace
   – Change occurring at continually differing rates

CREATING A WORD WALL

2. Start to create your own Word Wall that you can add to as you go through the course. On a large piece of paper write down in two different colours:
   – words that will help you communicate more clearly and precisely what you mean, for example vocabulary of change and continuity
   – technical words to do with warfare (see pages 4–5).

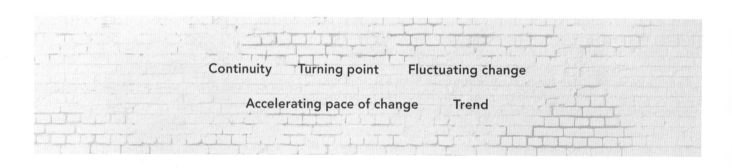

Now let's see how we can apply the language of change to two of the main developments in warfare. We will focus on the topic of weapons. The graph below illustrates changes in the technical sophistication of weaponry between c.1250 and the present.

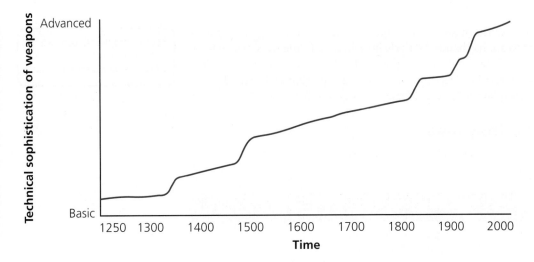

IDENTIFYING PATTERNS OF CHANGE IN WEAPONS AND THE COMPOSITION OF ARMIES

1. How would you describe the graph line during the Middle Ages?
2. Can you identify periods where there were turning points in the development of weaponry?
3. How would you describe the pace of change in weapons development from the 1950s?
4. In a sentence or two, describe the patterns of change shown in the graph.
5. Look back at your work on the four soldiers on pages 4–5. Can you suggest any reasons that explain the patterns of change that you have identified from the graph? (Hint: what types of weapons were introduced during periods of dramatic change?)
6. Look back at your work on the soldiers on pages 4–5. How would you describe, in a sentence or two, the patterns of change in the composition of English armies? (Remember that you can talk about the number, type and role of soldiers.)

1.5 Introducing the factors – explaining why change did (and didn't) happen

Now that you have identified some of the main changes and continuities in the Big Story, you may want to ask 'why'? Why did weapons change relatively little in the Middle Ages, but change so rapidly in the twentieth century? Why did the role of the cavalry decline in importance? Why did the size of armies change so much? This page introduces the **factors** that will be used throughout the book to help you explain the reasons for changes and continuities.

> Factors are the reasons we will use to explain why there were changes or continuities.

The factors and what they mean

The three main factors are illustrated in the table below. The table shows the developments in warfare that each factor explains.

Factor	Explains developments in:
Science, technology and communications	• weapons technologies • methods of transport • methods of armaments manufacture • communications technologies
Governments and individuals	• the funding and development of new weapons technologies • the recruitment of combatants • the organisation of armies • the choice of tactics It is important to remember that governments have changed dramatically in the 750 years covered in this book. For example, government was controlled by kings in the Middle Ages, and is led by democratically elected politicians today. In the Middle Ages and the Early Modern Period the king usually led the Army in battle.
Attitudes in society	The attitude of civilians towards war and how/whether it should be fought.

WHAT DO THE FACTORS MEAN?

1. How do you think each factor helps to explain changes in each of the following topics:
   – weapons
   – composition of armies (number, type and role of troops)
   – recruitment and training of combatants
   – the experience of civilians?

2. Can you suggest ways in which the factors might link to or influence each other?

Many of the factors relate to British society. This is because there is an important connection between warfare and British society. The deployment of troops on the battlefield depends on the manpower, weapons and supplies its government and population is able or willing to provide. Warfare shapes societies but is also shaped by them.

Using the factors to write explanations

The factors will help you explain the reasons for changes and continuities in warfare. It can be helpful to draw a diagram to help you visualise the factors and how they connect to the question you are trying to answer. The Factor Map below shows the factors and an example of a change or continuity question that you need to explain. The three factors are connected to the question in the diagram.

These connections remind you that it is important to explain how the factors explain the changes in warfare, not just to describe the factors.

Look at the diagram. What type of language is used to demonstrate how the factors explain the changes in weapons in the twentieth century?

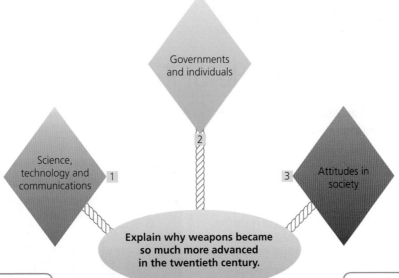

Governments
and individuals

2

Science,
technology and
communications

1

3

Attitudes in
society

Explain why weapons became
so much more advanced
in the twentieth century.

1: Rapid advances took place in science, technology and communications in the twentieth century. This included the development of radio, nuclear and digital technologies. **This led to** many new types of weapons that made use of these new technologies.

2: Governments invested an increased amount of money in the military in the twentieth century, particularly during the two world wars (1914–18 and 1939–45). This investment **contributed to** more rapid development of new weapons. It is no coincidence that particularly large numbers of new weapons were developed during the world wars, for example, the tank in the First World War, and the nuclear bomb in the Second World War.

3: In the later twentieth century attitudes in society in Britain became increasingly critical of war, especially as people were horrified by the deaths of civilians and British military personnel. **This encouraged** the development of new weapons designed to limit casualties, such as precision guided missiles and drones.

LINKING FACTORS ?

Can you suggest any reasons why the factors that are shown as linked together in the Factor Map might influence each other?

And before you turn over!

You are now in a very strong position to begin looking at each period in detail. You have a good understanding of the Big Story of warfare between c.1250 and the present. You know the main topics that make up the nature and experience of warfare, you know the main changes and continuities that took place, and so will be able to build more detailed knowledge onto this framework. You've also been introduced to the factors explaining change and can think about how they might link and be used to form good explanations. And remember, if you are confused at all, admit it – it is only when you make problems visible that they can be overcome.

2 Medieval warfare and British society c.1250–c.1500

When you think of warfare in the medieval period, you probably imagine armoured knights and archers, with fierce hand-to-hand combat between knights on horseback as the decisive force on the battlefield. How far was this true? And, if it was, did warfare remain relatively unchanged throughout the Middle Ages?

2.1 Case study: The Battle of Falkirk, 1298

Let's begin this chapter on the battlefield at Falkirk in 1298 to find out what fighting was like at the beginning of our period.

Who fought at Falkirk?

The Battle of Falkirk was fought between the large army of King Edward I of England, and the smaller Scottish forces of the nobleman William Wallace. The Scots were fighting against English efforts to impose control over Scotland. The two armies met in countryside near Falkirk in Scotland on 22 July 1298. The graph below shows the composition of the two armies.

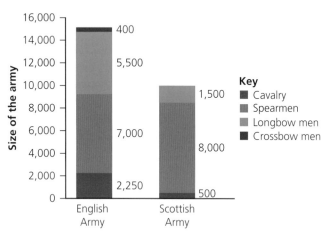

▲ The composition of the English and Scottish forces at Falkirk

KING EDWARD I (1239 – 1307)

Edward I, like most kings in the Middle Ages, personally commanded his troops in battle. He would have fought on horseback, alongside the other **knights**. His role as commander would have been to select the most suitable ground for battle, to organise his troops and to rally their morale often by actions of personal bravery.

Edward I, like all knights, wore chainmail armour, made of linked rings (chains) of iron which provided protection against cuts, but was little use against crushing blows from heavy swords. Arrows could penetrate chainmail if they hit with sufficient force. In battle he would have worn a 'great helm' – a heavy, cumbersome solid metal helmet – this provided protection but would have contributed to the difficulties of communicating effectively on the battlefield.

What happened at the Battle of Falkirk?

DID EDWARD I LEAD THE ENGLISH ARMY EFFECTIVELY AT FALKIRK?

You will now find out what happened during the Battle of Falkirk, and judge how well Edward I led the English Army. To do this, you are going to rate the effectiveness of five key decisions made by Edward I during the battle. Read each decision and rate each one according to whether you think it was:

- a good decision that was likely to succeed

- an okay decision that might succeed
- a poor decision that was unlikely to succeed.

When making your judgement, try to think of the possible advantages and risks of each decision. Don't worry that you don't know the outcome of each decision when you rate it.

Decision 1

The Scottish forces had taken up position at the top of the ridge. William Wallace had ordered the spearmen to form large rings, known as **schiltrons**, which provided the best protection against charging **cavalry**. The schiltrons were enormous with some 2000 spearmen in each ring. The battle began with Edward I's decision to order some of the English mounted knights to charge up the hill to attack the Scottish cavalry (not yet the Scottish archers or spearmen).

Rate this decision.

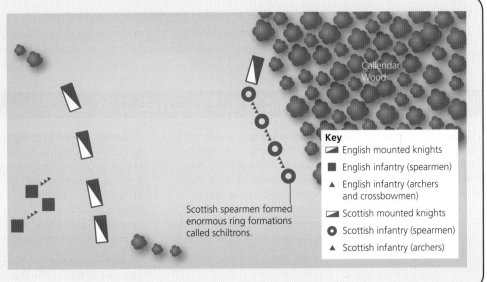

Scottish spearmen formed enormous ring formations called schiltrons.

Key
- English mounted knights
- English infantry (spearmen)
- English infantry (archers and crossbowmen)
- Scottish mounted knights
- Scottish infantry (spearmen)
- Scottish infantry (archers)

Decision 2

The English cavalry charge succeeded. The Scottish cavalry, hugely outnumbered, fled from the battlefield. It would now be easier for the English cavalry to attack the Scottish archers. King Edward I's next decision was to order his remaining cavalry (about 1350 men) to attack the Scottish longbow men who were positioned at the top of the hill between the schiltrons (rings) of spearmen.

Rate this decision.

Decision 4

The English cavalry charged repeatedly against the schiltrons but could not break them. The spearmen were packed so tightly in the rings that there was no way for the English horses to break through without being impaled. Scottish archers inside the schiltrons also fired arrows at the charging knights. Edward I decided to order the English longbow men forward to fire arrows at the schiltrons.

Rate this decision.

Decision 3

The English cavalry charge against the Scottish archers succeeded despite being disorganised. Many knights valued the opportunity to show off their individual bravery and did not co-ordinate their advances; their heavy helmets also made communication difficult. The vulnerable Scottish archers were cut down with swords, fled from the battlefield or took shelter inside the schiltrons. With the majority of Scottish archers removed, Edward I decided that the English cavalry should charge against the four enormous schiltrons of Scottish spearmen (there were about 2000 men in each ring).

Rate this decision.

Decision 5

Large numbers of English longbow men fired thousands of arrows into the schiltrons. The Scottish spearmen did not wear armour or helmets and were vulnerable to the arrows. As individual spearmen fell, gaps began to appear in the schiltrons which weakened their structure. Edward I decided that the English cavalry and infantry should break their way into these gaps and fight the Scottish spearmen at close quarters.

Rate this decision.

The outcome

The English cavalry broke through the gaps that had appeared in the schiltrons and hacked the spearmen down with swords. Once the schiltron formations were broken, the Scottish spearmen were very vulnerable; their spears were too long and unwieldy to be used in hand-to-hand combat. English spearmen broke through too, throwing rocks and other missiles into the schiltrons. The Scottish spearmen fled from the battlefield, seeking shelter in Callendar Wood, but thousands were cut down as they fled.

It is impossible to known the exact number of casualties on each side as no reliable records were kept and contemporary chroniclers tended to exaggerate massively. But the Scottish losses are likely to have been considerable, probably between 2000 and 5000 dead; the English significantly less. The battle had taken no more than a few hours.

The English actions at the Battle of Falkirk showed that the cavalry charge could be one of the most decisive forces on the early medieval battlefield. But, it also showed that cavalry had their limitations; without the archers, they could not overcome the schiltrons.

WILLIAM WALLACE, BORN C.1270, EXECUTED 1305

William Wallace was a Scottish nobleman and leader of those Scots fighting against English attempts to impose control over Scotland. Wallace was a skillful military leader. He realised the Scottish forces were numerically weaker than the English armies and so preferred to use tactics of raid and ambush that made use of the Scots' superior knowledge of the landscape, rather than fighting in battles where the larger size of the English armies put the Scots at a disadvantage.

However, the English Army took him by surprise at the Battle of Falkirk and he had little choice but to fight. He wisely chose to position his troops on the elevated ground and to arrange his spearmen into large schiltron formations. What little we know of Wallace suggests he was also a charismatic individual who inspired his troops. At Falkirk he is reputed to have said just before the battle began: 'I have brought you to the ring, now dance the best you can!'

He was finally captured and executed (hanged, drawn and quartered) by the English, as a traitor, in 1305.

REASONS FOR THE OUTCOME OF THE BATTLE

1. Draw a series of six basic pictures to show the main stages of the Battle of Falkirk.
2. Describe the role of William Wallace at the Battle of Falkirk.
3. Describe the role of Edward I in determining the outcome of the Battle of Falkirk.
4. 'The decisions made by Edward I were the main reason for the English victory at the Battle of Falkirk.' How far do you agree with this statement? Explain your answer.

   You might like to refer to:
   - the effectiveness of Edward I's decisions
   - the size and composition of the two armies (particularly the larger size of the English Army)
   - the positioning of the two armies at the start of the battle.

What was the civilian experience of the Battle of Falkirk?

At first it might seem as if civilians had little to do with the Battle of Falkirk. But, the majority of infantrymen in both armies were not professional, permanent soldiers but civilians, usually agricultural labourers, recruited from the nearby counties and compelled to serve the armies. English infantrymen received payment for their service, usually 2*d* (pence) a day (less than the pay of a skilled craftsman but more than that of an unskilled agricultural labourer).

The wider military campaign, of which the Battle of Falkirk was part, showed the significant extent to which civilians could be affected by war. The Battle of Falkirk, like most battles, was not decisive, and there followed a series of raids by the English Army across the countryside of Scotland in which fields and towns were burned, looted and destroyed. This devastation had an enormous impact on the civilian population who suffered violence and the loss of homes, livestock and crops.

2.2 Your Enquiry Question: patterns of change

The Battle of Falkirk has given you some understanding of what warfare was like at the beginning of the Middle Ages. This is a good starting point for your task in this chapter, which is to identify what changed and what stayed the same in warfare during the period between c.1250 and c.1500 and to answer the big Enquiry Question:

'There were few major changes in warfare in the Middle Ages.' How far do you agree? Explain your answer.

As you work through this chapter you will find it useful to organise your notes in such a way that you can easily identify patterns of change. The **Knowledge Organiser** table below will help you do this.

Beginning your enquiry

1. Make a large (A3) copy of the table below. Read pages 10–12 again.
2. List the weapons used at Falkirk in the first row of your table in the 1250–1350 column.
3. Describe briefly the composition of the English Army at Falkirk (include information about size, and the proportion (relative number) of cavalry and infantry) in the first column.
4. Describe the experience of civilians in the Battle of Falkirk and in the military campaign of which the battle was part in the final row of your table.

   Leave the recruitment and training of combatants row empty for now. You will be able to complete this table as you work through the rest of the chapter.

Topic	1250 – 1350	1350 – 1500
Weapons		
Composition of armies (number, type and tactics of combatants)		
Recruitment and training of combatants		
Experience of civilians		

As you work through the chapter and add to the Knowledge Organiser, you will be looking for patterns of change and continuity. You will also compare the pattern of change between the different topics: was there less change in weapons than in the composition of armies? Was there greater continuity in the civilian experience of war than in recruitment and training?

5. In this chapter you will also read about the factors that explain the changes and continuities in warfare. It will be useful to keep a record of the role of these factors. To do so, create three separate factor sheets or cards, like the one below, one for each of the factors:
   - Science, technology and communications
   - Governments and individuals
   - Attitudes in society

Key features of Science, technology and communications, c.1250–c.1500	Impact of this feature in explaining changes and continuities in warfare

At key points as you work through the chapter you will be reminded to fill in these factor sheets.

2.3 How much did weapons change in the Middle Ages?

There was considerable continuity in the main weapons used in the Middle Ages. The more important weapons are described below.

Swords

Swords were the main weapon used by knights in hand-to-hand combat throughout the Middle Ages. But swords did change during the period. In the thirteenth century swords were broad and flat for dealing crushing blows against knights wearing chainmail armour. From the late fourteenth century swords became thinner and more sharply pointed, designed to thrust between the joins of plate armour.

◀ A thin, pointed sword typical of those from the late fourteenth century

Staff weapons

▲ Spears being used in battle by mounted knights

Staff weapons were based on a 'staff' which simply means a wooden pole. They often had a sharpened wooden end or a metal blade attached, such as in a spear or pike. Most of the effectiveness of the weapon came from the placement of spearmen close together to form an impenetrable wall or circle (like the schiltrons at Falkirk – see page 12). They were little use in hand-to-hand combat, however, as they were too unwieldly.

Longbow

The longbow was used throughout the Middle Ages. The bow itself changed little. It had a range of just over 350 metres, and was highly accurate up to 200 metres. Steel, bodkin-shaped arrow heads could penetrate even plate armour if they hit with sufficient force and at a 90-degree angle. The main impact of arrows in battle, however, was not in piercing shots (although there are plenty of examples of soldiers being hit in an unprotected part, most often the face). Instead, a storm of arrows fired repeatedly by a large group of archers would have delivered weakening and disorientating blows – much like being punched, severely, over and again. A skilled archer could fire up between eight and twelve arrows per minute.

Bows required considerable skill and strength to operate. To pull back the bowstring of a standard longbow was the equivalent of pulling back a weight of 45 kg (that's the weight of 45 litre bottles of milk!). This is known as the draw-weight of a bow. The skeletal remains of bowmen show deformities of the spine and shoulder from repeated use of the bow.

Crossbows

Crossbows could fire bolts at tremendous force. By the end of the period, bolts fired from metal crossbows penetrated even plate armour. These bows were so hard to draw back that a mechanical device (called a cranequin) had to be used. This made their rate of fire slow, often only two bolts a minute.

▲ A crossbow from the Middle Ages

METALLURGY: THE SCIENCE OF METALS

In the mid-fourteenth century new methods of manufacturing steel were developed that, for the first time, enabled it to be produced in large enough quantities to make the production of steel plate armour possible. Previously it had only been possible to produce steel in small quantities for arrow heads or the cutting edge of swords. Steel was ideal for armour because it was both hard and shatter resistant. Iron, for example, long used in the manufacture of weapons, was no good for plate armour because it was brittle.

Cannon

Cannon were first used in Europe around 1320. They were a new type of weapon, using gunpowder as the powering force to fire a **projectile**. Projectiles were initially stone shots and then, from the fifteenth century, cast iron cannon balls. Cannon were at first made from rolls of sheet iron, bent into a tube shape and reinforced with iron bands – a method that was both time-consuming and costly. There were therefore few cannon until the 1400s. From the fifteenth century it became increasingly possible to manufacture cast iron cannon by pouring liquid iron into moulds. This was quicker and cheaper and more cannon were produced.

From the 1400s, new types of gunpowder became available which increased the reliability of cannon, and reduced (but did not eliminate) the danger of the cannon itself exploding on firing! This was because of the development of gunpowder that burned more slowly, creating a more powerful and reliable explosion in large guns like cannon.

The earliest cannon had relatively short range and poor accuracy in comparison to **siege engines** such as large catapult and **trebuchet** that were already in use against castles and fortifications. Cannon were not used with great frequency; typically they were fired less than twelve times a day during a **siege**. But gradual improvements in their rate, range and accuracy of fire contributed to them being used more regularly from the 1370s.

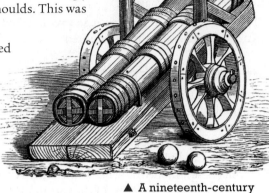

▲ A nineteenth-century wood engraving of a medieval cannon

Throughout the Middle Ages cannon were most often used in sieges where their shot was useful in bringing down walls; they were only rarely used on the battlefield, and then usually to fire a series of opening shots at the start of the battle. This was partly because cannon were so difficult to transport, requiring several horses and only being able to move at slow speeds. They could not be easily manoeuvred in battle.

Small cannon (or handguns) were also developed from the 1350s and, by the later medieval period, were increasingly used, although they frequently required at least two people to fire. Their shot could penetrate even plate armour, but they remained secondary to bows and crossbows, largely because of their limited accuracy and range, and the danger of them exploding.

CANNON: A TURNING POINT IN WARFARE?

Did the introduction of cannon into Europe represent a turning point in warfare? In some ways it did. Cannon used gunpowder, a completely new technology from other weapons of the time, and the impact of cannon (and other gunpowder weapons) was to be long lasting. But, in other ways, cannon did not rapidly transform the nature of warfare for much of the Middle Ages. Technological problems limited their effectiveness, the numbers produced were small and their impact on the battlefield was relatively minor.

HOW MUCH DID WEAPONS CHANGE?

1. What weapons do you think were the greatest danger to knights:
   a) at the beginning of the period, c.1250?
   b) by the end of the period, c.1500?

   Explain your answer by referring to the capabilities of the weapons and armour.

2. Describe the main changes in weapons during the Middle Ages.

3. Add information about weapons to the first row of your Knowledge Organiser table (see page 13). Where a weapon remained unchanged throughout the period, you can write your entry across all the dates to show continuity. Where there was change, write the change under the appropriate date.

4. Write a few sentences in the final column to describe the pattern of change in weaponry during the Middle Ages. Think about the extent and pace of change: was change gradual or rapid?

5. Add information to your factor sheet on Science, technology and communications. Write about the changes in the science of making metal and the impact this had on weapons.

2.4 Was there any change to the composition of English armies, c.1250–c.1500?

Weapons changed only a little and gradually during the Middle Ages, so you might expect there to be little change in the composition of armies; however, by 1500 there had been two significant changes:

- The vast majority of infantry men were longbow men.
- Knights usually fought dismounted.

The size of the English armies

The number of troops in the English armies fluctuated considerably during the Middle Ages. This was mainly because there was no permanent army. Armies were summoned and assembled from the knights and population as a whole when there was a need.
The numbers summoned, and hence the army's size, depended upon the seriousness of the threat.

Infantry: the increased role of archers

Infantry made up the largest proportion of armies throughout the Middle Ages and made up usually at least 75–90 per cent of the army. What did change was the type and skill of the infantry. At Falkirk the majority of infantry were untrained agricultural labourers, armed with basic spears, stones or even farm implements. By the late fourteenth century, the majority were longbow men. Although many were not professional, permanent soldiers, bowmen had to be skilled to operate a longbow effectively in battle (see page 14).

The longbow played an increasingly important role in battle during the 1300s. New battlefield formations typically placed archers on the **flanks** (with knights in the centre) of the battlefield. Battles often began with large numbers of archers firing a hail of arrows into enemy knights advancing on horseback or on foot. This could be devastating and highly effective in weakening an enemy, before they were able to engage in hand-to-hand combat with your own knights. The increased importance of infantry, especially archers has been termed by some historians as a 'military revolution'.

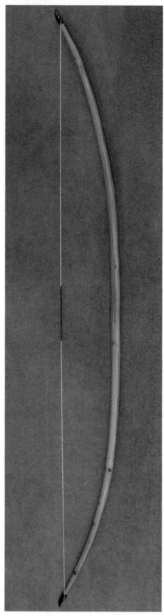

▲ A longbow made from yew tree

Decline in the role of mounted knights

Mounted armoured knights had a decisive role in battle in the thirteenth and early fourteenth centuries – remember the importance of the charges of knights on horseback at the Battle of Falkirk.

There was, however, a decline in the role of the mounted knight in battle from the mid-fourteenth century. At this time, new formations in English armies tended to use knights fighting dismounted in the centre of the battlefield (flanked by archers). Their plate armour gave them significant protection and this type of hand-to-hand combat fitted well with the emphasis on military prowess and bravery in chivalric culture (see box).

Mounted raids

Mounted knights, and mounted archers, continued to have an important role in raids, which were a crucial part of military campaigns. These raids were carried out by troops on horseback, and were often referred to as *chevauchée* (meaning horse charge or raid). The raiders destroyed and burned farmland and villages in large areas of enemy territory. The strategic purpose of these raids was to deny the enemy valuable resources and weaken their morale.

Positions of command

Knights were usually commanded in battle by **bannerets** (the military rank above knight). Positions of military command were linked closely to the social structure, with command given to men from the wealthiest and most privileged noble families who usually held the hereditary titles of earl and

▲ Battle of Poitiers at Maupertuis (1356), Boethius Master. The artist emphasises the brutality of hand-to-hand combat

duke (duke was the highest hereditary title, usually reserved for members of the royal family). For example, at the Battle of Falkirk the mounted knights were divided into groups led by King Edward I himself, the Earl of Surrey and the Earl of Lincoln.

The fact that these men got their positions of command due to social status did not necessarily mean that they were incompetent commanders, given the emphasis on military prowess in elite chivalric culture (see box).

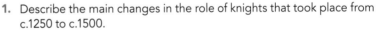

CHIVALRY

Chivalry was a code of conduct important to the culture of the **social elites** in the Middle Ages. It stressed the values of military skill, service and loyalty. It also had an impact on the way war was fought. Missile weapons (arrows and bolts) were despised as cowardly and unchivalrous, whereas hand-to-hand combat was regarded as brave. This contributed to knights continuing to use the sword and favouring dismounted hand-to-hand combat.

The shared chivalric culture meant that knights on opposing sides treated each other with respect. The convention was that if a knight surrendered to another knight on the battlefield, then he would be captured and ransomed rather than killed. There was a clear financial advantage to this 'noble' convention too!

HOW MUCH CHANGED IN THE COMPOSITION OF ARMIES?

1. Describe the main changes in the role of knights that took place from c.1250 to c.1500.
2. Describe the main changes in the number and role of archers that took place from c.1250 to c.1500.
3. Describe the main continuities in the composition of armies (number, type and tactics of troops) during the period c.1250 to c.1500.
4. Add information about the composition of armies to the second row of your Knowledge Organiser table (page 13). Include information about the number, type and tactics of troops.
5. Write a few sentences in the final column to describe the pattern of change in the composition of armies during the Middle Ages. Think about the extent and pace of change (was change gradual or rapid?).
6. Add information to your factor sheet on Attitudes in society. Write about the continuities in the values of chivalry and the impact this had on warfare.

2.5 How much change was there in the recruitment and training of knights?

As you have seen there was no permanent, standing army in England in the Middle Ages. This meant that the king had to recruit **combatants** to fight in his armies when there was a need. The methods used to recruit knights were very different to those used for the infantry. Let's begin by looking at knights.

Who were knights?

Knights, such as Sir Giles of Trumpington, came from the wealthy social elite, with land worth at least £40 a year (the equivalent of over 20 years' income for a prosperous peasant family). Such men probably made up no more than 4 per cent of the overall population.

The knights of the Royal Household

The knights of the Royal Household were the king's private army, and were paid by the king. The Household usually numbered around 50 knights. Each knight had their own following of knights and archers (called their **retinue**) who they could call upon to fight. This meant that the size of the Royal Household army could quickly be expanded. Household troops provided about one third of the knights at the Battle of Falkirk, which was fairly typical.

The Royal Household, however, was not large enough to fight a full military campaign, or even battle. So how did the king recruit more knights to fight for him?

What methods could kings use to recruit knights?

The king had a number of options for recruiting knights, but most of these relied on the fact that military service and military prowess were highly valued and respected in the chivalric elite culture of the Middle Ages. In consequence the social elite had a strong sense of their duty to provide military service.

> **HOW DID THE KING RECRUIT KNIGHTS?**
>
> Rank each of the following three recruitment options in order of your preference (you can choose more than one favourite option as kings often used a combination of methods). Give reasons for your choices, so think about the advantages and disadvantages of each option.

A FEUDAL SUMMONS

A **feudal summons** was issued by the king to all noblemen who had received land directly from the crown. It required them to fight for the king for a 40-day period. They were also expected to bring with them a set quota of men to fight with them in their retinue.

The feudal summons had once been the standard means of recruiting knights. Feudal summons created what can be referred to as 'medieval feudal armies'. But a feudal summons was unsatisfactory if the king needed men to go on military campaign for longer than 40 days (as was increasingly the case). A king could also not be completely confident in the number of knights that would turn up to fight following a feudal summons; by the fourteenth century sometimes less than one sixth of those supposed to respond actually answered the summons.

A GENERAL SUMMONS

A general summons was issued by the king and appealed to all knights to volunteer to fight on the basis of their loyalty to him. It offered them no direct payment. Knights usually responded to a summons for two reasons: the strong culture of military service and because they hoped they would be rewarded by grants of land from the king, or make financial gains through **ransoms** or plunder. It was probably no coincidence that more volunteers came forward for wars against France where the financial gain was greater than for wars against Scotland. But a king could never be confident or certain of how many would respond to a general summons.

AN INDENTURE (A CONTRACT)

The king could make a contract with an individual knight, which stated that the knight agreed to provide military service to the king for a fixed period of time in return for the payment of wages by the king. The rate of pay per day was usually 2 shillings for a knight, 1 shilling for a **squire** and 4 shillings for a banneret (the social/military rank above a knight). This rate of pay was decent, but hardly enough to be the main motivation for knights performing military service. Often the payment only just covered the costs of going on campaign – the knight was expected to provide horses and equipment himself.

The big advantage of contracts was that the king knew who was going to turn up to fight. The king could also have more control over the types of troops recruited; during the fourteenth century mounted archers were increasingly preferred and this was specified in contracts. Contracts were expensive, however, because the king did have to make payments in return for service. Large numbers of contracts also required a sizeable government bureaucracy to write up and keep records (all of which had to be done by hand), and arrange payments. This was only possible on a large scale from the fourteenth century onwards when government bureaucracy and royal financial resources grew significantly.

AN INDENTURE

An example of an indenture is shown below. It was made between Sir Thomas Tunstall and King Henry V in 1415. Read it and answer the following questions.

1. For what length of time was the contract valid?
2. How many, and what type of, men was Thomas to supply in his retinue?
3. How much was Thomas to be paid in wages from the king?
4. What other money was Thomas entitled to receive from the king?
5. What potential types of profit does it mention Thomas might make from going on campaign? Are they entitled to keep such profit?

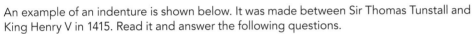

This indenture, made between the king and Sir Thomas Tunstall, bears witness that the said Thomas is bound towards our lord the king to serve him for a whole year … Thomas shall have with him in the expedition for the whole year six men-at-arms, himself included, and 18 mounted archers. He will take wages for himself at 2 shillings per day … In the event that Thomas goes in the company of the king into the kingdom of France, he shall take as wages for each of the men-at-arms 12d per day, and for each of the archers 6d per day, during the year. If the expedition is to France then Thomas shall take the customary regard [a bonus payment common after the 1340s] for himself and his men-at-arms.

Thomas shall be obliged to be ready at the sea coast with his men well mounted, armed and arrayed … Thomas shall have shipping for himself and his retinue, their horses, harness and provisions, at the expense of the king, and also return shipping …

If it happens that the [king of] France, or any of his sons, nephews, uncles or cousins shall be captured in the expedition by Thomas or by any person of his retinue, the lord king of England shall have whoever are captured and shall make reasonable [payment] with Thomas or with the person who made the capture. With reference to other profits or gains of war the lord king shall have one third of the gains of Thomas as well as one third of a third part of the gains of the men of his retinue gained during the expedition, relating to gains of prisoners, booty, money, all gold, silver, and jewels worth more than 10 marks.

In witness of these matters, Thomas has affixed his seal.

The indenture got its name because of the indented edge which was made to separate two halves of the same contract which had been written twice on the same piece of paper. A copy was kept for future reference by both knight and king and the two halves could be placed together to confirm they were genuine.

Was there a change in the methods of recruiting knights?

At the beginning of the period, feudal summons were used with reasonable frequency. Edward I (1239–1307) issued at least nine feudal summons during his reign (although not for the Falkirk Campaign, which was the result of a general summons). However, by the end of the Middle Ages, feudal summons were no longer used. Indentures became the main method of recruiting knights. By the 1400s almost every knight on campaign had an indenture, whereas at the time of the Falkirk Campaign just 560 knights (about one quarter of the knights) were contracted troops. Indeed, the first record of any sort of indenture is from 1270.

There was certainly a significant shift in the methods of recruiting knights during the Middle Ages, but it was gradual, with the different methods of recruitment overlapping as transition to an almost fully indentured system took place.

The training of knights

Chivalric culture placed great importance on military prowess and individual knights took the development of their military skills seriously. Opportunities to practise these skills were plentiful in the tournaments and jousts that were popular entertainments for the social elites. Tournaments were small-scale mock battles in which groups of mounted soldiers fought each other; knights would be captured but (usually!) not killed. Jousts were contests between two knights in which each attempted to unseat the other from their horse using their lances.

These tournaments encouraged an emphasis on individual bravery and prowess, rather than fighting together effectively as a unit in battle. This contributed to a lack of sophistication and co-ordination in tactics on the battlefield.

DID THE RECRUITMENT OF KNIGHTS CHANGE?

1. Describe the main changes in the recruitment of knights during the Middle Ages.
2. Were there any continuities in the recruitment of knights in the Middle Ages?
3. Summarise the main information about the recruitment of knights in the relevant columns of your Knowledge Organiser (see page 13).
4. Add information to your factor sheets on Governments and individuals and Attitudes in society. Write about the changes in government bureaucracy and finance and the impact this had on recruitment, as well as the impact of chivalry and changes in attitudes towards recruitment.

2.6 How much change was there in the recruitment and training of infantry?

You have learned that increasingly more skilled infantry were used in the armies of the later Middle Ages (see page 17). We might therefore expect there to have been a shift in the way in which infantry were recruited to achieve this.

How were infantry recruited in the thirteenth century?

In the thirteenth century most infantry were recruited by the local sheriffs (individuals responsible for law enforcement in each county). It was the duty of every local man to provide military service if needed, so sheriffs **mustered** local men and selected those most suitable to serve as foot soldiers. Sheriffs, however, frequently accepted bribes from those wishing to avoid military service, so those sent to war were often the weaker or less popular members of the village. To improve the system, from 1277 the selection process was often supervised by Commissioners of Array, knights sent from the Royal Household to assist in the recruitment process.

This system of recruitment could result in very large numbers of infantry (sometimes in the tens of thousands), but they were usually unskilled and inexperienced. Most would have been agricultural labourers with no training and armed with basic spears or even farm implements. The large-scale **desertion** of foot soldiers was also, unsurprisingly, a constant problem. Foot soldiers did receive pay for their service, at 2*d* (pence) a day; this was more than the pay of an unskilled agricultural worker, but less than that of a skilled craftsman.

How were infantry recruited by the end of the Middle Ages?

By 1400 most foot soldiers were archers, who were men of considerable skill (see page 14). Bowmen were typically from the middling ranks of society, such as small landholders for whom the respect, wages and potential profits of going on a military campaign would have been an incentive. Most archers were actually recruited as mounted archers (paid at a rate of 6*d* per day) as this gave them greater mobility on campaign, although they usually fought on foot in battle.

These men had usually made an agreement or contract with an individual knight to serve as part of his retinue in time of war. Remember how Sir Thomas Tunstall promised to serve with eighteen mounted archers (see page 19).

Government tried to increase the pool of bowmen that might be available by passing laws from 1363 making it compulsory for all men aged between 16 and 65 to practise every Sunday at the butts (an archery firing range).

The Commissions of Array and sheriffs did continue to muster men, but from the 1340s this tended to only be for local defence, for which men could be compelled to serve without pay.

The geographical spread of recruitment was uneven throughout the Middle Ages. Recruitment tended to focus on the regions closest to the fighting. Areas of intense recruitment were Wales, Cheshire and the northern counties of England.

DID RECRUITMENT OF INFANTRY CHANGE?

1. Describe the main changes in the type of infantry troops recruited in the Middle Ages.
2. How far did the methods of recruiting infantry change during the Middle Ages?
3. Summarise the main information about the recruitment of infantry in the relevant columns of your Knowledge Organiser table (see page 13).
4. Add information to your factor sheet on Governments and individuals. Write about the actions of the Government to encourage the recruitment and training of archers.

▲ Archery practice

2.7 What was the impact of war on civilians?

> 1. List the ways in which civilians might have been affected by war from what you know about the nature of warfare in the Middle Ages.

Civilians as soldiers

We know that civilians were directly involved as recruits in combat. In the early part of the period, social elites were expected to fulfil their feudal duties by performing military service for 40 days (see page 18). Ordinary labourers could also be compelled to serve as foot soldiers (see page 21). Overall, probably no more than 10 per cent of the adult male population were directly engaged in foreign war at any one time.

Victims of raids

Civilians could be victims of military raids in which land, livestock and property were looted, burned and destroyed.

Raids were more common in the north of England, Scotland and Wales. England was not entirely safe from raids during the **Hundred Years War** (see page 24), which was fought between England and France (1337–1453) even though the fighting took place in France. French troops raided England's southern coast on a number of occasions, striking at Southampton, Portsmouth, Winchelsea and the Isle of Wight. The largest raids, during the Hundred Years War, however, took place in France. A particularly destructive raid in 1355, known as the *grande chevauchée*, led by the Black Prince (King Edward III's son), destroyed 500 settlements and devastated 18,000 square kilometres of territory.

The purpose of these raids was to weaken the enemy by limiting his resources and ability to fight as well as undermining civilian morale and encouraging internal revolt. Civilians were not the accidental victims of war; they were deliberately targeted for strategic reasons. Raids also provided an opportunity for **plunder** – troops were often very keen to get their hands on valuable possessions (the percentage of plunder they could keep was frequently even written down in military contracts, see page 19).

It was sometimes possible for people to 'buy' safety from raiding parties by paying 'protection money' or *patis*, but this was often costly.

Civilians might also suffer if their town was besieged. Widely accepted 'rules' said that if a town surrendered it would not be pillaged, but if they held out then the besiegers were entitled to sack (loot and destroy) the town if they finally gained entry.

> 2. Can you identify what is being looted from the picture of a raiding party?

▲ Raids were a common part of warfare in the Middle Ages. They had a strategic purpose, but also provided the opportunity for plunder.

Feeding and sheltering soldiers

In the Middle Ages it was not possible for armies to transport all the food supplies they needed with them. Armies had to 'live off the land' which meant getting food and shelter from the population in the areas through which they marched. Civilians were expected to provide food and shelter for troops, which was an unpopular burden on the population.

Large armies, and their horses, needed a lot of food. To meet this need, kings had the right to compulsorily buy up food; a right known as **purveyance** or prise. It was one of the most unpopular consequences of war for civilians. The crown did not pay good rates when it paid at all (and payments were often made very late). This contributed to food shortages and resultant inflation in the price of foodstuffs.

Paying for war: taxation

Wars were expensive. Kings had three main ways of funding them:

- Loans from wealthy individuals
- Direct taxation: people paid an amount in tax that was a proportion of the value of their property. A king could only collect direct taxes with the approval of Parliament.
- Indirect taxation: an amount of money was added as a tax to the cost of goods that were imported or exported.

Taxation became increasingly regular in the Middle Ages, and was often used specifically to fund wars. But particularly high tax demands could spark serious revolt. In 1381 when the government attempted to impose a **poll tax** to fund the increasing costly Hundred Years War which was not going well for England, it sparked widespread revolt in the southern counties. This became known as the Peasants' Revolt. The poll tax was a new and particularly unpopular type of tax since it was a tax on the person rather than on his property, which was widely regarded as unfair to the less well off.

How much did civilians know about wars?

In the 1200s, most civilians would have known very little, if anything, about the detail of wars involving English armies. Most people were illiterate and the main way of communicating news was through the sheriffs, who might make announcements in market places, and the clergy preaching in the churches. There were certainly royal orders stating that news of victories be announced in public places, but beyond this, there was little way for ordinary people to obtain anything like up-to-date news. By the 1400s, with literacy rates rising, the population, especially in London, was well-informed of news of English armies in France. Their reactions to defeats played a major part in political events.

HOW WERE CIVILIANS AFFECTED BY WARFARE?

1. Describe three ways in which you think warfare most seriously impacted civilians in the Middle Ages.
2. Was there any change in how civilians experienced warfare during the Middle Ages?
3. Summarise the main information about the civilian experience of warfare in the Middle Ages in the relevant columns of your Knowledge Organiser (see page 13).
4. Add information to your factor sheets on Governments and individuals and Attitudes in society about the impact of continuities and changes in these factors to warfare.

2.8 Case study: the Battle of Agincourt, 1415

Let's now look at the Battle of Agincourt which took place in 1415 to make a judgement about how much had changed in the nature of warfare towards the end of the period.

Who fought at Agincourt?

The Battle of Agincourt was fought, in northern France, between the armies of England and France. It was part of the Hundred Years War (1337–1453) that was sparked by the claims of successive English kings to be recognised also as kings of France. The English King Henry V led a military campaign to France in 1415. His army successfully captured the port of Harfleur after a five-week siege, and then marched through Normandy. However, they found their route to Calais blocked by a much larger French Army. The English Army was trapped; they had to fight. The battle that resulted was the Battle of Agincourt.

HOW LIKELY WAS AN ENGLISH VICTORY AT AGINCOURT? **?**

Decide how likely you think an English victory was at each of the six main stages of the Battle of Agincourt described on these two pages. At each stage, shade in a bar like the one below to show how likely you think the English Army was to succeed. Write a few sentences to explain your judgement at each stage.

Low   50/50   High
Likelihood of English victory

Stage 1: Numbers

The English Army was considerably outnumbered, especially in knights, by the French Army (see bar graph). The English Army was also running seriously short of food supplies.

Stage 2 : Positions

King Henry V arranged his army in a standard formation of blocks of dismounted knights in the centre, flanked on each side by large groups of longbow men (see map). He chose to fight on fields of recently ploughed ground (this was very soft, especially because of heavy rains, which made it extremely difficult to walk across). Woodland protected the English Army's **flanks** and also narrowed the battlefield where the English were positioned. Henry V ordered his archers to make long, sharpened stakes from wood and ram these into the ground in front of them to act as a barrier against a cavalry charge. Having placed his army in a defensive position, Henry V hoped the French Army would attack.

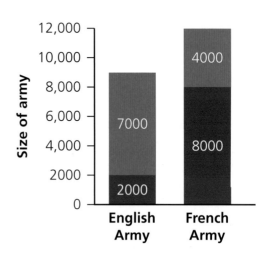

Key
- ■ Knights (English knights and the majority of French knights fought dismounted)
- ■ Infantry (longbowmen for the English and longbow and some crossbowmen for the French)

▲ The approximate size of the armies at Agincourt. Exact numbers are not known. These figures are based on recent research by the historian Anne Curry.

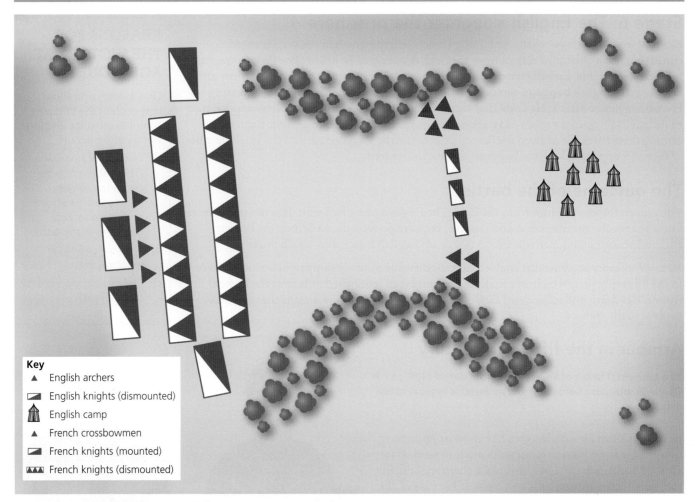

Key
- ▲ English archers
- ◪ English knights (dismounted)
- ⌂ English camp
- ▲ French crossbowmen
- ◪ French knights (mounted)
- ▲▲▲ French knights (dismounted)

▲ A plan of the battlefield at Agincourt

Stage 3: The English bowmen fire

Despite Henry V's hopes, the French Army did not attack. The English Army was not strong enough to attack the French, but could not afford to wait as they were running out of supplies and the French might be joined by reinforcements. Henry V advanced his army a small distance so that the French Army was within longbow range. The large numbers of English archers began firing a storm of arrows into the French Army. The French had no way to defend themselves against the intense and unrelenting rain of arrows – the French crossbowmen, who could have fired on the archers, were positioned too far to the back to be used.

Stage 4: The French cavalry attack

The French cavalry rode across the muddy ground to attack the English archers (who were still protected behind their stakes). The French cavalry attacks failed to defeat the English longbow men and withdrew, churning up the muddy fields even more.

Stage 5: The French dismounted knights attack

The French dismounted knights attacked the English dismounted knights. They struggled in their advance, slowed and tired by walking in armour in ankle deep mud, under a constant barrage of arrows which disorientated and weakened them. To make things even worse, the battlefield narrowed just before the position of the English Army, which meant the large number of French knights became bunched together. This crush made it difficult for them to wield their double-handed swords in the fierce hand-to-hand combat with the English knights. Many knights who stumbled or fell were trampled or drowned in the mud by the weight of the crush. A second group of French knights joined them, worsening the crush. The English longbow men, no longer able to fire arrows for risk of hitting their own men in the crush of close combat, joined the fighting with daggers and stones. The French casualties were large, with thousands killed or taken prisoner.

Stage 6: The English slaughter the prisoners

Henry V sent a messenger to the remaining French knights who had not yet advanced, threatening that they must retreat from the field, or expect to be killed. The French knights began to retreat, but a small French force had made their way behind the English Army and attacked the English **baggage camp.** Henry V feared this would encourage the retreating French knights to attack. He knew that the worn-out English Army did not have enough men to defend itself against a renewed attack and to guard the prisoners to prevent them from arming themselves. He ordered the French prisoners to be slaughtered, and the small number of French troops attacking the baggage camp were defeated.

The outcome of the battle

The French forces withdrew from the field. The English Army had won. It is not possible to know the precise numbers of casualties as there were no records made, but the French suffered serious losses, perhaps over 3,000 dead; English losses were much lower.

Henry V's victory at Agincourt enabled him to renew his military campaigns against France in the following years which eventually led to him being recognised as heir to the French throne. His death and subsequent English military defeats, however, meant that this was never actually realised.

> ### REASONS FOR THE VICTORY AT AGINCOURT
>
> Give evidence to show how each of the following contributed to the English victory at Agincourt:
>
> a) The role of Henry V (Think about how he chose the terrain, positioned his troops and made tactical decisions in the battle.)
> b) The role of English longbow men.
> c) The mistakes/problems of the French.

Armour in the fifteenth century

The memorial brass of Robert Staunton, dated 1458, in ▶ Castle Donington, Leicester, shows armour typical of the time

By the fifteenth century knights like those at Agincourt would have worn plate armour suits made of steel. Plate armour had gradually come to replace chainmail during the fourteenth century. This was possible because of the development of methods of steel production (see page 14).

Plate armour offered greater protection than chainmail armour, particularly in deflecting crushing blows and most arrow hits (see page 14). It was heavy – a complete suit was about 30 kg (that's the weight of 30 litre bottles of milk) – but, as the weight was distributed around the body it did not hugely impede movement. A padded jacket was worn beneath the plate armour, for comfort and to help absorb some of the force of sword and arrow hits.

The helmet was the heaviest, and most uncomfortable, piece of this armour. By the time of Agincourt the most commonly worn style were bascinet helmets which protected the entire face with a hinged, moveable, pointed visor. Bascinets offered greater visibility and ventilation than the older style great helm helmets.

▲ A great helm

▲ A bascinet

> 1. What are the main differences between the armour shown in this image to that depicted on the brass of Sir Giles of Trumpington from the 1290s (on page 4)?
> 2. How effective was the protection provided by plate armour?

Was the Battle of Agincourt typical?

The English victory against the odds at Agincourt might seem unusual, but English armies had actually achieved similar successes using very large numbers of bowmen in other key battles in the Hundred Years War, at Crécy (1346) and Poitiers (1356). In many ways Agincourt was typical of how English armies fought at the time. The composition of the army was dominated by longbow men at a ratio of three longbow men to one knight. Troops fought in the new formations typical of the time – knights fighting dismounted in the centre of the battlefield with archers on the flanks.

The recruitment of the men who fought at Agincourt was also relatively typical. All the English troops had signed indentures (contracts) in which payment was promised in return for their military service. But as Henry V was unable to make many of the cash payments in advance, he instead offered royal jewels as a guarantee of his intention to pay (he never did fulfil all the payments in cash). Typically, too, the counties of northern England (particularly Cheshire and Lancashire) as well as Wales provided particularly large numbers of archers. Positions of command were, as usual, given to the highest-ranking noblemen, such as the Duke of York (a grandson of King Edward III).

What was very unusual was Henry V's order to slaughter the prisoners. However, as we have seen, this was probably driven by practical considerations, rather than a disregard for the importance of the convention of respecting and ransoming prisoners.

The wider military campaign of which Agincourt was a part was also typical of warfare of the time. It had begun with the five-week siege of Harfleur in which the English armies made use of cannon firing stone shot, alongside traditional wooden stone-hurling siege engines. The eventual surrender of Harfleur followed the conventions of the time, in which a treaty was made, and the inhabitants of the town were permitted by the English Army to leave with the possessions they could carry. On the English Army's march through Normandy there were the common complaints that the soldiers took food and burned homes, although it seems that Henry V's army was more restrained than was typical. The English Army transported much of its food supplies and Henry V issued decrees (orders) forbidding his soldiers to pillage and loot beyond their need for food or to attack the civilian population.

HOW MUCH HAD WARFARE CHANGED BY THE LATE MIDDLE AGES?

1. In what ways was the Agincourt **campaign** (not just the battle) typical of warfare by the late Middle Ages? Write about:
   - weapons
   - the composition of the army (number and type of troops, as well as their tactics)
   - recruitment and training of combatants
   - experience of civilians.

2. Make a copy of the Venn diagram opposite to record what had changed and what had stayed the same between the Battle of Falkirk in 1298 (see pages 11–12) and the Battle of Agincourt in 1415. Try to include information about: weapons, composition of armies, recruitment, and the experience of civilians.

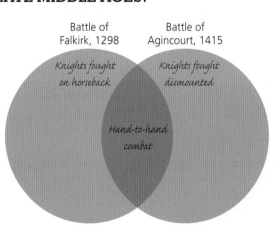

2.9 Communicating your answer: making judgements

Let us return to the big Enquiry Question for this chapter:

'There were few major changes in warfare in the Middle Ages.' How far do you agree? Explain your answer.

This question asks you to reach a judgement about how far you agree. This type of question is worth 16 marks in the exam – that's a lot of marks for one question, so it's worth pausing to think about how we might answer a question like this. The activity below helps you to reach a judgement about how much warfare changed during the Middle Ages.

HOW MUCH CHANGE? ?

1. Use your Knowledge Organiser to place each of the topics below on a continuum line to show the extent of change in each.
   - Weapons
   - Composition of armies (number, type and tactics of troops)
   - Recruitment and training
   - Experience of civilians

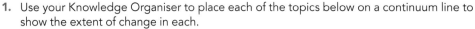

No changes   Moderate changes   Major changes

2. It is important to have your answer clear in your mind before you begin to plan and write your answer. Write a paragraph summarising your answer to the enquiry question, using your completed continuum line to help you. See page 174 for language that will help you show how far you agree with a statement.

Structuring your answer

There are two main ways you could organise your answer.

Approach 1: for and against

This is probably the simplest way to structure your answer.

- **Paragraph 1**: give evidence to **support** the statement in the question – that there were few major changes in warfare in the Middle Ages.
- **Paragraph 2**: give evidence to **counter** the statement in the question – that significant changes actually took place in warfare during the Middle Ages.
- **Paragraph 3**: write your overall judgement – weighing up the evidence to write how far, overall, you agree with the statement.

Approach 2: by topics

Use the four topics to structure your answer. For each topic you choose to include (you do not need to write about all of them), write a paragraph evaluating the extent to which there was change.

Finish with a conclusion giving your overall judgement. You could comment here on whether some topic areas had more change than others.

Supporting your points

Whichever approach you choose you need to support your judgements with evidence. This means using examples to prove your judgements. Look at the example below. How does it use evidence?

There was little major change in weapons during the Middle Ages. The sword and longbow were the main weapons used both at the Battle of the Falkirk in 1298 and at the Battle of Agincourt over 100 years later in 1415. Although the shape of swords altered during this period from broad, flat blades to longer and more tapered blades by the end of the fourteenth century, these were not major changes. The longbow remained unchanged throughout the period.

Although there had been a major change with the introduction of cannon into Europe in the 1320s, its impact on warfare was gradual. Despite cannon coming to have an increasingly important role in sieges, they only rarely, and in very small numbers, appeared on the battlefield in this period.

You will find further guidance on writing answers in the Writing Guide on pages 174–75. And remember to use words from your Word Wall to help your write accurately and with confidence.

Now write your answer to the enquiry question.

2.10 Explaining why

Some questions will ask you to explain why changes took place in warfare. Here is an example of such a question:

Explain why changes took place in the recruitment of combatants in the Middle Ages.

To answer **'explain why'** questions you need to write about the causes of change. The factors can help you explain changes and continuities in warfare:

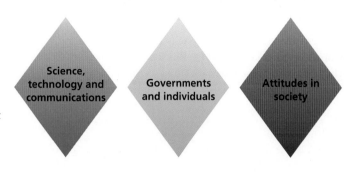

Using connectives

When you write about a factor in an 'explain why' question, it is not enough just to say that the factor of government for example, brought about changes in recruitment. You need to explain how it caused change. To do so, it is helpful to use connective phrases, these are phrases that encourage you to connect the factor to the change in warfare that you are explaining. The visible learning box below shows some examples of connectives.

Visible learning

This meant that … using connectives to tie in what you know to the question

When talking or writing about a factor, you cannot just say that it affected medicine. You have to prove that the factor affected medicine. You can do this effectively by using some of the golden words and phrases below such as 'this meant that …', 'this led to' and 'this resulted in …'

We call these words and phrases connectives because they connect what you know to the question and prove they are strongly linked.

Identify how connectives have been used in the paragraph below to explain why there were changes in the recruitment of combatants:

One change that took place was the increasing number of combatants recruited through the use of indentures (contracts) by the fifteenth century. This was partly the result of changes that took place in government. government bureaucracy grew considerably in the fourteenth century, this led to more combatants being recruited through indentures since government now had the larger number of officials required to write and record the indenture documents. Government also became wealthier as a result of increased taxation during the fourteenth century. This meant that it became possible for government to pay more troops wages that were a key part of all indenture contracts.

Revisiting the Word Wall

We can now add a new group of words to our Word Wall. These are words that help you to think, talk and write effectively when you are answering questions. You use them to:

- link your answer strongly to the question
- make your argument clear, for example, when writing about which factors were the most important, or explaining how factors were linked together
- show that there is evidence to prove your argument.

Now add the connective phrases shown in the visible learning box above to your Word Wall. Also add words that help explain the nature of your judgement such as, 'mainly agree', 'mainly disagree', or 'to a large extent' or 'to some extent'. Use a different colour to that previously used on your Word Wall. Use this colour from now on for all words that help you write effectively when answering questions.

You are now ready to write answers to 'explain why' questions such as those in the practice box below. You will find it helpful to refer to the factor sheets you made as you worked through this chapter (see page 13). These will remind you of the role of each factor in bringing about changes in warfare.

Practice questions

1. Explain why changes took place in the recruitment of combatants in the Middle Ages.
2. Explain why there were continuities in the impact of warfare on civilians during the Middle Ages.
3. 'The composition of armies changed little in the Middle Ages.' How far do you agree? Explain your answer.

2.11 Visible learning: Revise and remember

You are probably wondering why this section is here. It's a long time until the exams; it must be a mistake. But it's not a mistake. Take a look at the graphs below; they give you some clues about why this section is here.

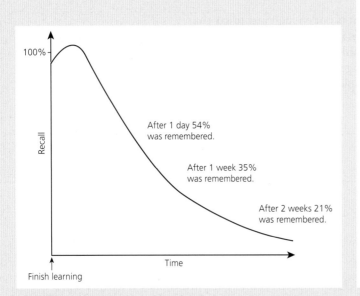

▲ Graph 1 The Ebbinghaus Curve of Forgetting. That sounds impressive but the graph is alarming. We forget the detail of what we study very quickly.

▲ Graph 2 How do you stop yourself forgetting?

It would seem it is never too early to start the revision process! Successful students begin planning their revision while they are studying the topic and do not leave revision until close to the exam. This page helps you start that revision process. So, how can you revise?

1. Build up summaries on Knowledge Organisers

In this chapter you have created a Knowledge Organiser table that summarises what changed and what stayed the same, and Factor Maps. These will be very useful to return to in your revision.

2. Set questions yourself

Work in a group of three. Each of you should set four revision questions on warfare in the Middle Ages. Use the style of questions as above. Then ask each other the questions – and make sure you know the answers!

3. Test yourself

You need to work at making your knowledge stick to your brain! The more you recap what you have learned and **identify what you're not sure about**, the more chance you have of success. Answer these questions, identify what you don't know and keep repeating this.

1 What weapon was first introduced to Europe in the 1320s?	2 How many arrows a minute could typically be fired by a skilled longbow man?	3 List two ways in which advancements in the production of steel in the Middle Ages led to changes in armour/weapons.	4 What were schiltrons?
5 What was an indenture?	6 List three ways in which a king might recruit knights in the Middle Ages.	7 Explain two ways in which a typical foot soldier by the end of the Middle Ages differed from a typical foot soldier at the beginning of the period.	8 What was the name of the King of England who led the English troops at the Battle of Agincourt?
9 How did the English archers protect themselves at the Battle of Agincourt?	10 Identify three ways in which civilians might be affected by warfare in the Middle Ages.	11 What did you find hardest to understand in this chapter? How are you going to help yourself understand it?	12 Name one thing that you learned in this chapter that surprised you or that you now think differently about. Explain why.

4. Revise and remember: the Big Story

As you work through this book it will be important to keep in mind the Big Story between c.1250 and the present. This is because you will be trying to identify patterns of change across periods as well as within them. It will be useful to create a big chart that summarises the key developments for each time period.

Make your own giant copy (on A3 paper) of the table below and fill in the first column (you will complete the rest as you go through the book). Think of it as a giant Knowledge Organiser. You don't need to add lots of detail – you have your other Knowledge Organisers for this. Just add the key points.

	1250–1500	1500–1700	1700–1900	1900–present
Weapons				
Composition of armies (number, type and tactics of combatants)				
Recruitment and training of combatants				
Experience of civilians				

3 Warfare and British society in the early modern period, c.1500–c.1700

Major changes took place in warfare between c.1500 and c.1700. Most importantly, this was the period when gunpowder weapons came to dominate the battlefield, a change that influenced many other aspects of war. Developments in science and technology enabled this shift by producing guns that were more useable and reliable. But was the factor of Science, technology and communications the only factor that brought about major changes? This chapter explores why significant changes took place in the early modern period.

3.1 What was warfare like in 1500?

The picture gives an impression of what battle was like at the beginning of the early modern period. It depicts the Battle of the Spurs fought in France in 1513, involving English troops. Look closely at the picture and answer the questions below.

WHAT WAS BATTLE LIKE IN 1500? ?

Using the picture of the Battle of Spurs, answer these questions:

1. What weapons were being used?
2. How were the troops fighting? (What were their tactics?)
3. What type of armour and clothing was worn?
4. What proportion (approximately) of the soldiers were armed with gunpowder weapons (cannon or handguns)?
5. What similarities and what differences are there with what you remember about the nature of battles in the Middle Ages?

The picture shows that gunpowder weapons (cannon and handheld guns) were already being used at the beginning of the period, but only in small numbers. By 1700 they would dominate the battlefield. Developments in science and technology were crucial in enabling this change, so this chapter's Enquiry Question focuses on the role of science and technology in explaining changes in warfare.

'Developments in science and technology were the main reason for significant changes in warfare between c.1500 and c.1700'. How far do you agree? Explain your answer.

To answer this question we need to find out:

- what changed in warfare between c.1500 and c.1700
- what factors explain these changes.

To help you organise your notes as you work through this chapter, set up another Knowledge Organiser. Make a large (A3) copy of the table below and record your notes on this as you work through this chapter.

Knowledge Organiser

Topic	What were the main changes that took place c.1500–c.1700?	In what ways did science and technology contribute to these changes?	How did other factors contribute to these changes?
Weapons			
Composition of armies (number, type and tactics of combatants)			
Recruitment and training of combatants			
Experience of civilians			

◀ The artist Georg Lemberger's impression of the Battle of the Spurs fought in France in 1513. It was painted for the German Emperor Maximilian in 1515.

3.2 How much, and why, did weapons change, c.1500–c.1700?

Gunpowder weapons became the dominant weapon on the battlefield during this period. This was a major change. It was a shift that took place gradually but fully by 1700. The key changes that took place were as follows:

- Guns replaced traditional missile weapons like longbows and crossbows.
- By the 1640s two thirds of the infantry in English armies were armed with guns – this proportion was even higher by 1700.
- Cavalrymen were increasingly armed with pistols.
- Artillery (cannon) were used in larger numbers in battle.

How did science and technology contribute to changes in weapons?

Gunpowder was centuries old, and cannon and basic handguns had existed from the Middle Ages, but they had not been the main weapons in battle. Why did guns come to dominance in early modern warfare? The main reason was developments in science and technology that enabled guns to be produced that were more powerful and more reliable to use.

From the Middle Ages basic handguns (called hand cannon) used gunpowder to fire a round lead or stone ball (called shot). But these were very bulky, liable to explode in the user's face, incredibly inaccurate and probably required two men to fire. They were, understandably, not widely used.

Matchlock muskets

The more widespread use of firearms from the sixteenth century was because of the technological innovation of the matchlock mechanism used to fire the guns (see diagram on page 35). The **matchlock musket** had key advantages over early handguns, mainly that they could be fired by a single man and were less likely to explode in his face!

The musket, however, was not nearly as accurate as the longbow and had a much slower rate of fire. But it did have advantages over the longbow which explain why it rapidly replaced that weapon. The diagram below outlines these advantages.

By the fifteenth century crossbows had a similar ability to muskets to pierce plate armour, also required only basic training and actually had a better rate of fire than muskets. But these crossbows (made of metal and wood) and their bolts were actually more expensive to produce than muskets, suggesting cost was another factor in why the musket came to overtake the crossbow in usage.

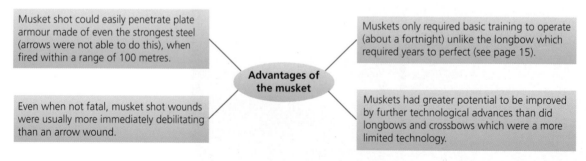

Musket shot could easily penetrate plate armour made of even the strongest steel (arrows were not able to do this), when fired within a range of 100 metres.

Muskets only required basic training to operate (about a fortnight) unlike the longbow which required years to perfect (see page 15).

Advantages of the musket

Even when not fatal, musket shot wounds were usually more immediately debilitating than an arrow wound.

Muskets had greater potential to be improved by further technological advances than did longbows and crossbows which were a more limited technology.

▲ Advantages of the musket

How (well) did early muskets work?

Let's have a closer look at how early matchlock muskets actually worked. The basic operation of the matchlock musket is shown in the diagram below.

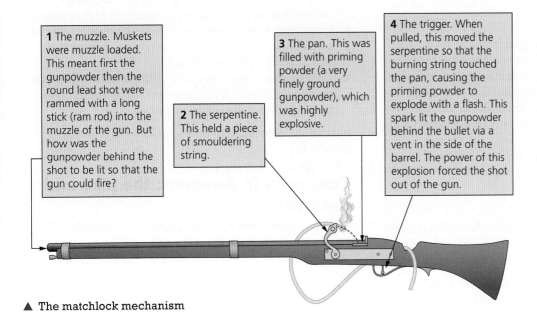

1 The muzzle. Muskets were muzzle loaded. This meant first the gunpowder then the round lead shot were rammed with a long stick (ram rod) into the muzzle of the gun. But how was the gunpowder behind the shot to be lit so that the gun could fire?

2 The serpentine. This held a piece of smouldering string.

3 The pan. This was filled with priming powder (a very finely ground gunpowder), which was highly explosive.

4 The trigger. When pulled, this moved the serpentine so that the burning string touched the pan, causing the priming powder to explode with a flash. This spark lit the gunpowder behind the bullet via a vent in the side of the barrel. The power of this explosion forced the shot out of the gun.

▲ The matchlock mechanism

THE LIMITATIONS OF MATCHLOCK MUSKETS ❓

Look at the diagram and list three possible problems that might occur when using matchlock muskets in battle.

Limitations of matchlock muskets

You probably thought of several problems with matchlock muskets.

- It was difficult to keep the smouldering cord alight in wet or damp weather.
- The explosion from the primer did not always successfully light the gunpowder in the barrel of the gun and so the gun failed to fire. It was not unusual for as many as four out of ten musket shots to fail to fire in the 1600s.
- The reload time was lengthy, especially since the barrel had to be regularly cleaned to remove gunpowder deposits. Typically only one shot every two to three minutes was possible.
- Their effective range was around 100 metres (much shorter than the longbow).
- They could not be fired very accurately at a target.

'A flash in the pan'
You may have heard this phrase to describe something that despite a showy or bright beginning actually amounts to very little (think of the careers of one-hit wonders!). The phase originates from describing when gunpowder in the primer exploded but failed to light the gunpowder in the barrel of the gun (which therefore didn't fire).

How did science and technology contribute to further changes to weapons?

Flintlock muskets

Flintlock muskets were introduced from the 1610s. The flintlock mechanism created the spark needed to ignite the gunpowder by a piece of flint striking against steel when the trigger was pulled. They were quicker, less dangerous and slightly more reliable than matchlocks. But they were more expensive. In the 1630s the only troops armed with them were the small number chosen to guard the gunpowder stores (to avoid the obvious danger of smouldering cords near a lot of gunpowder!).

Pistols

Pistols were much smaller and lighter than muskets, and had shorter barrels. They could be operated with only one hand which meant they could be, and were, used by cavalry.

It only became possible to operate a firearm with a single hand after the invention of the wheellock firing mechanism in around 1500 (matchlocks required two hands). This worked by the trigger releasing a small wheel that had been wound around a spring. When the wheel rotated it gave off sparks that ignited the priming powder in the pistol. But wheellock pistols were expensive, complicated and unreliable. They were replaced by the snaphaunce pistol from the 1560s, which was an early flintlock design, using a spring-loaded flint to strike sparks. Proper, more reliable, flintlock pistols were introduced from the 1610s. But the pistols remained relatively unreliable and had a short range and limited accuracy.

HOW MUCH, AND WHY, DID WEAPONS CHANGE, c.1500–1700?

1. Describe four of the main changes that took place in weapons during this period.
2. Add these changes to the first column of your Knowledge Organiser table (see page 33).
3. Explain the developments in science and technology that enabled these changes. Add them to the second column of your Knowledge Organiser table.
4. What other factors contributed to determining changes in weapons in this period (clue: think about cost – individuals and governments would have to pay for many of these weapons). Add these to the third column of your Knowledge Organiser table.
5. Describe the extent and pace of change that took place in weapons in this period in a paragraph. Remember to use vocabulary from the Word Wall you created on page 6 to help you talk more precisely, and to back up what you say with examples.

Cannon

Technological developments affecting cannon included:

- England's cast iron industry had grown from the sixteenth century (see page 14), which created new possibilities to manufacture cannons on a large scale.
- Innovations in cannon design made it possible to more easily alter the rate and range of fire, so making them more useful on the battlefield.
- Lighter weight cannon, called field guns, were developed that could be more easily transported by horses, again making them more useful in battles.

But cannon continued to have a limited range and poor accuracy.

Continuity in weapons: the pike and the sword

The limitations of matchlock muskets explains why muskets did not immediately replace traditional weapons. Pikes continued to be very important. The picture of the Battle of Spurs on pages 32–3 shows a large proportion of pikemen, and by the 1640s typically one third of English infantry were equipped with pikes.

Swords (and sometime lances) continued to be the most useful cavalry weapons, despite most cavalrymen also carrying pistols.

▲ A pikeman   ▲ A pike

3.3 How, and why, did the composition of the army change c.1500–c.1700?

The major changes that took place in weapons during this period had a significant impact on the composition of armies. Armies were made up of:

- **Infantry** (the biggest proportion of armies). Infantrymen were composed of a combination of musketeers and pike men. The proportion of musketeers increased steadily through the period, so that by 1700 almost all infantrymen were armed with muskets.

- **Dragoons** (a small proportion of the army). These were mounted infantry, armed with muskets. They usually rode into position but then fought on foot (it was unfeasible to fire a matchlock musket from horseback). They had smaller horses and more basic equipment than the cavalry (dragoons did not wear armour), and so were cheaper to recruit and maintain.

- **Cavalry** (typically made up about a third of the army). They were armed with swords and pistols. They no longer wore suits of armour (there was little point limiting mobility since the suits of armour provided little protection against shot), but instead wore simply plate armour breastplates.

- **Artillery** (very few in number).

There were some similarities to the composition of armies in the Middle Ages. These included the main division of armies into cavalry and infantry, with the infantry making up by far the largest proportion. But there were substantial differences: the type of infantry were different; pike men and musketeers replaced longbow men, and artillery was a new addition to the battlefield.

▲ A musketeer

THE COMPOSITION OF ARMIES, c.1500–1700

1. Describe the main changes that took place in the composition of armies in this period. Add them to the first column of your Knowledge Organiser table (see page 33).

2. Explain the scientific and technological developments that contributed to these changes. Add them to the second column of your Knowledge Organiser table.

3. Were there any other factors that contributed to determining changes in the composition of armies in this period? Add these to the third column of your Knowledge Organiser.

How did changes in weapons impact on tactics?

The changes in weaponry had an impact on the tactics used in battles.

WHAT WERE TYPICAL BATTLE TACTICS C.1500–C.1700?

For each of the four situations in the boxes below, select the option that you think is the best way to **deploy** (position and use) troops for battle. Give reasons for your choice. You may find it helpful to refer to some of the strengths and limitations of the weaponry (see pages 34–5).

1 How would you deploy musketeers?

a) In a continuous long thin line (about two men deep) across the length of the battlefield.

b) In squares of six rows. The front row fires, then marches to the back to reload while the second row moves forward to fire, and so on.

The front row fires then moves to the back to reload

The second row moves forward to fire

▲ The Dutch Countermarch

2 How would you deploy pikemen?

a) In a continuous long thin line (about two men deep) across the length of the battlefield.

b) In squares of six rows.

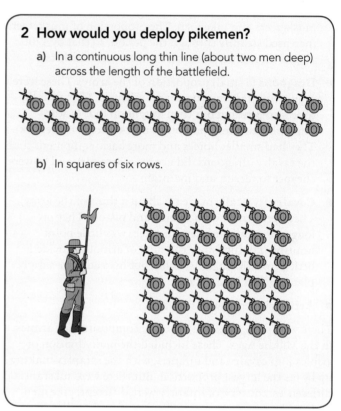

3 How would you deploy cavalry?

a) At the centre of the battlefield in front of the infantry.

b) On the flanks (sides of the battlefield).

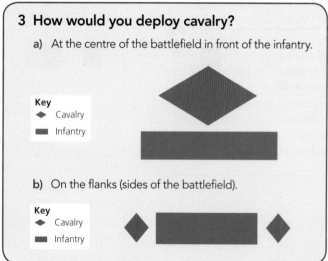

4 How would you deploy artillery?

a) In a group at the front of the battlefield.

b) In pairs between groups of infantry.

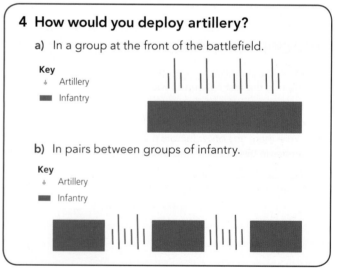

A big change in tactics?

If you chose to deploy your musketeers and pike men in squares, with your cavalry on the flanks, and artillery in pairs between groups of infantry, then you chose the tactics typically used in the early modern period. This was very different from the typical deployment of an army in the Middle Ages, with archers on the flanks and lines of knights (mounted or dismounted) in the centre.

Why did tactics change?

Tactics were driven by the capabilities (including the limitations) of the weapons used. These are explained in the diagram below.

How did individuals influence changes in tactics?

Although changes in tactics were driven by the capabilities of new weaponry, it was individuals who came up with the tactical ideas. The use of musketeers in squares to achieve continuous fire was developed from the 1590s by Prince Maurice of Nassau from the Netherlands. This became known as the Dutch countermarch (see diagram on page 37).

A variation of these tactics was developed by King Gustav Adolf of Sweden from the 1620s. The Swedish armies deployed musket squares in rows six deep. The first row would kneel down, the second crouch above them and the third row stand. This meant that the front three rows could fire altogether to create a more forceful volley of fire. These rows would then withdraw to the back to reload while the remaining three rows moved forward to fire. This was known as the Swedish salvo.

The tactics developed by these individuals were widely known, as both the Dutch and Swedish armies produced training manuals designed to instruct soldiers in these tactics (since they required considerable drill training to be effective). These manuals were translated into several languages, including English.

Square formations had several advantages:

1. Musketeers could keep up continuous fire (despite long reload times) by moving to the back to reload while other rows moved forward to fire.

2. Musketeers increased their chances of hitting their target by firing as a group (the accuracy of individual muskets was poor).

3. Pike men in squares could defend against an attack from any side; a wall of pikes was a strong defence against a cavalry charge.

4. Pike men could fight against other pike men by using their combined weight to push against each other in a tactic that was called the 'push of pike'. During this manoeuvre, the pikes were usually raised in the air so their points were not used. Eventually one group of pike men would break formation and be defeated.

5. Squares of pike men were usually placed on the battlefield between squares of musketeers. Pike men could quickly move in front of the musketeers to protect them from a cavalry or pike charge.

6. Squares gave greater flexibility; if one square was defeated, then another square unit could be moved to fill its space. This was unlike the long lines of dismounted knights or infantry from the Middle Ages which, when ruptured, could quickly lead to the collapse of the entire army.

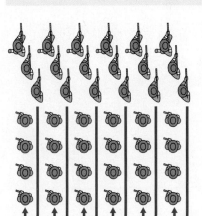

The first row kneels down

The second row crouches above them

The third row stands

These rows then withdraw to the back to reload

The remaining three rows move forward to fire

The first three rows

◀ **The Swedish salvo**

Add information about the factors that contributed to changes in the composition and tactics of armies in this period to the third column of your Knowledge Organiser.

3.4 How, and why, did the recruitment and training of combatants change, c.1500–c.1700?

The significant change in recruitment that took place in this period was a shift towards more permanent, professional and better-trained armies. But this shift did not take place until the 1640s. For the first part of this period, the recruitment and training of troops remained much the same as it had been in the Middle Ages.

Continuity in recruitment

The traditional methods of recruitment continued to be to send Commissioners of Array (royal officials) into the counties to assist in the muster of local civilian men for the armies (see page 22). The recruits were not professional soldiers and received their equipment and pay out of local taxes.

The local **militias** (sometimes called Trained Bands) were also an increasingly important part of defence. They were made up of small groups of local men (usually of moderate wealth) who purchased their own weapons and trained together for the purpose of providing local defence. But they were not a national army; in fact they frequently refused to fight outside their local areas.

Were the English Civil Wars a catalyst for change?

Enormous pressure was placed on the traditional recruiting system when civil war broke out in 1642. The Civil Wars were fought between the supporters of King Charles I (Royalists) and Parliament between 1642 and 1649. Both sides tried desperately to enlist men, and the need to find more efficient ways to recruit and train combatants undoubtedly accelerated the pace of change in recruitment and training.

At first both sides used traditional methods: the King sent Commissioners of Array and Parliament sent officials to appeal for the support of the local militias. But these measures tended to create lots of local armies that were often reluctant to fight outside their immediate localities. They also failed to provide sufficient numbers of recruits.

▼ Modern re-enactors in the costume of infantrymen from the New Model Army

Both sides resorted to **conscription** (compelling men to fight) in the areas that they controlled. Parliament introduced conscription in 1643; the Royalists in 1644. Although this did lead to an increase in troops, they were poorly trained and desertion was a huge problem. It was not uncommon for one third of infantry units to desert.

Both sides produced propaganda pamphlets to encourage men to volunteer to serve in their armies. This was one of the first times this was possible, as it made use of the relatively recent development of the printing press to mass produce pamphlets. Many pamphlets told exaggerated stories of atrocities committed by the enemy.

But the significant change in recruitment came when Parliament reorganised its army in 1645, creating the **New Model Army**. It was new because it was a shift towards a more professional, national, and permanent or **standing army** (an army that exists even in peacetime).

What was new about the New Model Army?

A more professional army

- Parliament passed the Self-Denying Ordinance in 1645 which removed incompetent military leaders who had gained their command solely due to their elite social status or because they were Members of Parliament. They were replaced by those with military experience like Thomas Fairfax who was made commander-in-chief of the New Model Army.
- **Drill training** (frequently repeating set manoeuvres) was given greater emphasis.
- Discipline of troops was enforced more strictly.
- Infantry troops were paid a reasonable wage – 8**d** (pence) a day – which encouraged better discipline. But even in the New Model Army wages were often in **paid in arrears**. More taxes were imposed in areas controlled by Parliament to help fund the wages and equipment of the New Model Army. But, at least 50 per cent of the infantry in the New Model Army were conscripts (not professional soldiers).

A national army

- The separate local parliamentary armies were merged together to create a national army of 22,000 men.
- It was funded by national rather than local taxes.
- All infantry were issued with a basic standard uniform for the first time: a russet (orangey-red) coat.

A standing army

- It was intended to be a more permanent army and it continued to exist even after the Civil Wars had ended.

A standing army after 1660

The New Model Army contributed significantly to Parliament's victory in the English Civil Wars. King Charles I was executed as a traitor to his own country in 1649, and Parliament (and later Oliver Cromwell) ruled without a monarch until 1660 when the monarchy was restored. Although the new king, Charles II (Charles I's son) disbanded the New Model Army in 1660, the existence of a permanent army (even in peacetime) continued as he established a new, small standing army. England has had a permanent standing army ever since.

King Charles II's original army was tiny – only a few regiments totalling a few thousand troops. Its small size was partly due to the fact that people were suspicious of an army that existed in peacetime, fearing that it may be used against the English people, and because of the increased taxes required to fund it.

Changes in government made possible the creation of a permanent standing army; in particular the increase in the government's financial revenues (mainly raised through increased taxation) which made it possible for the government to afford to pay the wages of permanent troops. The English Civil Wars accelerated the emergence of a standing army in England since military need prompted Parliament's creation of the New Model Army. But with standing armies emerging in other European countries at this time, it was likely England would have established a standing army around this time even without the Civil War.

How much did individuals contribute to changes in recruitment?

Oliver Cromwell, one of Parliament's leaders during the Civil Wars, was hugely important in the creation of the New Model Army and therefore in the shift towards a more permanent professional army.

OLIVER CROMWELL, 1599–1658

Oliver Cromwell, was a Member of Parliament (MP) and one of the Parliamentary leaders during the Civil Wars. He was also a skilled cavalryman, was vital to the creation of the New Model Army, and became the leader of its cavalry.

Cromwell insisted upon the importance of drill training and strict discipline among his troops. He believed commitment and skill should be more important in the promotion of commanders than their social status. He is said to have declared that 'I would rather have a plain russet-coated captain that knows what he fights for, and loves what he knows, than that which you call a gentlemen and nothing else.' He was a key figure in pushing to remove incompetent leaders from Parliament's armies, helping to draw up the Self-Denying Ordinance to this end in 1645 (see page 40).

In his religious beliefs he was a **Puritan** (a strict Protestant) and he believed fervently that the Civil Wars were a godly fight against Charles I, whom he condemned as a corrupt, unjust tyrant.

Did new weapons encourage changes in recruitment?

Developments in the science and technology of weapons, and the changes in tactics they encouraged, contributed to the shift towards more professional, permanent standing armies. We learned on pages 37–8 that muskets became widely used, but they had serious limitations in their rate, range and accuracy of fire had led to tactics that deployed soldiers in square formations flanked by pike men. However, square formations were only effective in battle if soldiers were well drilled and disciplined in manoeuvring in these formations. It's harder than you might think to march around in tight square formation, changing rows to reload and fire while keeping the structure. Discipline and constant drill practice was crucial, and this could be more easily achieved by professional, standing armies than in armies that were assembled of civilian-soldiers only in times of war.

Overall, significant changes in the recruitment and training of armies in the seventeenth century came about as a result of developments in the science and technology of weapons as well as the influence of government and individuals.

HOW MUCH, AND WHY, DID THE RECRUITMENT AND TRAINING OF COMBATANTS CHANGE, C.1500–C.1700?

1. Describe three things that made the New Model Army different from previous English armies.

2. Explain how Oliver Cromwell and King Charles II contributed to changes in the recruitment and training of combatants.

3. Describe the main changes that took place in recruitment and training of combatants in this period. Add them to the first column of your Knowledge Organiser table (see page 33).

4. Explain the technological developments that influenced these changes. Add them to the second column of your Knowledge Organiser table.

5. Were there any other factors that contributed to determining changes in recruitment and training in this period (think about government and individuals)? Add these to the third column of your Knowledge Organiser table.

3.5 Case study: the Battle of Naseby, 1645

The Battle of Naseby was a key battle in the English Civil Wars (1642–49). It took place in 1645 and was fought between the Royalist army of King Charles I and Parliament's newly formed New Model Army. Did the infantry's increased use of gunpowder weapons and pike men at this time mean that cavalry no longer played a decisive role on the battlefield? We are going to look at what happened at the Battle of Naseby and in particular to think about how important cavalry were determining its outcome. The engraving below shows the positions of the two armies just before the start of the battle.

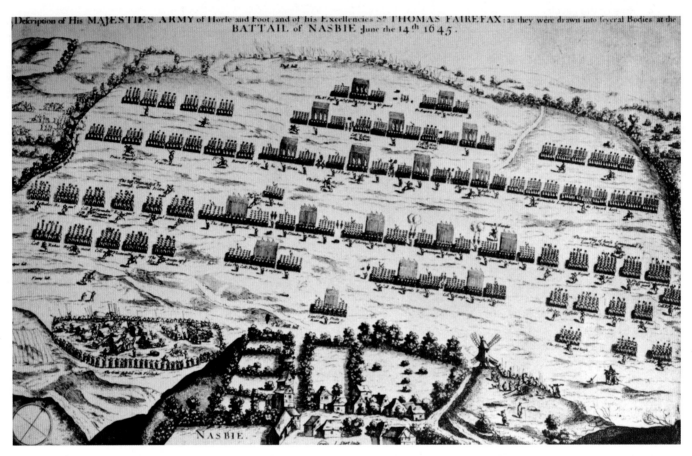

Description of His MAJESTIES ARMY of Horse and Foot, and of his Excellencies S.ʳ THOMAS FAIREFAX: as they were drawn into severall Bodies at the BATTAIL of NASBIE June the 14ᵗʰ 1645.

NASBIE.

▲ An engraving of the positions of the two armies at the start of the Battle of Naseby.

HOW IMPORTANT WERE THE CAVALRY AT NASEBY?

1. Look at the engraving above. Can you identify the:
   a) Royalists? b) Parliamentarians? c) pike men? d) musketeers?
   e) cavalry? f) dragoons (positioned on the left flank of the Parliament's army)?

1. On pages 43–4 you will read about the main stages of the Battle of Naseby. Decide at each of the six main stages whether:
   a) Parliament had the advantage
   b) Royalists had the advantage
   c) neither had the advantage.
   Give reasons for your answers.
2. Use your answers to Activity 2 to choose which of the following was most decisive in explaining the outcome of the battle:
   a) Role of the artillery
   b) Role of the infantry
   c) Role of the cavalry

Stage one: Numbers

The cavalry on both sides were experienced and skilled troops. The Parliamentarian cavalry were well trained and disciplined with experience of fighting together under their able military leader Oliver Cromwell (see page 41). The Royalist infantry had more battle experience.

Both sides struggled to raise and maintain infantry which explains why, unusually for the period, the numbers of cavalry were almost the same as infantry at Naseby (see graph).

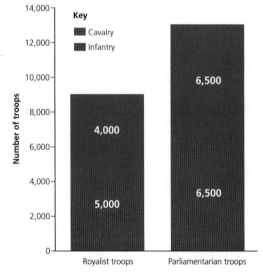

▲ The number of troops in the Royalist and Parliamentarian armies at the Battle of Naseby (figures not exact but based on best estimates).

Stage two: Positions

The two armies were positioned opposite each other on opposing grass ridges with a shallow dip of land between them. The Parliamentary troops were positioned on a slightly higher ridge. They were protected on their flanks (sides) by thick hedges and rough, boggy ground. This location had been chosen by Oliver Cromwell. A low ridge just in front of the Royalist troops provided them with some protection.

Stage three: Artillery

The battle began when the Royalists advanced. The Parliamentarians fired about five of their artillery but most of the cannon balls overshot the advancing Royalist infantry. The armies were so close that there was no time to fire more artillery before the infantry engaged, making further use of artillery unwise as it would have endangered their own men. Most of the Royalist artillery had not been moved into position by the time the battle began, so was not used.

Stage four: Cavalry (1)

A swift and forceful Royalist cavalry charge, led by Prince Rupert (the nephew of King Charles I and leader of the Royalist cavalry at Naseby), stormed up the slope on the left-hand side of the battlefield. The Royalist cavalry, armed with pistols and swords, succeeded in chasing off the field at least 1000 (but not all) of the Parliamentary cavalry on the left-hand side of the battlefield.

Stage five: Infantry

The musketeers from both sides, probably in Swedish salvo formation (see page 38), fired a volley of shots as the infantry advanced. But the armies were so close that there was only time for one volley before the infantry met. Hand-to-hand combat followed with musketeers using the butts of their muskets as clubs and the pike men engaging in the 'push of pike' (see page 38). Although outnumbered, the more experienced Royalist infantry began pushing the Parliamentary infantry back.

The fighting was described by Sir Edward Walker, a Royalist who fought at the Battle of Naseby:

> The foot [infantry] on either side hardly saw each other till they were within shot, and so only made one volley; our falling in with sword and butt end of the musket did notable execution, insomuch as I saw their colours* fall and their foot in great disorder.
>
> * Colours mean flags that represent each army in a battle.

Stage six: Cavalry (2)

The Parliamentarian cavalry on the right of the battlefield, led by Oliver Cromwell, charged towards the Royalist cavalry. These were Parliament's best cavalry troops, known as the Ironsides – they were well equipped, well trained and well disciplined. Using swords and pistols they defeated and then chased the outnumbered Royalist cavalry on the right from the field.

Oliver Cromwell quickly regrouped his cavalry following the charge and led them against the flanks of the Royalist infantry. The Royalist infantry began to collapse. The Royalist cavalry led by Prince Rupert could not defend the infantry as they had not regrouped after their first charge but had ridden off to loot the Parliamentary **baggage train** at the rear of the battlefield. They did not return for at least an hour.

The Royalist historian Edward Hyde, the Earl of Clarendon, was frequently critical of Prince Rupert's leadership of the Royalist cavalry. He wrote:

> though the King's troops prevailed in the charge and routed [defeated] those they charged, they never rallied themselves again in order, nor could be brought to make a second charge again the same day … whereas Cromwell's troops … rallied again and stood in good order till they received new orders.

The Royalist cavalry reserve did not help the Royalist infantry either, possibly because they misinterpreted a signal on the battlefield believing it to be an instruction to leave the field.

The outcome of the Battle

The Royalist infantry quickly collapsed with no real assistance from the Royalist cavalry. Parliament's New Model Army was victorious at Naseby. Almost all the Royalist infantry were captured, as was a huge amount of Royalist gunpowder and firearms. Exact numbers of casualties are not known, but perhaps as many as 1000 Royalists were killed and about half that number of Parliament's troops. The battle had lasted about three hours.

POOR COMMUNICATIONS

Communicating effectively on the battlefield was difficult and continued to depend on gesture and voice commands. These were made even harder by the use of muskets and artillery which created noise and thick black smoke. It was frequently even difficult to tell friend from foe once battle had begun, especially as uniforms were not generally worn. Combatants often tried to wear some distinguishing object on their bodies for a battle, such as a leafy branch or piece of white cloth. They also used agreed secret words, which could be shouted if there was imminent danger of being killed by a member of their own side.

The role of Oliver Cromwell

Oliver Cromwell had an important role in determining the outcome of the battle. He was sure only to engage in battle once he knew that his troops outnumbered their Royalist opponents, and helped to select their starting position. His cavalry – the Ironsides – proved themselves to be skilled, determined and disciplined, charging against Royalist troops and then quickly rallying to charge again (something the Royalist cavalry failed to do). This was largely because of his training and leadership; many of these cavalrymen had been commanded by Cromwell since 1642.

Cromwell led by example: he was personally involved in the midst of the fighting. His passionate religious conviction in the 'right' of his cause against Charles I (see page 41) contributed to his determination and bravery as a commander.

Were the cavalry decisive?

Parliament's cavalry, particularly the Ironsides led by Oliver Cromwell, were probably the main reason for Parliament's victory at the Battle of Naseby. This revival of the cavalry's decisive importance in battle seems like a return to the earlier Middle Ages, and a change from the later Middle Ages when knights tended to fight dismounted. The cavalry's importance at Naseby was made possible because the technical limitations of muskets meant that they lacked accuracy, rate and range of fire. Had guns been more sophisticated, cavalry would have stood little chance, as we will see in Chapter 4. However, even at Naseby the cavalry alone could not have won the battle; they needed the infantry too.

REASONS FOR THE OUTCOME OF THE BATTLE

1. How did Oliver Cromwell contribute to Parliament's victory at the Battle of Naseby?
2. Rank the following in order of their importance in determining the outcome of the Battle of Naseby:
   – artillery
   – infantry (musketeers and pike men)
   – cavalry.
   Explain your rankings.
3. Explain how far the Battle of Naseby was typical of battles of this time. Refer to the following in your answer:
   – weapons
   – composition of armies (numbers, type and role/tactics of troops)
   – duration of battle.

3.6 How much, and why, did the experience of civilians change, c.1500–c.1700?

For much of the period c.1500–c.1700, civilians in England were not directly affected by warfare or coastal raids. However, civilians were hugely affected during the Civil Wars, 1642–49. Although the Civil Wars impacted people's lives on a much larger scale than previous wars, the type of burdens it imposed on people were similar to those in the Middle Ages.

The village of Myddle during the Civil Wars

We are going to read about how one village experienced the Civil Wars. Myddle was a small village of 350 residents near Shrewsbury, and the following account was written by Richard Gough who was a schoolboy during the Civil Wars. As an adult, he recorded the impact of the Civil War on where he grew up.

> Out of the three towns of Myddle, Marton and Newton, there went [voluntarily to fight for the King] no less than 20 men, of which 13 were killed in the wars … And if so many died out of these three towns, we may reasonably guess that many thousands died in England in that war …
>
> There was but few that went out of this village to serve the Parliament, and of them, there was none killed (as I know of) nor wounded except John Mould … he was shot through the leg with a musket bullet which broke the bone in his leg and slew his horse from under him. His leg was healed but was very crooked as long as he lived.
>
> [Royalist soldiers] made excursions very often into Myddle, and took away cattle, provision and bedding, and whatever they pleased.
>
> There happened no considerable act of hostility in this village during the time of the wars, saving only one small skirmish in Myddle, part of which I saw, while I was a schoolboy. [Our teacher] commanded us boys into the church, so that we could not see the whole action. [Royalist soldiers were in the village when there also by chance came several of Parliament's soldiers who were also garrisoned nearby. One of Parliament's soldiers shot a Royalist soldier] through the body with a **carbine** shot and he fell down. The other Royalist troops fled and two were taken prisoner. [The soldier who had been shot] was carried into Allen Chaloner's house … [our teacher] was sent to pray with him. I went with him and saw the man lying on his bed with much blood running along the floor. In the night a troop of [Royalist] horsemen came and took him to their garrison where he died the next day … The two soldiers captured were both hanged.

HOW DID THE CIVIL WAR AFFECT MYDDLE?

1. Describe at least three ways in which the civilians of Myddle were affected by the Civil Wars.
2. Look at the source on page 48. Can you identify the following items that have been pillaged by the looting Civil War soldier shown in the picture:
   - roast chicken
   - duck
   - string of sausages
   - cauldron (large cooking pot)?
3. How typical were the experiences of the civilians of Myddle during the Civil Wars? Read page 47 to help you to answer.

How much, and why, did the experience of civilians change, c.1500–c.1700?

The story of Myddle is useful in showing how a small village experienced the Civil Wars. But was the experience of Myddle typical?

Providing food and shelter for combatants

The most consistent burden on the villagers of Myddle during the Civil Wars was the **requisitioning** (forcible taking) of foodstuffs to feed the armies. This was typical. Armies at the time frequently 'lived off the land', meaning they did not carry sufficient food supplies with them, so civilians were expected to provide combatants with food. Civilians were also expected to provide **quarter** (accommodation) in their homes, known as **billeting** the troops. Soldiers, especially badly paid ones, were usually not good guests and often stole what they could. Billeting was one of the most unpopular burdens during the Civil War.

Civilians were supposed to receive payment as compensation, but this was rarely paid in advance. Instead 'free quarter' tickets were issued that could be redeemed for payment later, but payment was sometimes never made.

Looting

Looting was extremely common. Badly paid, poorly disciplined soldiers frequently took any opportunity to steal.

▲ This woodcut from the Civil War shows a common view of the pillaging soldier carrying the objects he has looted

Taxation

Increased taxation imposed by the government to fund the wars was a big burden on civilians. These taxes included excise taxes on the purchase of a wide range of foodstuffs (including salt and beer). Although these taxes were an exceptional response to the needs of war, more regular and higher taxes had become increasingly accepted by 1700.

Both sides also confiscated the property of their wealthy opponents, and forced wealthy individuals to pay compulsory loans.

Casualties

Many towns, particularly large ones where troops were **garrisoned**, experienced direct violence on a much greater scale than Myddle. About 150 towns suffered major attacks or were besieged during the Civil Wars. Deaths in sieges made up just over 10 per cent of the total Civil Wars deaths (many, but not all, of those who died in sieges would have been soldiers).

Conditions in sieges could get desperate. During the eleven-week siege of Colchester in the summer of 1648 the besieged Royalist troops and the local population ate horses, cats and dogs, and even candles and soap. In these conditions diseases, like plague, were common. If a besieged town refused to surrender but was eventually captured, then the victorious soldiers were permitted to loot and destroy much of the town in revenge. The rape and murder of civilians was not uncommon.

Estimates for the soldier and civilian casualties caused by the English Civil Wars, including those due to both combat and disease, was 180,000. This was about 3.6 per cent of the population, a proportion greater than the First World War (2.6 per cent) and the Second World War (0.6 per cent).

Propaganda

There were considerable attempts to inform, persuade and appeal to people about the events of war during this period. Both sides made use of the relatively newly invented printing press to mass produce pamphlets and weekly newsbooks. Many told exaggerated stories of atrocities.

▲ Parliamentary propaganda woodcut produced during the Civil Wars

Although there was considerable variation in the extent to which different areas suffered in the Civil Wars, overall the ways in which civilians experienced war in this period was not hugely different to the Middle Ages. What was different was the intensity of their experience during the Civil War.

THE EXPERIENCE OF CIVILIANS

1. Describe the main ways in which war impacted on civilians in this period.
2. Write a brief paragraph explaining the main continuities in the civilian experience of warfare in this period.
3. What were the main changes, if any, that took place in the civilian experience of war during this period? Add them to the first column of your Knowledge Organiser table (see page 33). If there were mainly continuities write a brief note to explain this.
4. Explain what factors influenced any changes in the civilian experience of warfare. Add them to the second and third columns of your Knowledge Organiser table.

Identifying the main reasons for change

Let's return to the key enquiry question for this chapter:

'Developments in science and technology were the main reason for significant changes in warfare between c.1500 and c.1700.' How far do you agree? Explain your answer.

This question asks you to make a judgement about whether science and technology were the **most important** factors in causing changes in warfare during the early modern period. This means you need to think about prioritising the factors; which were the most important, and which were the least important in causing change? The activity below will help you think about this.

PRIORITISING THE FACTORS

Use the Knowledge Organiser you completed throughout the chapter to help you answer these questions (see page 33).

1. Place the three factors in order from the most to the least important in explaining the changes which took place in each of the following topics:
   - weapons
   - composition of armies
   - recruitment and training of combatants
   - experience of civilians

2. Explain how important each of the factors was in creating changes in warfare. Use one or more of the following phrases to help you write a brief answer to this question.
   - … was the main / most important cause of …
   - … played a significant / important / major role in …
   - … was of some importance in…
   - … was of equal importance with …

   This brief answer is now your overall answer to the question.

Supporting your judgement

Whatever factor, or factors, you think are most important, you need to give a reason for your judgement. You can't just say that one factor was most important; it won't be convincing. To help you prove that one factor was particularly important you could:

- compare two factors and show how one factor is more important than the other in bringing about a change
- show how the factor led to changes in lots of topic areas
- demonstrate that without the factor changes would not have taken place
- show how one factor links to lots of other factors (the most important factors usually have the most links to other factors).

Look at the two explanations opposite. For each, which factor does it think was most important in bringing about change, and how does it try to prove this.

Science and technology was the most important factor in explaining changes in tactics, in particular the shift from linear to square battle formations. This was because square tactics were a response to the technical strengths and limitations of the new matchlock muskets. Square formations helped to counter the problem of the slow reload time of matchlock muskets by enabling continuous fire by having rows of men firing and then rotating to the back of the square to reload. Individuals were important in developing particular tactical formations, such as Prince Maurice of Nassau's Dutch countermarch. But the general shift away from linear tactics was determined more by developments in science and technology.

Government and individuals were the most important factors in bringing about the change towards more professional, permanent armies during the early modern period. Without the increased revenues that governments raised through taxation from the seventeenth century, it would not have been possible to fund and pay the wages of a permanent professional army. Government and individuals were more important than attitudes in society in leading to this change, because at this time attitudes in society were largely hostile to the idea of a permanent, standing army, resenting its expense, fearing that it may be used by the ruler against the people, and tending to see England's best defence in its Royal Navy.

Revisiting the Word Wall

> x factor was more important than y factor because...
>
> x and y factors were equally important because...
>
> x factor was important but not sufficient on its own to explain changes because...
>
> without x factor then change would not have taken place because...

The phrases shown on the Word Wall are useful in helping you to explain the relative importance of factors. Add them to your own Word Wall. You should write them in the colour used for words that help you to answer questions more clearly and effectively.

Making links between factors

The factors often worked together to bring about changes in warfare. It is often helpful to talk about how the factors link together in an explanation. The activity below will help you to do this.

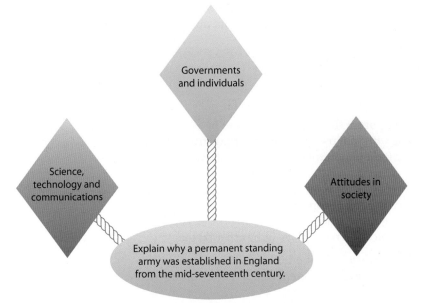

Practice questions

Look at the question in the factor map.

1. Make your own copy of the diagram.
2. Draw arrows between the factors to show where you think a factor might have influenced another factor.
3. Annotate the lines to explain the links between the factors.
4. Do you think all the factors were of equal importance in explaining the change in the weapons used by infantrymen or do you think one factor was particularly important? Remember to explain your answer.

3.7 Communicating your answer

Before you begin writing your answer to the big enquiry question, it is important to plan how you are going to organise your answer. Let's remind ourselves of the question:

Developments in science and technology were the main reason for significant changes in warfare between c.1500 and c.1700. How far do you agree? Explain your answer.

It is another **how far** question, which means you need to reach a judgement about how far you agree that science and technology was the most important factor in causing changes to warfare. You will need to show that you can weigh the evidence **for** and **against** the statement. You might find that you 'mainly agree' with the statement or 'mainly disagree', or that you agree to 'a large extent' or 'to some extent'. The thinking you did on page 49 on deciding which factors were most significant will help you reach a judgement.

It is a good idea to discuss your ideas about which factors were the most important with a partner. Talking can really help you to clarify your own thinking, because it helps you to think carefully about how you explain your ideas when you try to communicate them to somebody else.

How does talking help?

Some people think that students are only working effectively if the classroom is quiet. This is wrong. Experience shows that students write better answers if they have first talked through their answer with other people. Talking helps us organise ideas in our minds, choose the right words and decide what evidence we need to prove a point.

Visible learning: What is an argument?

An argument in history is not a punch up! Argument describes your view or judgement about what or why something happened in history – supported by evidence to show why you think this is. Some words can be particularly helpful in making your argument clear, such as the words you added to your Word Wall on page 51. Further powerful words that help you write more effectively can be found on page 174.

Organising your answer

Remember there are two main ways of organising your answer to a **how far** question.

- Approach one is to write a paragraph in **support** of the statement, followed by a paragraph to **counter** the statement, before finishing with your own judgement in the conclusion. This might include which factor you think was most important or how the factors worked together.
- Approach two is to structure your answer by all (or some) of the main topics: weapons, composition of armies, recruitment and training of combatants, experience of civilians. For each topic that you decide to include write a paragraph evaluating the extent to which changes were brought about by science and technology or by other factors.

The second approach enables you more frequently to talk about how the factors might work together (link together) to bring about changes in different topics. The examiner will be impressed if you can do this.

You will find more guidance in the Writing Guide on pages 174–175.

Now write your answer to the big enquiry question.

Practice questions

1. Explain **one** way in which the role of mounted soldiers was similar in the Battle of Falkirk (1298) to the Battle of Naseby (1645).
2. Explain why cavalry continued to have a significant role in battle throughout the early modern period?
3. 'The invention of the matchlock musket transformed the nature of warfare in the early modern period'. How far do you agree with this statement? Explain your answer.

3.8 Visible learning: Revise and remember

1. Test yourself

Remember how important it is to test yourself to help make everything you have learned stick in your brain? Have a go at answering these questions, and don't be surprised if you spot a few questions from the previous chapter too (we need to keep refreshing our knowledge to help us remember!).

1 What weapon was first introduced to Europe in the 1320s?	2 Explain two ways in which a foot soldier might be recruited in the Middle Ages?	3 What was the name of the gun used by most infantrymen by the seventeenth century? Why was it given this name?	4 What was the typical rate of fire of one of these guns?
5 What type of soldier made up about one third of infantrymen in English armies by the seventeenth century?	6 What was the shape of a typical infantry formation by the seventeenth century? Explain two reasons for this.	7 In what year was the New Model Army established? Explain two things that made it new.	8 What was the name of the leader of Parliament's cavalry at the Battle of Naseby?
9 Explain one way in which Parliament's cavalry helped them to win the Battle of Naseby.	10 Identify three ways in which civilians were affected by war in this period.	11 What did you find hardest to understand in this chapter? How are you going to help yourself understand it?	12 Name one thing that you learned in this chapter that surprised you or that you now think differently about. Explain why.

2. Set questions yourself

Work in a group of three. Each of you set revision questions on warfare in the early modern period. Then ask each other the questions – and make sure you know the answers!

3. Revise and remember: the Big Story

Remember that it is important as you work through this book to keep in mind the Big Story between c.1250 and the present. This is because you will be trying to identify patterns of change across periods as well as within them. Return to the big chart you began on page 31 to summarise the key developments for each time period.

1 Fill in the second column of your chart for the period 1500–1700. Remember you don't need to add lots of detail – you have your other Knowledge Organisers for this. Just add the key points.

	1250–1500	1500–1700	1700–1900	1900–present
Weapons				
Composition of armies (number, type and tactics of combatants)				
Recruitment and training of combatants				
Experience of civilians				

4 Warfare and British society c.1700–c.1900

In 1700 soldiers went to war with basic and inaccurate guns and cavalrymen still wielded swords in cavalry charges. By 1900, powerful artillery dominated the battlefield, ending the era of cavalry charges. Did these changes take place gradually or suddenly over a short space of time? This chapter explores both the extent and pace of change between c.1700 and c.1900.

4.1 How much had changed since 1700?

A SOLDIER IN 1800

As you read about William Lawrence, below, think about the following questions:

1. What aspects about soldiers, their weapons, uniform and tactics, are **similar** to the period 1500–1700?

2. What aspects about soldiers are **different** from the period 1500–1700?

3. How would you describe the **extent** of the change? Look on your Word Wall for helpful vocabulary.

A soldier in the spotlight: William Lawrence (infantryman)

William Lawrence was born in 1791 in a village in Dorset. His father worked as a farm labourer. William and his six siblings had no opportunity to go to school. He volunteered for service in the British Army, a permanent standing army, and received regular wages of 1 shilling a day. Lawrence's decision to enlist was mainly motivated by a desire to escape poverty and personal difficulties.

Lawrence was given the uniform and equipment of an infantryman. He received a short period of training, before being sent to fight the French armies in Portugal and Spain. For most of the years that Lawrence served as an infantryman, Britain was at war with France, which was ruled by Napoleon Bonaparte. Lawrence fought at the Battle of Waterloo in 1815. It was after this battle, when he was stationed in France, that he met a young French flower seller. They married and she returned to England with him. He recorded his experiences as a soldier in his autobiography.

Bayonet: a thin, sharp blade that fitted onto the end of the musket which still allowed the gun to be fired. Used since the late eighteenth century.

Knapsack: contained a soldier's essential kit – a blanket, waterproof and basic rations.

All soldiers were issued with a **red tunic**. Red was easy to see on the battlefield but this didn't matter since soldiers fired in, and at, big formations – a soldier was not targeted individually. On smoky battlefields red helped identify friendly troops. British infantry were known as Redcoats.

Brown Bess musket: used by most infantrymen from 1720s to 1840s. It was:

- muzzle-loaded with a flintlock firing mechanism (see page 36)
- capable of two to three shots a minute
- relatively inaccurate so soldiers fired volleys in large groups to increase the chance of hitting opposition troops
- liable to misfire
- used solid round lead balls as ammunition
- produced black smoke on firing.

◀ A redcoat infantry soldier, c.1800

54

4.2 Your enquiry: measuring the extent and pace of change

What we have learned about William Lawrence suggests that few major changes had taken place in the weapons, uniform and tactics of ordinary soldiers since the end of the early modern period that you learned about in the previous chapter. The **extent** of change was limited. This implies that the **pace** (speed) of change was gradual; changes that did occur tended to be incremental (slowly building on each other) rather than sudden.

The big Enquiry Question for this chapter will explore how far it is fair to say the pace of change was gradual during this period. It asks:

'The pace of change was gradual in the nature and experience of warfare during the period 1700–1900.' How far do you agree with this statement? Explain your answer.

Visible learning

Pace of change

It is worth reminding ourselves of the ways in which the pace of change can be described. The graph below illustrates some of the main types of pace of change.

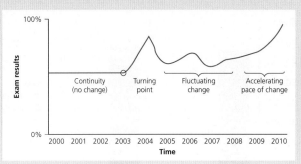

WHAT CHANGED?

1. Before you can identify patterns in the pace of change, you will need to find out what actually changed. As you work through the chapter, use the Knowledge Organiser table shown below to record your notes (making a copy of it on A3 paper). For each topic write your notes in or across the date section(s) that apply. For example, if a new weapon was introduced in 1850, write the entry for this weapon in the 1850 section. Or if a weapon was used throughout the period 1700–1800, write your notes about this weapon across these dates, as in the example entry for the Brown Bess musket shown below.

Knowledge Organiser

Topic	1700	1750	1800	1850	1900
Weapons	The Brown Bess musket was used by most infantry between 1720 and 1840 – it had a limited range, rate of fire and accuracy (typically two to three shots per minute).				
Composition of armies (number, type and tactics of combatants)					
Recruitment and training of combatants					
Experience of civilians					

2. In this chapter you will also read about the factors that explain the changes and continuities in warfare. It will be useful to keep a record of the role of these factors. To do so, create three separate factor sheets or cards, like the one below, one for each of the factors:
    –   Science, technology and communications   –   Governments and individuals
    –   Attitudes in society

Key features of Science, technology and communications, 1700–1900	Impact of this feature in explaining changes and continuities in warfare

At key points as you work through the chapter you will be reminded to fill in these factor sheets.

4.3 Case study: the Battle of Waterloo, 1815

Let's begin our enquiry for this chapter one hundred years into the period, at the Battle of Waterloo which took place on 18 June 1815.

Who fought at the Battle of Waterloo?

The Battle of Waterloo was fought in what is now Belgium, between the French Army, led by Napoleon Bonaparte, and an Allied Army of British, Dutch, Belgian and Prussian (German-speaking) troops who were commanded by the British officer Arthur Wellesley, the Duke of Wellington. It was the final battle of the **Napoleonic Wars** against France.

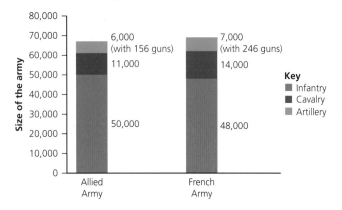

▲ The number of troops from each side at the Battle of Waterloo

▶ A nineteenth-century cartoon entitled 'A Wellington Boot – or the Head of the Army'. Wellington was made Commander-in-Chief of the British Army in 1827. Wellington boots were named after him as he wore and made popular this style of knee-high boot.

Wellington's strategy at Waterloo was to wait for the French to attack. It was a sensible strategy since Napoleon's troops outnumbered his. Wellington knew that his army would have to hold back a French attack alone before **Prussian** troops could arrive to provide help. Wellington personally chose the battlefield at Waterloo because he believed the landscape had good defensive features. The map shows the key features on the battlefield and the positions of troops at the beginning of the battle. Can you see how Wellington might have used the features of the battlefield to his advantage?

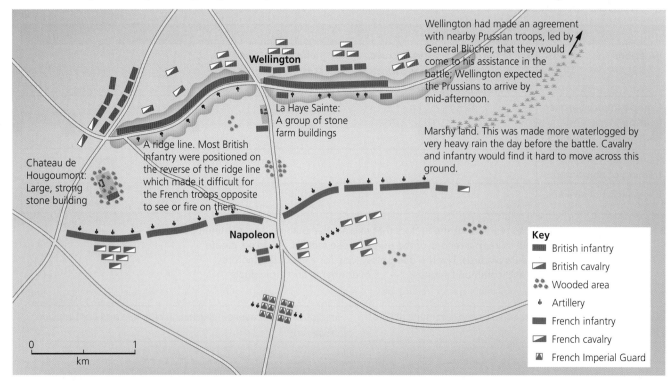

▲ The Battlefield at Waterloo showing the positions of the troops at the beginning of the Battle

Was Waterloo Wellington's victory?

The Allied Army won the Battle of Waterloo and Wellington was celebrated as a hero. What was his contribution as an individual to the outcome of the battle? In order to evaluate how far Wellington's decisions contributed to victory, you are going to rank his actions at key stages during the battle.

Stage 1: Positioning his troops

Wellington was concerned that the French would not just attack from the centre but would try to attack around his **flanks** (sides) too. With this in mind, Wellington:

- placed a small number of troops to the east of the battlefield
- placed a substantial number of troops on the west of the battlefield
- sent troops to occupy and reinforce Chateau d'Hougoumont and La Haye Sainte
- placed the majority of his troops in the centre of the battlefield behind the ridge line.

Stage 2: The French attack Chateau d'Hougoumont

At 11.30 a.m. a large force of French infantry attacked Chateau d'Hougoumont. If successful, this attack would have allowed the French to attack Wellington's more vulnerable flanks without the danger of being attacked by the Allies within Hougoumont. The French sent more and more troops to Hougoumont throughout the battle. Wellington decided to:

- send some reinforcements to Hougoumont, but did not take many troops away from their positions in the centre of the battlefield.

Stage 3: French artillery bombardment

Despite fierce fighting Hougoumont was never captured by the French. At 1 p.m. large numbers of French artillery began firing at the centre of the British lines. The French artillery were not as effective as they might have been as heavy rain the previous day had made the ground wet so that the cannon balls did not bounce along the ground. Napoleon had delayed his opening attack by several hours in the hope the ground would dry out. Wellington responded to the artillery bombardment by:

- ordering the infantry in the centre of the battlefield to lie down on the reverse side of the ridge.

HOW GOOD WERE WELLINGTON'S DECISIONS AT WATERLOO?

Wellington's actions at key stages of the battle are described on pages 56–7. At each stage decide if you think Wellington's actions were:

a) not good

b) okay but could have been better

c) good

d) excellent/inspired.

Give reasons for your choices.

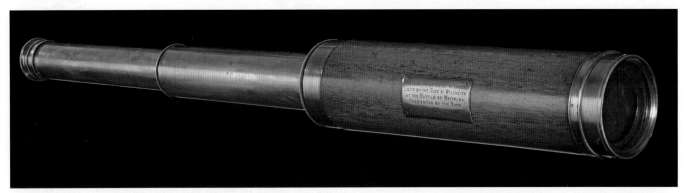

▲ Wellington's telescope. The battlefield was 2.5 kilometres wide and Wellington needed a telescope to make out the movements of troops in the distance. Using this telescope Wellington would have seen a line of infantry at 1.5 kilometres as a solid black line; a line of cavalry as a dotted line. Wellington's orders were written in pencil on a piece of goat skin (so that they could be erased and reused) and sent by messenger on horseback.

Stage 4: The French infantry attack

Behind the ridge, the British infantry had been relatively well protected from the French artillery fire. Then, at 1.30 p.m., 18,000 French infantry advanced towards the British infantry lines. Wellington ordered:

- the Allied artillery to fire
- the Allied infantry to stand in lines and fire with bayonets fixed (see box below)
- the Allied cavalry to charge, swords drawn, at the French infantry after they had begun to retreat.

INFANTRY LINES

Infantry usually fired in line formations two men deep. This was in order to maximise firepower by having a large numbers of soldiers firing at once. Soldiers no longer had to stand in several rows to fire and reload as technological improvements had reduced the reload times of muskets. Each soldier could now fire up to three times a minute.

Stage 5: The French cavalry charge

The French infantry attack failed, but half of the Allied cavalry were lost in the charge against them.

At 4 p.m., 5000 French cavalry began a series of repeated charges against the Allied infantry. Wellington's response was to order:

- the infantry behind the ridge to form thirteen hollow squares
- the Allied artillery to fire as the cavalry approached.

INFANTRY SQUARES

Infantrymen made square formations of four men deep to defend against cavalry charges. The front two rows held their muskets at a 45-degree angle with bayonets pointing outwards like pikes, while the standing two rows fired volleys of shot. The centre of the square provided protection for officers issuing commands, and the wounded. Square formations were, however, vulnerable to artillery fire.

Stage 6: The fall of La Haye Sainte

The Allied infantry's discipline and determination ensured that all of the thirteen squares held firm and the French cavalry eventually stopped the charges. However, elsewhere on the battlefield the French did make advances. At 6 p.m. the French took control of La Haye Sainte. This left the centre of Wellington's army vulnerable. At this critical moment Wellington acted by:

- sending reinforcements to strengthen the line near La Haye Sainte
- making himself visible to the troops by riding up and down the line, despite the danger to himself, stating that 'I, and every Englishman on this field, must stand and die on the spot which we now occupy'.

Stage 7: The charge of the French Imperial Guard

After the fall of La Haye Sainte, Wellington's exhausted infantry began to waver. But help came when Prussian troops began to arrive on the battlefield, forcing the French to divert troops. Napoleon knew it was his last chance for victory and ordered his elite Imperial Guard infantry to advance on the centre of the Allied line. Wellington acted by:

- ordering the Allied artillery to fire on the Imperial Guard as they advanced
- instructing the British infantry to stand up in lines and fire when the Imperial Guard were close.

BRITISH ARTILLERY

A 6-pounder artillery gun was the most common British artillery piece at Waterloo. It had a range of just over 500 metres, required a crew of eight men, was **muzzle-loaded** and could fire about two shells per minute.

Artillery was becoming increasingly important at this time, which was reflected in the establishment of a Royal Regiment of Artillery from c.1700, and gunners were well trained. But artillery numbers still remained small and Wellington's use of artillery was quite old fashioned. He did not concentrate his guns in one place, but spread them out along the battlefield. He used artillery to support the infantry rather than the French method of using artillery to fire large-scale concentrated bombardments.

Shrapnel shells were also used at Waterloo. These were a hollow metal shell filled with a mixture of metal balls and powder and a crude time fuse. The shell exploded shortly after it was fired, releasing the metal balls, causing devastating injuries to infantry. The shrapnel shell was the invention of the British-born Henry Shrapnel in 1784, and was first used by the British Army in 1803.

Armour breast plate of a French cavalryman shot ▶ through with a cannon ball.

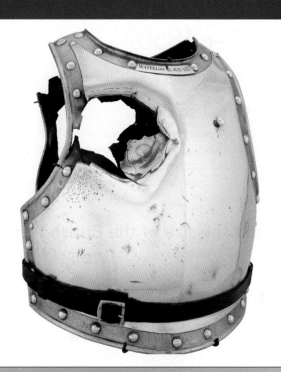

The outcome of the battle

The Imperial Guard struggled through the Allied artillery fire, but was forced back by gunfire from the Allied infantry. The French Army was defeated. Casualties were substantial. French losses were estimated at 25,000; Allied at just over 23,000. This meant that one in three of the Allied troops became a casualty during the battle. Large losses were typical given the tactics of using maximum firepower at close range.

What does Waterloo tell us about the nature of warfare, c.1700–c.1800?

We can use the Battle of Waterloo to inform us about the nature of warfare (the weapons, composition and tactics of armies) in the period 1700–1815. This is because there had been little change in weapons between 1700 and 1815. Remember, flintlock muskets had been invented in the seventeenth century; they just became more widely used from 1700. Bayonets too were in use from 1700. The basic capabilities of artillery guns also remained the same during this period. You can therefore use information from the Battle of Waterloo to tell you about the weapons and tactics of warfare c.1700–c.1800.

THE NATURE OF WARFARE, c.1700–c.1800

1. Look over how you rated Wellington's decisions (page 55). To what extent did Wellington as an individual contributed to Allied victory?

2. Explain why infantry tended to be deployed in either line or square formations (see page 57).

3. Fill in the weapons row of your Knowledge Organiser table (see page 55) based on the knowledge you have about the weapons used at Waterloo. You can write most of your information across the dates 1700 to 1800 as we know there was little change between these dates.

4. Fill in the composition of armies row of your Knowledge Organiser table, again based on the knowledge you have about the weapons used at Waterloo. You can write most of your information across the dates 1700 to 1800 as we know there was little change between these dates. Try to include information about:
   - artillery
   - infantry
   - cavalry.

4.4 What methods were used to recruit combatants, c.1700–c.1850?

The methods of recruiting combatants remained largely unchanged for most of this period.

Professional soldiers

By 1700 soldiers were professional soldiers, which meant that being a soldier was their job, and, for most, their only means of earning a wage. This was possible because England had a permanent standing army, even in peacetime (remember this was established in 1660, see page 40). This became the British Army in 1707 when the kingdoms of Scotland and England were joined.

How did the size of the British Army change?

The size of the British Army fluctuated during this period, as the graph below shows.

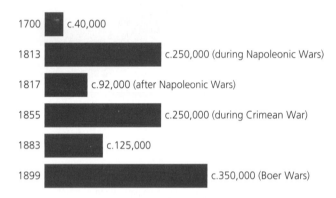

1700	c.40,000
1813	c.250,000 (during Napoleonic Wars)
1817	c.92,000 (after Napoleonic Wars)
1855	c.250,000 (during Crimean War)
1883	c.125,000
1899	c.350,000 (Boer Wars)

▲ The approximate size of the British Army, 1700–1900

CHANGES IN THE SIZE OF THE ARMY

1. Why do you think there were increases in the numbers of troops at certain times?
2. How would you describe the overall pattern of change in the approximate size of the British Army?

The British Army was initially small. People were suspicious of a large army, fearing the king may use it against the people as had happened in the English Civil Wars (1642–49). Its basic size gradually grew through the period although it remained small in comparison with the armies in other European countries. This was partly because the British tended to see the Royal Navy, not the Army, as their main defence and as the most useful means of controlling their overseas Empire. Peaks occurred in army size when Britain was involved in foreign wars and needed to recruit many more soldiers, for example during the Napoleonic Wars (1803–15), the Crimean War (1853–56) and the Boer Wars (1899–1902).

What motivated men to join the infantry, c.1700–c.1850?

Let's begin by looking in more detail at the circumstances which led to the enlistment of our soldier in the spotlight, William Lawrence, in about 1806 (see the page opposite). These methods of recruitment were largely unchanged since 1700.

1. Over 90 per cent of recruits to the British Army were illiterate *in the first half of the nineteenth century (approximately 30 per cent of the male population were illiterate).*

2. Recruiting parties (usually made up of a group of about three soldiers) were sent to local fairs and public houses to try to attract recruits.

3. As an incentive, anyone bringing a new recruit to enlist was given a bounty, usually of about two guineas.

SOLDIER IN THE SPOTLIGHT – WILLIAM LAWRENCE: ENLISTMENT

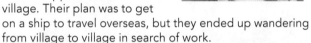

William Lawrence was the child of a farm labourer. He had no formal education and worked as a ploughboy until he was fourteen years old. By then his father had saved enough money to send him as an **apprentice** to a builder in a different village. But William was not treated kindly, went hungry and was flogged. He decided to escape along with another apprentice from the village. Their plan was to get on a ship to travel overseas, but they ended up wandering from village to village in search of work.

Then, by chance, William saw some soldiers and commented that he would like to become one. A farm worker took him to a **public house** where there was an army sergeant who gave the farm worker two guineas for bringing William, and gave five guineas to William for agreeing to become a soldier. William was then dressed in a soldier's coat and, with ribbons tied to him, was paraded around other pubs to persuade others to enlist. Lawrence spent almost all of his five-guinea bounty on drink and entertainment that night.

The next day William was taken to the town hall to swear before a **magistrate** a formal oath to commit to becoming a soldier. When asked his occupation, William lied, saying that he was a farm labourer, apprentices were one of the few groups not permitted to enlist. William then received his uniform and began drill training.

4. Bounty was the money paid to a man when he enlisted. The amount varied; by 1806 it was often twelve guineas – a substantial sum (about 40 per cent of the yearly income of an agricultural labourer).

5. Many recruits spent their bounty almost immediately on drink and entertainment.

7. The majority of recruits were labourers (see pie chart, page 62).

6. New recruits had to swear an oath of loyalty committing to army service to a judge before they were formally accepted into the army. This had to be done within four days of enlisting, but officially not within 24 hours in order to give the new recruit a chance to sober up and possibly change his mind! If a man did change his mind before he swore the oath, he would have to pay back the bounty money and pay an additional 20 shillings. This additional money was known as 'smart money' – this was because at this time 'smart' was used to mean a sharp, stinging pain – which may have been how the extra payment made men feel! Many could not afford to pay and so were forced to continue to enlist. The term of service men agreed was 21 years, a lifetime commitment.

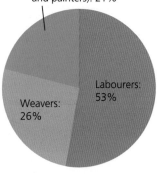

Other (including shoemakers, tailors, butchers, blacksmiths and painters): 21%

Labourers: 53%

Weavers: 26%

▲ The working background of members of the 64th Staffordshire Regiment, 1806–29. The proportions of trades in this regiment were typical. Unemployment and low wages in this period that affected the agricultural and weaving trades help explain the high proportions of men from these backgrounds.

It could be difficult for the British Army to attract recruits. Life in the British Army was harsh, with strict discipline, including floggings, low pay and monotonous drill training, and that was if you survived battle and disease on campaign! What's more, the commitment to the Army was for life – with recruits agreeing to serve for 21 years.

Unsurprisingly, the Army was seen by many civilians as the last resort for those who had little else. Even the Commander-in-Chief of the British Army, the Duke of Wellington, said ordinary British infantryman were:

> the scum of the earth. People talk of their enlisting from their fine military feeling – all [nonsense] – no such thing. Some of our men enlist from having [committed criminal] offences – many more for drink.

It is important to remember that he was not talking about the officers, who were recruited quite differently, but about ordinary infantrymen. How fair were Wellington's comments?

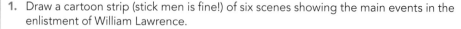

▲ A recruitment party of the 33rd Regiment of Foot, 1814. A print by R. Havell from 1814. It shows a recruiting party gathering recruits outside a pub. A flat oatcake is depicted on the sergeant's sword to represent the plentiful food that was promised to recruits once they enlisted in the Army.

REASONS FOR RECRUITMENT

1. Draw a cartoon strip (stick men is fine!) of six scenes showing the main events in the enlistment of William Lawrence.
2. List as many possible reasons as you can to explain why William Lawrence enlisted in 1806.
3. How far do you think William Lawrence's experience of recruitment was typical?
4. Was William Lawrence a typical recruit? Give reasons for your answer.

Other methods of recruitment, c.1700–c.1850?

Recruiting parties were the main way of gaining recruits during this period, but other methods were used.

The Militia

Soldiers were recruited from the Militia. The Militia was an organisation whose members were equipped and trained to provide basic local defence. From 1757 counties had to provide lists of men aged 18 to 45 from which men were selected by ballot to serve in the Militia for a period of five years. Militiamen were not part of the army and were not expected to serve overseas.

Traditionally, special permission had to be granted by Parliament each time the army recruited men from the Militia. But this was ended in 1809 when recruitment from the Militia became more regular. Militiamen were encouraged to transfer to the regular army by a bounty payment which was larger than the bounty paid to volunteer recruits to the army. Between 1805 and 1815, 100,000 Militiamen joined the regular army.

Kidnap!

Some men were forced to join the army. Victims were often made drunk and then held captive until they swore the oath to enlist. Kidnappers were known as crimps. Their incentive was the bounty money given to those who brought men forward to enlist. Crimps were most active in the 1790s and 1800s when there was particular need for recruits during the Napoleonic Wars.

Desertion

Unsurprisingly, **desertion** was a constant problem. Most desertions took place soon after the men had enlisted and before they had actually joined their regiments. Between 1803 and 1812 just over 53,000 men deserted; in the worst year of 1805 there was one desertion for every 157 recruits. Desertion was an offence punishable by death, although it was only really imposed on soldiers who deserted to the enemy in a campaign. Many deserters had public sympathy, as the painting on the front cover of this book, *Searching for the Deserter*, suggests. Painted in 1868, it shows a desperate deserter hiding from pursuing troops in a family home.

How were officers recruited?

Officers (including cavalrymen) were recruited very differently from infantrymen. They were from the wealthy upper middle and aristocratic classes. The position of an officer in the army was seen as an appropriate career for the younger sons of the **aristocracy** and **gentry** (the eldest son would inherit the family estate).

The purchase system

Positions as officers were traditionally bought for money, in what was known as the **purchase system**. It was customary for parents to purchase a commission (a position/rank) as an officer for their sons. A lieutenant commission could typically be purchased for upwards of £1000. This did not mean that officers were not brave or skilful, but it meant that they might well *not* be, especially since there was no formal training requirement or qualifications needed; officers were expected to learn through experience. Nepotism (favouring one's own family members) was also common. In the 1850s five of the aide-de-camps (military secretaries) were the nephews of the Commander-in-Chief, Lord Raglan.

Promotions were usually either purchased or were based on seniority (the length of period an officer had served). There was very little opportunity, although it did occasionally happen, for men from the ranks (non-officers) to become officers. During the Napoleonic Wars, however, 4.5 per cent of officers were promoted from the ranks. This was unusual and a consequence of the need to replace officers killed during the Wars. One officer remarked, 'soldiers are but soldiers, and officers are soldiers and gentlemen'. This system of recruitment was not reformed until the 1870s.

DESERTION AND RECRUITMENT

1. Look carefully at the image on the front cover of your textbook. It is trying to tell a story. Write a paragraph explaining what you think the story might be (try to include historical information about the way soldiers were recruited into your story).

2. Identify two disadvantages of the purchase system.

3. Fill in the recruitment row of your Knowledge Organiser table (see page 55). Remember to include details about how infantrymen and officers were recruited.

4.5 Case study: the Battle of Balaclava, 1854

We have seen that little major change took place in warfare from 1700 until the Battle of Waterloo in 1815. Was there similarly little change in the almost 40 years that followed before the next major European war, the Crimean War (1853–56)?

Who fought in the Crimean War?

In the Crimean War the armies of Russia fought against the Turkish forces of the **Ottoman Empire**, Britain and France (known as the Allies). The war was the result of the Russian Empire's attempt to take control of the Black Sea from the Ottoman Empire. This action was resisted by the Ottoman Empire, France and Britain, who regarded Russian expansion as a threat to their own power.

The Allies believed that taking control of Russia's main port and naval base on the Black Sea, at Sevastopol, was their best strategy for winning the war. But Sevastopol was well defended with fortifications and large numbers of artillery. An Allied attack against Sevastopol failed in early 1854, after which the Allies began a lengthy siege of the city, digging numerous trenches to provide infantry with protection from Russian artillery bombardments.

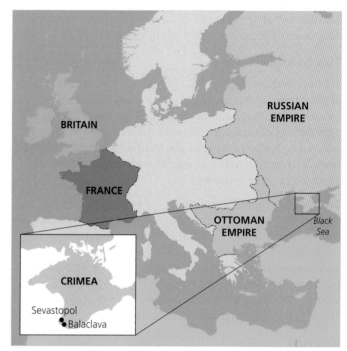

▲ The location of the Crimea

Was there anything *new* about the Crimean War?

The Crimean War is seen by some as the first 'modern war'. This is because it was one of the first conflicts to make use of new technologies that were being developed in the Industrial Revolution at this time.

Steam technologies

The Crimean War was the first war to demonstrate the military use of the relatively newly developed technologies of steam ships and steam engine railways (the first commercial railway had only opened in Britain in 1830, between Liverpool and Manchester).

Steam ships were used to transport men, weapons, ammunition and food supplies to the Crimea more quickly and reliably than would otherwise have been possible. They were, however, also still equipped with sails since they couldn't carry sufficient coal to power their steam engines for the entire journey. Supplies for the troops besieging Sevastopol were unloaded at the small port of Balaclava (see map).

The Crimean War was also the first war in which the military made use of steam railways. The British constructed a small purpose-built railway in 1855 to transport supplies from the port of Balaclava to their troops in the hills around Sevastopol. The 11 km of track were vital to move supplies, since the thin, hilly track roads became almost impassable in winter. This had contributed to severe shortages and terrible conditions for troops sheltering in the trenches around Sevastopol during the harsh winter of 1854–55. Deaths from disease (particularly cholera, typhus and dysentry) far outnumbered numbers killed in enemy action which made up just 8 per cent of the British military deaths during the Crimean War.

◀ Weapons supplies unloaded at Balaclava port. Notice the steam funnel on one of the ships. The fact that this is a photograph is another new development – the Crimean War was the first war in which photographs were taken. But this picture also shows some things did not change: notice the sailing ships and the cannon and cannon balls, which were traditional weapons.

Electric telegraph

Developments in communications technologies meant that the Crimean War was one of the first wars in which it was possible to communicate events that happened overseas back to Britain faster than a human messenger could carry them. This was because of the invention of the electric telegraph in the 1830s, which allowed coded messages to be sent as electrical signals along a cable (as **Morse code**, for example). For the first time messages could be received from far away within hours. But this did not have much impact on communications on the battlefield which remained, as before, dependent on gesture, written messages, flags and bugle calls.

▲ An electric telegraph machine invented by Emile Baudot (1845–1903)

Weapons

A substantial change had also taken place in the guns used by infantrymen by the time of the Crimean War. Infantrymen were no longer equipped with muskets, but instead with rifles which had been introduced on a large scale from the 1840s. Rifles got their name from the 'rifling' or grooving on the inside of the gun barrel, which cause the bullet to spin and therefore travel straighter, thereby increasing range and accuracy. Earlier guns without grooves were called 'smoothbore'. A comparison of the capabilities of muskets and rifles are shown in the table below.

	Effective range (not maximum) in metres	Rate of fire per minute
Brown Bess musket	(50 m) Poor accuracy	2–3 shots
Enfield Rifle c.1850	(500 m) Reasonable accuracy	3–4 shots

Rifles used the new **percussion cap** firing mechanism (invented in 1820). The spark to fire the gun was created when the trigger caused a metal hammer to strike a foil cap made of a highly flammable chemical mixture. Percussion cap guns were more reliable, even in wet weather, than flintlock guns. But rifles continued to be muzzle loaded and were therefore reasonably time-consuming to reload.

Artillery, however, continued to be smoothbore, limiting their range and accuracy since the technology did not yet exist to create rifling in larger guns.

Cavalrymen carried pistols, although they continued to use swords frequently on the battlefield. This was because pistols still had a very short range and limited accuracy.

HOW MUCH WAS NEW BY THE CRIMEAN WAR?

1. Identify four new technologies that were used in the Crimean War and explain how they were used.

2. Identify three ways in which what we know about the Crimean War so far shows similarities with how wars had been fought previously.

3. Add information to your factor sheet on Science, technology and communications. Write about the changes in the technology of weapons and the impact this had on warfare.

The Battle of Balaclava: change in the nature of warfare?

The Battle of Balaclava was one of the major battles of the Crimean War, and was fought on 25 October 1854. Did it show that changes had taken place in the nature of warfare?

Balaclava was initiated by a Russian attack on Turkish-held **redoubts** (small strongholds containing large guns) near Balaclava. It soon broadened to include British cavalry and infantry troops who were positioned in the area around Sevastopol.

The images below depict different stages of the Battle of Balaclava. You will find out more about what happened in the battle on page 67.

▼ Artists' impressions of scenes from the Battle of Balaclava

BALACLAVA SIMILAR OR DIFFERENT?

Look at the two images of the Battle of Balaclava above.

Does the nature of the battle look similar to or different from battles from earlier in the eighteenth and nineteenth centuries? Think about the weapons used, the composition of armies and tactics (see pages 64–65). Give reasons for your view.

What happened at the Battle of Balaclava?
The main stages of the Battle of Balaclava are described below.

BATTLE OF BALACLAVA ?
Identify the phase of the battle that is being depicted in each of the images on the previous page.

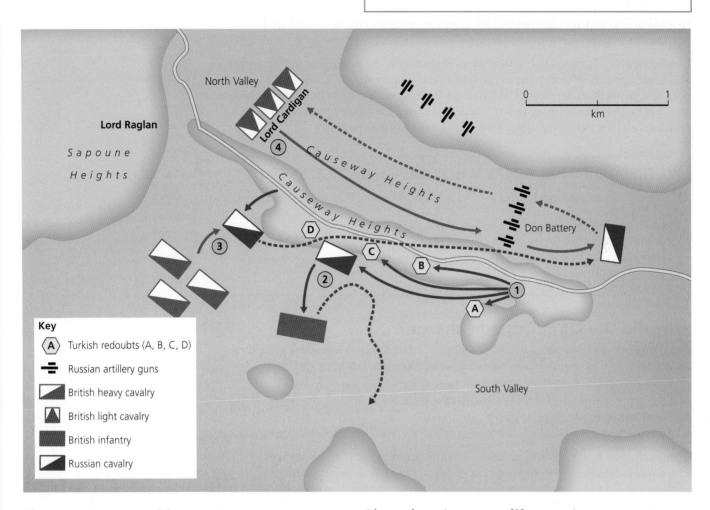

Key

(A)	Turkish redoubts (A, B, C, D)
≡	Russian artillery guns
◱	British heavy cavalry
◪	British light cavalry
▮	British infantry
◩	Russian cavalry

Phase one (see arrow [1] on map)
A Russian attack succeeded in taking control of the Turkish-held redoubts and Causeway Heights just before dawn. The Russians made preparations to tow away the captured guns.

Phase two (see arrow [2] on map)
At 8.30 a.m., 2,300 Russian cavalry attacked 700 British infantry and Turkish forces. The British infantry, and some of the Turks, formed a line two-men deep and fired repeated rifle volleys towards the approaching Russian cavalry. A nearby British artillery battery fired **grapeshot**. The Russian cavalry retreated. This phase of the battle became known as the Thin Red Line, from the outnumbered infantrymen in line formation.

Phase three (see arrow [3] on map)
At 9.15 a.m., 300 British **heavy cavalry** charged uphill, using mainly swords but also pistols, at 2000 Russian cavalry who had just appeared on the battlefield. The Russian cavalry retreated back over the Causeway Heights.

Phase four (see arrow [4] on map)
At 11 a.m. the British Brigade of **light cavalry** charged with swords and pistols down the North Valley towards the Russian Don Battery in an attempt to capture the Russian artillery guns. They were fired on by the Don Battery to their front and from the hills on both sides of the valley. Those that reached the Don Battery were confronted by Russian cavalry and had little choice but to return up the valley. Less than half of the 673 who began the charge returned uninjured; 113 were dead. This phase became known as the Charge of the Light Brigade.

The outcome of the battle

The Russians claimed the Battle of Balaclava as a victory. They had captured the redoubts and the Causeway Heights, and took seven of the large guns back to Sevastopol as trophies. However, the British infantry and the British heavy cavalry had shown superiority over the Russian troops with which they had engaged. But the tragic Charge of the Light Brigade cost the British enormous losses and soon became what was most remembered about the Battle of Balaclava.

The Battle also suggested that artillery was beginning to have a greater impact in battle and could limit the effectiveness of the traditional cavalry charge. Russian artillery bombardments from Sevastopol had also made it necessary for the British to dig extensive trenches for protection (see page 64). This type of trench warfare foreshadowed, on a smaller scale, the trench fighting of the First World War (see page 81).

WATERLOO TO BALACLAVA: HOW MUCH HAD CHANGED?

1. Compare the Battle of Balaclava and the Battle of Waterloo. How similar or different were:
   a) the use of infantry
   b) the use of cavalry
   c) the use of artillery.

2. Add notes to your Knowledge Organiser table (see page 55) about the composition of armies c.1850.

Why did the Light Brigade charge?

The Charge of the Light Brigade was virtually suicidal. This has inevitably prompted questions as to why it took place. Blame has been placed on key individuals:

- Lord Raglan (commander of all British troops in the Crimea)
- Lord Lucan (commander of the Cavalry Division)
- Lord Cardigan (the Light Brigade's commander)
- Captain Nolan (a messenger sent to carry Lord Raglan's instructions during the Battle).

Ultimately, the charge was a mistake caused by miscommunication on the battlefield, which was partly due to incompetent leadership, and partly to personal animosities between the key individuals. It showed how limited communications technologies on the battlefield could lead to tragic errors. To understand what went wrong, look at the cartoon strip on pages 68–69, which shows the main stages in the lead-up to the Charge of the Light Brigade. Then answer the questions below.

Cavalry to advance and take advantage of any opportunity to recover the Heights. They will be supported by the infantry which have been ordered to advance on two fronts.

1. Raglan on Sapoune Heights (with a clear view of the a battlefield) sent a message to Lucan in the South Valley around 10.15 a.m.

2. Lucan did not advance as he could not see any infantry (they had been delayed).

Lord Raglan wishes the cavalry to advance rapidly to the front, and try to prevent the enemy carrying away the guns.
Troop of horse artillery may accompany.
French cavalry is on your left.

Lord Raglan's orders are that the cavalry should attack immediately.

There, my lord, is your enemy; there are your guns.

Attack, sir! Attack what? What guns, sir?

3. Raglan saw the Russians prepare to tow away the redoubt guns. He sent Nolan with another message for Lucan.

4. Captain Nolan was highly critical of Lucan's leadership, regarding him as always too reluctant to attack. Lucan could not see the Don Battery or the redoubts as his view was obscured by hills.

Attack? Certainly, sir; but allow me to point out to you that the Russians have a battery in the valley in our front, and batteries and riflemen on each flank.

I know it, but Lord Raglan will have it. We have no choice but to obey.

5. Lucan rode to the South Valley and ordered Cardigan's Light Brigade to attack the Don Battery. Lucan and Cardigan were brothers-in-law and despised each other. Cardigan could see the Don Battery but he could not see the Russians towing away the guns from the redoubts.

6. Cardigan ordered the Light Brigade to attack down the valley. As they set off, Captain Nolan appeared and rode across their path gesturing with his arm. He tried to shout something but was struck by shrapnel and fell dead. Had Nolan realised the Light Brigade were about to attack the wrong guns? Was he trying to warn them?

WHO WAS TO BLAME? ?

1. Did Lord Raglan intend the Light Brigade to charge towards the Don Battery?
2. How did obscured views on the battlefield contribute to the mistaken charge?
3. How did unclear communications contribute to the mistaken charge?
4. How did personal animosities between the individuals involved contribute to the mistaken charge?
5. Which of the individuals involved do you think was most to blame for the Charge of the Light Brigade? Give reasons for your answer.

4.6 How did recruitment and training change after 1850?

Britain was on the winning side in the Crimean War but there was not much about its performance to be celebrated. The war revealed problems of poor command, tactics, mismanagement of supplies and outdated artillery.

The Crimean War: catalyst for change?

During and after the Crimean War pressure for military reform increased, primarily to improve military effectiveness.

A **Royal Commission** was set up by the Government in 1858 to investigate mismanagement and recruitment problems during the war. The investigation condemned:

- the mismanagement of supplies and resources. There had been a failure to provide British troops with essential supplies during the winter of 1854.
- the failure to recruit sufficient numbers of men to fight in the Crimea at the beginning of the war; the army of only 25,000 that was initially sent took almost every trained soldier in Britain.

Such findings resulted in growing pressure for reform in military recruitment and training. However, change did not occur immediately after the Crimean War, mainly because of conservative **vested interests** within the military and Parliament, where positions of power were held by a relatively small number of people, all from privileged, wealthy families who had little incentive to introduce reforms. Britain's victory at Waterloo in 1815 had also encouraged enormous belief in the great ability of the British Army which had led to complacent attitudes undermining the need for reform – such attitudes were slow to erode. Public pressure was of limited impact, not least since only a little over 5 per cent of the population were eligible to vote by the 1860s. It would take a further decade before reforms began.

Prussia: another catalyst for change?

When reforms came they were less due to the Crimean War than motivated by the desire to keep up with Prussia, which was increasingly perceived as a potential political and military threat in Europe. The German-speaking kingdom of Prussia had built up a very strong military from the mid-nineteenth century. Their army was large, well organised, well trained and well equipped. It had won victories in a series of European wars in the 1860s and 1870s that had led to Prussia creating and assuming leadership of a united German nation.

Cardwell's reforms

Lord Cardwell, War Minister 1868–71, introduced a series of army reforms. These measures aimed to encourage greater **professionalisation** within the army by reforming the recruitment and promotions procedures. The measures included:

- the abolition of the **purchase system** (see page 63): promotion in the British Army was thereafter through merit.
- an increase in Government control over the army, since the army Commander-in-chief was made directly responsible to the Government.
- the reduction of the **enlistment period** from 21 to 12 years (divided between six years' **active service**, six years in the **reserve**). This was to encourage more recruits and to ensure a trained reserve of men.
- an end to paying of bounty money for recruits (see page 61).
- the simplification of the structure of the army with the creation of 66 local regimental districts, one in each area of the country. Each area was to have two **battalions**: one to be sent overseas, the other to stay at home.
- the abolition of flogging as punishment during peacetime (it was still permitted on active service abroad).
- the abolition of **branding** as a punishment, although it had been rarely used.

CHANGES TO RECRUITMENT ?

1. Copy the continuum line below and mark on it where you think each of the reforms to recruitment and training might be best placed.

|————————————|————————————|

little change   moderate change   substantial change

2. How would you describe the *extent* of changes to recruitment and training that took place in the 1870s? How much really changed? How much stayed the same?

3. Return to your Knowledge Organiser (see page 55) and add information to the row for recruitment and training for the 1870s.

4. Add information to your factor sheets on Governments and individuals and Attitudes in society. Write about the changes in these factors and how they impacted on warfare.

4.7 How much did weapons change after 1850?

If we were to draw a graph of the pace of change in weaponry during the period 1700 to 1900, it might look a bit like this:

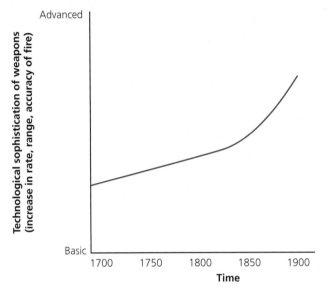

The graph shows an accelerating pace of change in weaponry after 1850. Increasing numbers of weapons were produced with increased rate, range and accuracy of fire. Many technological developments made this possible.

An increased rate of fire was achieved by the technological innovation of guns that could be loaded at the **breech** (not the muzzle). This reduced reload time considerably, increasing the rate of fire.

▲ A gun that can be loaded at the breech

Increased accuracy and range was achieved by using **rifled** (grooved) barrels to control the spin of the bullet. Rifling had been used in rifles since the 1830s but became possible in artillery from the 1860s. The biggest artillery could achieve ranges of 10 kilometres by 1900.

These developments themselves depended upon other technical innovations:

Steel

The reason why it became possible to rifle artillery pieces was because of developments in casting steel. From the 1860s artillery pieces began to be cast out of solid steel as a result of new manufacturing methods that enabled large pieces of steel to be cast relatively cheaply. Cast steel guns were much stronger and more capable of being rifled than the cast iron pieces. The British industrialist Henry Bessemer was responsible for developing a process for cheaply mass producing large pieces of steel from the 1850s. This became known as the Bessemer process.

Brass cartridges

The reason why breech-loading guns became possible was due to developments in ammunition **cartridges**. Brass cartridges (developed from the 1830s) contained one bullet and gunpowder inside a brass case. Brass cartridges were quicker and less dangerous to reload and enabled effective loading at the breech, which had not been possible before when shot and powder was loaded separately.

▲ The first 'machine-gun'. It was invented in the 1860s. The gun had multiple barrels which were rotated by hand. It usually fired about 400 rounds per minute. The gun made use of breech-loading and the new brass cartridge technologies

Smokeless powder

Another important innovation was smokeless powder which became available from the 1880s. It massively improved visibility on the battlefield.

Mass production

The increasing use of factories for production from 1850 had the important result that a lot more weapons could be produced more quickly. Weapons, and ammunition, began to be available in much larger quantities than ever before.

Pace of change

A large amount of change took place in a relatively small amount of time. This was because many of the innovations built on each other. For example, the invention of the brass cartridge allowed for more effective breech-loading guns.

Visible learning: helping your memory

There are a lot of technical developments to remember here. Sometimes it can be useful to think of an acrostic when you need to remember lots of things. Try using the acrostic here:

B   breech-loaders

R   rifling

A   ammunition

S   steel casting

S   smokeless powder

The consequences of changes in weapons after 1850

The impact of these new weapons technologies would not be felt immediately since it took time, and importantly money, to fund the provision of armies with new weapons on a large scale. Governments were understandably initially reluctant to invest in new technologies in this way – military spending was not a priority and they were unsure of the reliability of new weapons.

However, this changed due to increasing tensions in European relations from the 1870s which were caused by the perceived threat of Prussian and then German military strength and growing imperial rivalries (see page 70). British Governments increased their military spending, as did other European Governments, as an arms race developed in the later years of the nineteenth century.

No one really knew for sure the impact on tactics on the battlefield that the increased firepower of these weapons would have. It seemed likely it would result in all of the possibilities listed in question 4 below. One man, Ivan Bloch, a Polish railway owner and writer, wrote his vision for the future of war in 1897:

> at first there will be increased slaughter on so terrible a scale as to render it impossible to get troops to push the battle to a decisive issue … everybody will be entrenched in the next war; the space will be as indispensable to the soldier as his rifle.

We will see in the next chapter how far his vision became a reality.

CHANGES TO WEAPONS AFTER 1850 AND THE IMPACT ON TACTICS

1. What was different about weapons by 1900 compared to before 1850?
2. Write a few sentences to describe the pace of change in weapons from 1850. Give reasons for the pace of change.
3. Add information about the developments in weapons to your Knowledge Organiser table (page 55) for the dates after 1850.
4. Which of the following do you think were a likely tactical consequence of the developments in weapons? You can choose more than one. Give reasons for your answer.
- An increase in the size of armies
- Artillery becoming more important on the battlefield
- Cavalry becoming less effective on the battlefield
- An increase in difficulty for infantry attacking in line formations
- An increase in the size of battlefields
- An increase in the use of trenches to protect infantry from artillery bombardment
5. Add information to your factor sheets on Science, technology and communications, and Governments and individuals. Write about how the changes in these factors impacted on warfare.

4.8 How much changed in the civilian experience of warfare, c.1700–c.1900?

No wars were fought in Britain between 1700 and 1900 so civilians did not have to deal directly with the impact of fighting. However, they were affected indirectly by war. Perhaps the greatest change was the increased information the public received about foreign wars due to advances in communications technologies.

Recruitment and conscription

Civilians provided recruits for the armies. In the Napoleonic Wars (see page 56) it is estimated that almost 10 per cent of the population fought at some point, with a death toll amounting to over 2 per cent of the population. The proportion of the population participating in the Crimean War was more modest, with the death toll accounting for 0.1 per cent of the total population.

Women were also recruited for service abroad, in the medical services, mainly as nurses. Florence Nightingale and Mary Seacole may have been the most famous during the Crimean War, but they were just two among many nursing volunteers from Britain.

Free food and quarter

The **requisitioning** of food and provision of accommodation to troops became less of a requirement during this period. This was partly because troops were increasingly accommodated in purpose-built barracks. The construction of barracks was initially slow; by 1800 there were only seventeen permanent infantry barracks. However, in just twelve years, by 1812, there were 168 barracks accommodating 133,000 men. This rapid increase in barrack building was encouraged by the huge increase in troops during the Napoleonic Wars (see page 56). Nevertheless billeting in inns and towns continued in the early nineteenth century, with civilians complaining of soldiers being drunk and fighting on the streets.

Taxes

Taxes became increasingly regular during this period. Taxes were particularly high in the early 1800s to fund the lengthy Napoleonic Wars (1803–15). During this time indirect taxes (taxes on products) were imposed on an unprecedented number of goods, from hats, ribbons and wigs, to windows, horses, carriages, newspapers and beer. A tax on income was imposed annually between 1802 and 1815 to help fund the Napoleonic Wars. This tax had first been introduced in 1799 when it required a payment in tax at a rate of 10 per cent on all incomes over £200 (incomes between £60 and £200 were also taxed but at lower rates). However, it was very unpopular, and no further income taxes were imposed after 1816 for many years.

Income tax was reintroduced in the 1840s, and during the Crimean War the rates temporarily doubled. However, as it was a tax only imposed on those with quite a high income, relatively few people actually qualified to pay.

Reporting the wars

This period saw significant changes in the amount of news civilians received about foreign wars. At the beginning of the period, however, communications remained slow and dependent on human messengers. Civilians did not receive up-to-date reports. Even in 1815, it took three days for news of the Battle of Waterloo to reach England – carried by a messenger on horseback and by ship.

By the time of the Crimean War (1853–56), the invention of the electric telegraph (see page 65) enabled much faster communication. But even short dispatches sent by electric telegraph took several days to be published. Longer articles were still sent by boat and took much longer. The article on the Charge of the Light Brigade, written by the most influential war correspondent of the time, William Howard Russell, for *The Times* did not appear until twenty days after the charge.

It is difficult to measure the impact that reports had on public attitudes. However, Russell's criticisms of mismanagement of resources in the Crimea did encourage public outrage and pressure for reform, contributing to the resignation of the Prime Minister Lord Aberdeen and his government in January 1855. Nevertheless, it should be remembered that the direct impact of newspapers was limited given that at least 30 per cent of men and 40 per cent of women were illiterate in the 1850s.

In addition, the impact of public opinion on politics was slight given that only a fraction of the population was eligible to vote. The **franchise** was broadened in 1884, but 40 per cent of adult males and all women were still unable to vote.

It is also important to remember that education and most media emphasised the glory and patriotism of serving in the British Army. The Army and the Royal Navy were crucial to the establishment and maintenance of the British Empire, which was a key source of national pride.

Photography

The Crimean War was the first 'photographed' war. But these photographs did not really help the public to 'see' the realities of the war. Firstly, the technological limitations of early cameras meant that only static scenes, not action shots, could be captured. Most photographs were posed portraits of soldiers in studios or beside guns. Roger Fenton, the main photographer of the war, deliberately chose relatively safe and reassuring subjects; there were no images of dead and wounded British soldiers.

The photographs themselves could not be printed directly into newspapers until the 1880s, instead they had to be copied by hand onto engraved printing plates. In fact, most newspapers continued to use war artists, not least because they could inject heroism and excitement into their pictures (see page 32).

By 1900, technology had improved so that greater action could be captured on camera and it was even possible to shoot basic (silent) moving film footage. Film and photographs had great potential to be used for propaganda purposes, and were increasingly made use of in this way. This is seen in the images taken during the Boer War (1899–1902). This war was fought in South Africa between the British and the Boer (Afrikaner) republics, and resulted in a British victory.

THE IMPACT OF WAR ON CIVILIANS ?

1. Identify aspects of the impact of war on civilians which:
   a) changed during the period c.1700–c.1900
   b) remained the same during the period c.1700–c.1900.

2. Fill in the row on the civilian experience of war in your Knowledge Organiser table (page 55).

3. Add information to your factor sheet on Attitudes in society. Write about the changes (or continuities) in Attitudes in society and how these impacted on warfare.

◀ 'The Dying Bugler's Last Call', photographed in 1899 by the professional firm of photographers Underwood and Underwood, during the Boer War, was most likely staged to evoke emotions of heroic sacrifice

The horror of war was captured more fully than ever before in such photographs of dead British troops at Spion Kop in 1900 during the Boer War. It showed a very different image of war than photographs from the Crimean War 50 years earlier ▼

4.9 Communicating your answers

Let's return to the enquiry question for this chapter.

'The pace of change was gradual in the nature and experience of warfare during the period 1700 to 1900.' How far do you agree with this statement? Explain your answer.

This question requires you to reach a judgement about the **pace** and **extent** of change. To help you reach a judgement you may find it helpful to think about timescales and topics. For example:

- do you agree with the statement for the period 1700–1850, but think that the pace of change increased significantly from 1850 to 1900?
- do you agree that the civilian experience of war demonstrated only limited change in this period, but that for weapons and tactics there was much greater change?

Remember to think about how you are going to organise your answer before you begin to write. As a **how far** question you will need to evaluate evidence **for** and **against** the statement, and reach your own judgement. You could structure your answer using **for** and **against** paragraphs followed by a conclusion in which you write your own judgement. Alternatively you could structure your answer by topics, evaluating the extent and pace of change as you go through each topic. Remember to use your Word Wall for helpful vocabulary. You will also find more guidance in the writing guide on pages 162–75.

Now write your answer to the enquiry question.

Using the factors to explain why

Now let's look at questions that ask you to 'explain why' changes did (and didn't) happen. Here is an example of this type of question:

Explain why there was relatively little change in the nature and experience of warfare, 1700–1850?

You can use the factors to help you explain the reasons for continuities in warfare. The activities below help you to think about how you might use the factors.

1. Make a copy of the table below.
2. Fill in the second column to show how each factor explains continuities in warfare 1700–1850.
   Use the factor sheets that you completed for each factor throughout the chapter to help you (see page 55).

Factor	How does the factor explain why there was relatively little change in warfare, 1700-1850?
Science, technology and communications	
Government and individuals	
Attitudes in society	

Explaining the connections

Remember it is not enough to just describe each factor and say that they led to continuities – you need to explain how the factors contributed to the continuities. You have already practiced using connective phrases to help do this (see page 29). Read the paragraph below and identify how it uses connectives to show how the factor explains continuities.

There were no dramatic technological innovations in artillery weapons for much of the period 1700 to 1850. Field artillery continued to be relatively small and smoothbore, which limited their power, range and accuracy. This meant that artillery rarely had a decisive role in battles. It also helps explain why the cavalry charge could still be effective in this period (for example, the charge of the British Heavy Cavalry at the Battle of Balaclava in 1854). This is because had artillery been more numerous with greater range and accuracy, successful cavalry charges would have been virtually impossible as they would have been blown apart.

1. Write some sentences to explain how the factors explain the lack of change in warfare 1700–1850.

How did the factors work together?

The factors often worked together to explain changes or continuities. It can be helpful to draw a factor map that you can annotate with arrows.

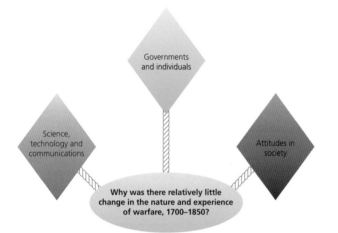

1. Make a copy of the factor map.
2. Draw arrows between the factors to show where you think a factor might have influenced another factor.
3. Annotate the lines to explain the links between the factors.
4. Do you think all the factors were of equal importance in explaining why there was relatively little change in warfare? Explain your answer.

The paragraph below describes links between some of the factors, showing how they worked together to limit change. Identify the factors it links and how they are linked.

The limited changes in weapons technologies in the period 1700 to 1850 were partly a result of government lack of investment in technological innovation (invention was carried out by individuals rather than sponsored directly by governments at this time). This lack of government investment was partly the result of attitudes of complacency following the British victory at the Battle of Waterloo in 1815, and so did not regard innovation and the development of new weapons as a priority.

Practice question

1. Explain **one** way in which the role of infantry was similar in the Battle of Naseby (1645) and at the Battle of Waterloo (1815).
2. Explain why changes took place in how wars were reported between 1700 and 1900.
3. 'There was little change in the recruitment of combatants in the period 1700 to 1900.' How far do you agree with this statement.

Organising your answer

Remember to think about how to organise your answer before you begin to write. You could organise your answer by using one paragraph for each factor and explain how each contributed to continuities between 1700 and 1850. Alternatively, you could use some, or all of, the topics to structure your answer. This would mean writing a paragraph on how the factors contributed to continuities in weapons,

followed by for example the composition of armies and so on. Remember that you need to have a conclusion in which you can show how the factors worked together or if there was a most important factor. Now answer the question:

Explain why there was relatively little change in the nature and experience of warfare, 1700–1850?

4.9 Visible learning: Revise and remember

Continuity or change in the nature of battle

You have now looked at battles in three different periods from 1000 to 1900. The technologies used to fight battles certainly changed a lot over this time, particularly with the introduction of gunpowder weapons. But some historians have argued that although the 'techniques' of battle changed radically, there was actually a lot of continuity in the 'nature' of battles. They argue that in terms of size of the battlefields, the duration of the battles, the composition of armies, and communications on the battlefield there were actually many similarities across the periods, especially between 1500 and 1900.

1. Make a copy of the summary table below.
2. Fill in information for each of the battles you have studied. The Battle of Naseby has been done for you.
3. Write a short paragraph to summarise the main continuities in the nature of battle.
4. Identify important **differences** in the nature of battles between 1500 and 1900 that are not included on this table (think about the role of artillery and the formation of infantry).

	Battle of Naseby (1645)	Battle of Waterloo (1815)	Battle of Balaclava (1854)
Main elements (composition) of army (e.g. infantry, artillery)	Infantry (mostly musketeers, some pike) Cavalry Artillery		
Communications on the battlefield	Handwritten messages carried on horseback Bugles Flags/signs Spoken command		
Close-quarter fighting	Yes		
Approximate duration of battle (minutes, hours, or days)	Three hours approximately		
Casualties (killed, wounded or missing) as a percentage of all troops involved in the battle	7% (very approximate)		

Test yourself

Remember that you need to make all that knowledge stick in your brain for the exam. The more you practise trying to remember things now, the more likely you are to remember them in the exam. Have a go at these questions – don't be surprised to read some from earlier chapters too – to help you remember them!

1 What was the name of the King of England who led the English troops at the Battle of Agincourt?	2 Explain two ways in which a typical foot soldier by the end of the Middle Ages differed from a typical foot soldier at the beginning of the period?	3 What was the shape of a typical infantry formation by the seventeenth century? Explain two reasons for this.	4 What was the name of the leader of Parliament's cavalry at the Battle of Naseby?
5 What was the name of the British commander at the Battle of Waterloo? And in what year did it take place?	6 What two main formations did the infantry use at the Battle of Waterloo?	7 How many years of service were most infantry recruits expected to give during the eighteenth and nineteenth centuries?	8 Explain two ways in which the Crimean War suggested a *new* type of warfare and two ways in which it showed continuities with previous wars?
9 List two of Cardwell's Army reforms. In what year did they take place?	10 Explain two innovations in weapons that took place between 1850 and 1900.	11 Identify two ways in which the civilian experience of warfare was different in 1700 and 1900 and two ways in which it was similar.	12 Name one thing that you learned in this chapter that surprised you or that you now think differently about. Explain why.

Set questions yourself

Work in a group of three. Each of you set revision questions on warfare between 1700 and 1900. Use the style of questions on page 29. Then ask each other the questions – and make sure you know the answers!

The Big Story

Now it's time to return to your chart summarising the main points of the Big Story. You have already completed the columns for 1250–1500 and 1500–1700. Now fill in the column for 1700–1900. Remember that you don't need to add lots of detail – you have your other Knowledge Organisers for this. Just add the key points.

	1250–1500	1500–1700	1700–1900	1900–present
Weapons				
Composition of armies (number, type and tactics of combatants)				
Recruitment and training of combatants				
Experience of civilians				

5 Warfare and British society in the modern era, c.1900–present

Warfare in the modern era has changed more rapidly in a relatively short space of time than during any other period. There have been substantial innovations in weapons, including tanks, nuclear weapons, precision guided missiles and unmanned aerial vehicles (drones). Science, technology and communications have driven many of these changes, but have they been completely responsible for changing the nature of warfare? This chapter will explore such questions.

5.1 The First World War: a different kind of war?

We will begin the modern era with the First World War (1914–18). In this war the armies of Germany, Austria-Hungary, Italy and their empires, fought against Britain, France, Russia and their empires.

How different was this war to the wars of the nineteenth century? Technological developments in weapons and rail transport meant this was a war on a much larger scale. It involved huge armies (4 million were in the British Army at its peak), with massively increased firepower and affected large sections of the civilian populations.

But, in some ways, it was not so very different to previous wars. Its great tragedy was, perhaps, the terrible juxtaposition of traditional and modern war: men with rifles and bayonets advancing towards modern machine guns. The men had little chance.

HOW DIFFERENT WAS THE FIRST WORLD WAR?

?

1. Identify what is being shown in each picture below. (Answers can be found on page 179.)

2. Does each picture suggest differences or similarities between the First World War and wars of the nineteenth century?

A

B

MILITARY SERVICE ACT
1916

EVERY UNMARRIED MAN
of
MILITARY AGE
Not excepted or exempted under this Act
CAN CHOOSE
ONE OF TWO COURSES:
(1) He can ENLIST AT ONCE and join the Colours without delay:
(2) He can ATTEST AT ONCE UNDER THE GROUP SYSTEM and be called up in due course with his Group.

If he does neither, a third course awaits him:
HE WILL BE DEEMED TO HAVE ENLISTED
under the Military Service Act
ON THURSDAY, MARCH 2nd 1916.

HE WILL BE PLACED IN THE RESERVE AND BE CALLED UP IN HIS CLASS,
as the Military Authorities may determine.

C

D

5.2 Case study: the Battle of the Somme, 1916

We will begin by looking in detail at one battle in the First World War, the Battle of the Somme, which took place in 1916.

BATTLE OF THE SOMME: A DIFFERENT KIND OF BATTLE? ?

1. Make a copy of the table below.

	Similarities to the nature of warfare in the nineteenth century	Differences from the nature of warfare in the nineteenth century
Nature of the battle including: • duration of the battle • size of battlefield • numbers of casualties • tactics		
Weapons		
Communications on the battlefield		
Composition of armies (number, type and tactics of combatants)		
Recruitment and training of combatants		
Experience of civilians		

2. As you read through pages 80–86 about the Battle of the Somme, add information to the table. You might find it useful to read through the pages first, without writing anything down, and then re-read the pages and record your notes.

The Western Front

The Battle of the Somme was fought in France. The majority of fighting in Western Europe during the First World War took place in France and Belgium. A German invasion in September 1914 had been halted by British, French and Belgian troops, but they had been unable to force the Germans to completely retreat. A **stalemate** had resulted, with neither side able to make a breakthrough. Both sides dug trenches as a means of providing protection from intense artillery fire (all sides had far greater numbers of artillery than they had had in previous wars). Eventually the trench lines extended from the English Channel to the Swiss border. These trench lines became known as the **Western Front**.

AN INFANTRYMAN AT THE SOMME

William Tickle was one of thousands of civilian men who volunteered to join the Army at the beginning of the war. He was about your age when he joined up. At just fifteen years old, he was too young to serve overseas (men had to be at least nineteen) but, like many, he lied about his age. New recruits received basic training before being sent to France and Belgium; many would have had little combat experience before the Battle of the Somme in the summer of 1916.

An infantryman like William Tickle would have worn a khaki uniform. (Khaki is a colour that had been worn by the British Army since the 1900s as it provided better camouflage than red uniforms.) At the Battle of the Somme a typical infantryman would have carried the following:

- a Lee-Enfield rifle – this was breech-loaded and capable of about fifteen rounds a minute, with bayonet attachment*
- 220 rounds of ammunition
- two grenades**
- wire cutters (to cut barded wire)
- emergency rations (typically a tin of corned beef and hard biscuits)
- gas mask (from 1915)
- two empty sand bags (for building trench defences).

*Bayonets were rarely used – bayonet wounds caused just 0.3 per cent of casualties. Soldiers made greater use of them as toasting forks!

**Early grenades were very basic and could explode in the thrower's hand. A more reliable grenade was developed from May 1915, called the Mills bomb.

The trenches

The trenches were often well defended and it became increasingly difficult for infantry to break the stalemate; neither side moved very far forwards or backwards from these positions until the end of the war four years later in 1918. The diagram below shows the common features of the trench system.

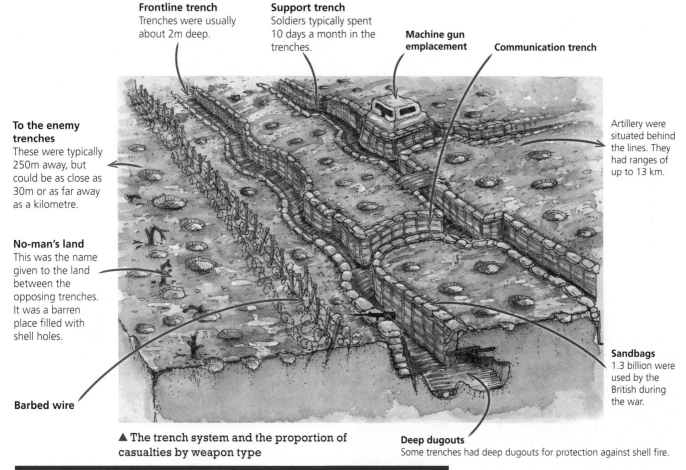

Frontline trench
Trenches were usually about 2m deep.

Support trench
Soldiers typically spent 10 days a month in the trenches.

Machine gun emplacement

Communication trench

To the enemy trenches
These were typically 250m away, but could be as close as 30m or as far away as a kilometre.

Artillery were situated behind the lines. They had ranges of up to 13 km.

No-man's land
This was the name given to the land between the opposing trenches. It was a barren place filled with shell holes.

Sandbags
1.3 billion were used by the British during the war.

Barbed wire

Deep dugouts
Some trenches had deep dugouts for protection against shell fire.

▲ The trench system and the proportion of casualties by weapon type

COMMUNICATING ON THE BATTLEFIELD

Laying telephone cables in a trench

Maintaining communication with troops once an attack was underway was difficult. Traditional communication methods continued to be used and included: human runners, **semaphore**, coloured flares, trained dogs and carrier pigeons (each tank carried two pigeons, see photo on page 79). Newer methods included the portable field telephone (pictured) which sent speech and Morse code messages through cables. But cables were difficult to lay during an attack and were frequently damaged by shells.

What happened at the Battle of the Somme?

The Battle of the Somme took place along a 30-km stretch of trench lines in northern France. The aim of the British and French attack was to achieve a decisive breakthrough of the German trenches to end the stalemate. The main stages of the battle are described below:

Stage 1: The artillery bombardment

The first phase of the attack was a massive, week-long artillery bombardment of the German trenches and their defences, using almost 500 heavy guns. It was hoped the shell fire would destroy the majority of the German trench defences and cut the barbed wire *before* the infantry attack began. **High explosive** and **shrapnel shells** were used. This was despite the limited effectiveness of shrapnel shells against trench defences; there were simply not enough high explosive shells produced at that stage in the war.

▲ Large guns like this 8-inch howitzer could fire shells several km, but they could not be aimed to hit with precision accuracy. Artillery gunners could not see their targets and relied on communication about where to aim from observation officers, usually by field telephone (see box on page 81). However, phone lines could often be cut by shell fire in battle.

Stage 2: Poisonous gas

In some places along the trench lines chemical weapons were used. Poisonous gases (mainly chlorine, which caused suffocation) were released from cylinders. This was blown by the wind towards the German trenches (later in the war gas shells were developed that could be fired from artillery). Gas had been first used in 1915 but it never made a big impact on the fighting since effective gas masks were quickly developed (also in 1915). Gas could be counter-productive since it could be as harmful to the side that used it as to the enemy, for example, if the wind changed direction or if gas lingered in territory where an advance was to be made. Gas attacks were hugely feared, in part because of the terrible effects of gas which included suffocation, blindness and blistering of the skin. There was huge fear about the future use of gas in war and in 1925 the Geneva Protocol, signed by 65 countries, outlawed the use of poisonous gas in warfare (although it has not been able to prevent its use entirely).

Stage 3: The detonation of mines

A series of large explosive mines that had been laid in tunnels dug by the Allies near the German frontline trenches were detonated early on the morning of 1 July 1916. Some of these explosions made craters of 50 m in diameter. The plan was that these would destroy key strong points and cause chaos in the German trenches shortly before the Allied infantry began their attack.

Stage 4: The infantry attack

An enormous infantry force of about 700,000 infantrymen was gathered for use at the Somme. The attack began at 7.30 a.m. when the first wave of infantry went 'over-the-top' of their trenches into **no-man's land**. The plan was for massed infantry to advance in successive waves, one after the other, to capture the German frontline trenches and begin a breakthrough.

The infantry would only have limited support from their own artillery. In some areas a **creeping barrage** was used in which artillery shells were fired to explode just ahead of the advancing infantry so that German troops would not be able to operate their guns. Although successful in places, the difficulties of communicating on the battlefield meant that there was often poor co-ordination between infantry and artillery. This meant that creeping barrages sometimes got too far ahead of the infantry rendering them useless, or in some cases, caused **friendly fire** casualties.

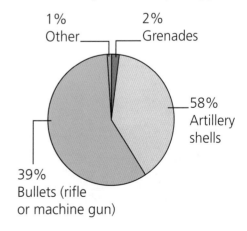

Proportion of casualties caused by each weapon type

1% Other

2% Grenades

58% Artillery shells

39% Bullets (rifle or machine gun)

Outcome of the first day: huge casualties

British troops did not achieve a swift and decisive breakthrough on the first day of the Battle of the Somme. Some troops achieved their objectives, but most found the German trench defences had not been destroyed by the artillery bombardment, and found themselves advancing towards a hail of machine gun bullets, under artillery fire and halted by uncut barbed wire.

Infantry losses were horrendous; there were almost 60,000 British casualties on the first day alone, including 20,000 deaths. This remains the highest British losses in a single day of combat.

William Tickle was among the dead. His body, perhaps hit by a shell, was never identified. His name, along with the names of over 72,000 other 'missing men' of the Somme is commemorated on the Thiepval Memorial to the Missing in France.

The battle continued

By 11 July 1916 most of the German front line had been captured by Allied troops. However, the Germans sent reinforcements and further Allied progress was minimal. Cavalry troops were only used to attack on two occasions during the Somme, and both times made no significant impact.

In September the British made the first use of the newly invented tank in an attack near the village of Flers. German troops initially retreated, horrified by these metal monsters, but soon launched a counter-attack and the British infantry were unable to retain the initial gains made by the tanks.

The role of tanks

Although tanks had shown their potential to assist infantry in an advance against machine guns, on the Somme they were unable to achieve a breakthrough. This was partly because tanks were:

- too few in number: only 49 were used at Flers
- technically problematic: many broke down and were only capable of a speed of 7 km per hour
- not used to their greatest tactical advantage: tanks were used in pairs, between lines of infantry on foot, whereas a massed tank advance might have been more effective.

▲ A British tank broken down on the Somme, 1916

The outcome of the Battle of the Somme

By the end of September 1916 the weather had become very wet, turning the battlefields into virtual swamps (see photo opposite). This made the logistics of supply very difficult; it became almost impossible to transport artillery and shells forward to support infantry advances, and without artillery support the infantry could not successfully advance.

When the Battle of the Somme finally ended on 18 November 1916, almost five months after it began, the Allies had gained just over 10 km at the maximum point of their advance. This was at a cost of over 400,000 casualties; 1 in 37 men were killed, and 1 in 19 were wounded. Proportionally this was less than the Battle of Waterloo (see page 59) where 1 in 20 troops were killed and 1 in 7 wounded, but of course the scale on the Somme was much greater (the deaths at Waterloo numbered 23,000; a fraction of the Somme campaign).

The Somme had become a battle of attrition – a battle in which both sides seek to wear down the enemy and their resources by sustained, lengthy bombardment. This is what the war would become; the slow, steady grinding down of the enemy with its consequent terrible slaughter of men. Almost one million soldiers from the British Army and British Empire were killed during the war; nearly one in every ten soldiers. However, the British Commander-in-Chief did not begin the Battle of the Somme as a policy of attrition. He had hoped that it would bring a breakthrough of German lines.

Was Haig accountable for the slaughter on the Somme?

Douglas Haig was Commander-in-Chief of the British Army during the First World War. He has been much criticised for his leadership of the Battle of the Somme. His critics condemn him for:

- being obstinately optimistic: continuing to send men over the top when there was little real hope of a breakthrough. Some of his generals, such as Henry Rawlinson, suggested more limited objectives, making a series of smaller gains might be more likely to succeed.

- failing to carry out adequate surveillance: being unaware that the majority of German trench defences were intact after the Allied artillery bombardment.

- being old-fashioned: remaining committed to the view that massed infantry advances could achieve a breakthrough against machine guns and artillery, and failing to make the best use of tanks or new tactics such as the creeping barrage.

But there are those who defend Haig, arguing that his tactical options were limited by available resources and technology. They point out that a high proportion of shells were duds or unsuitable shrapnel shells, and while Haig had been promised 150 tanks for the Somme offensive, only a fraction of this number was actually ready on time.

Haig was also under enormous political pressure from the British Government to achieve a breakthrough attack after two years of stalemate on the Western Front. The French military were also desperate for a British attack to force the Germans to divert resources away from their immense attack on the French at Verdun.

Ultimately, it was unlikely that any individual commander could have made a breakthrough at the Somme. Haig's culpability lies in his failure to recognise that the limitations of his resources made a breakthrough impossible, and that the attempt to do so meant an unacceptably high sacrifice.

▲ Douglas Haig

> ### WHAT HAPPENED DURING THE BATTLE OF THE SOMME?
>
> 1. Describe or illustrate the main stages of the Battle of the Somme between June and November 1916.
> 2. Explain why the British casualties were so high on the first day of the Battle of the Somme.
> 3. How significant was the impact of tanks in the Battle of the Somme?
> 4. Why has Haig's leadership at the Somme been:
>   a) criticised?   b) defended?

What was the civilian 'experience' of the Somme?

Although civilians in Britain were not directly affected by the Battle of the Somme, many of the troops who fought at the Somme were civilian-soldiers, ordinary men like William Tickle who had enlisted in the early weeks and months of the war.

Civilians in Britain were also affected by the huge demand for weapons and ammunition that battles like the Somme demanded (the week-long artillery bombardment before the Battle of the Somme used approximately 2 million shells). The production of **munitions** increased dramatically during the war and the Government encouraged large numbers of civilians to work in wartime industries. This included millions of women, whereas before the war such work would have been seen as 'men's work'.

◀ Women munitions workers making shells. By the end of the war 2.9 million women were employed in the munitions industry – three and a half times more than in 1914. It could be dangerous work; 109 women died during the war as a result of exposure to dangerous chemicals in the factories. The chemicals dyed their skin and hair yellow, earning munitions workers the nickname 'canary girls'. An explosion in the Silvertown Munitions Factory in east London in January 1917 also killed 73 and injured many more

Receiving news about the Battle of the Somme

Civilians received news about the Battle of the Somme from newspapers. Improved communications meant that reports came through relatively quickly. *The Times* newspaper printed a brief preliminary report on the first day of the Somme on 3 July, just two days after it happened. But reports were not entirely accurate, as this report suggests:

First Day's Results

It is now possible to get something like an accurate picture of the results of the first day's fighting in the battle which is now raging here … the success of the advance on this main section of the front is most heartening.

I have seen taken large numbers of German prisoners … I have also visited some of our wounded. They are extraordinarily cheery and brave. It is gratifying to know that an exceptionally large proportion of our casualties are very slight wounds, being injuries from shrapnel and machine gun fire … Our artillery fire had over most of the front been extremely destructive and very good … As always, however, there were places where individual bits of trench and stretches of the protecting barbed wire had miraculously escaped … causing our attacking infantry considerable losses.

▲ An extract from *The Times* on 4 July 1916 reporting the results of 1 July 1916

Censorship and propaganda

The information the public received about the war was tightly controlled, both for military reasons and to help maintain public support for the war. Journalists were not allowed in the trenches. They received information from official war correspondents appointed by the government and official photographers (from 1916 possession of a portable camera in front line trenches without permission was a **court martial** offence). The government imposed wartime **censorship**, forbidding newspapers to print information about troop movements or anything that was likely to harm public morale. Articles and photographs rarely lied outright, but presented a sanitised version of the truth; in images casualties were rarely shown and action shots tended to be posed because photographers did not have access to frontline fighting.

Cinema

Capturing moving (but silent) images on film and showing them in cinemas was a very new technology in the 1900s. 'Information films' showing the public images of the war on the Western Front were produced during the war. The most famous of these was the documentary film *The Battle of the Somme* which was shown in cinemas from 21 August 1916. As many as 20 million people watched the film in the first six weeks. It showed images from the trenches, including the detonation of mines before the attack and troops going over the top, but most action scenes were staged, and relatively few casualties were shown.

▲ Still from the film *The Battle of the Somme*

A DIFFERENT KIND OF WAR?

1. Now you have read the section on the Battle of the Somme, return to, and fill in, the table you created on page 80 to identify its similarities to and differences from the wars of the nineteenth century.

2. Summarise in a paragraph the extent to which the Battle of the Somme suggested that the First World War was a different kind of war from those in the nineteenth century.

3. What might be the problems of drawing conclusions about the First World War from the Battle of the Somme?

5.3 Identifying patterns of change in warfare in the modern era

Now we have a good idea about what warfare was like at the beginning of the modern era, we can begin to build up a picture of how much things have changed from the First World War to the present.

IDENTIFYING PATTERNS OF CHANGE

Use this Knowledge Organiser to record the information as you gather it.

1. Make a large copy (A3) of the table below.

2. Record information that you have learned about the First World War into the relevant date section of the table.

Topic	1900–1925	1925–1945	1945–1965	1965–present	What was the pattern (the pace and extent) of change?
Weapons, transport and surveillance					
Composition of armies (number, type and tactics of combatants)					
Recruitment and training of combatants					
Experience of civilians					

At key points as you work through the chapter you will be reminded to fill in this table further.

You will need a secure knowledge of what changed in order to tackle the big Enquiry Question of this chapter which focuses on the *reasons for* change:

'Developments in science, technology and communication were the main reason for rapid changes to the nature of warfare in the modern era.' How far do you agree? Explain your answer.

3. It will be useful for you to keep track of the role of factors in bringing about changes in warfare as you work through the chapter. Create three separate factor sheets or cards, one for each of the main factors:
   - Science, technology and communication
   - Governments and individuals
   - Attitudes in society

An example is given below:

Key features of Science, technology and communications, 1900–present	Impact of this factor in explaining changes and continuities in warfare

At key points as you work through the chapter you will be reminded to fill in these factor sheets.

5.4 How have weapons changed in the modern era?

The technical sophistication of weapons has decreased dramactically in the modern era.

Weapons have tended towards increased:

- precision (accuracy)
- rate and range of fire
- manoeuvrability in combat.

An infantryman's equipment by 2000 was very different from the Lee-Enfield Rifle, bayonet and Mills Bombs of soldiers like William Tickle in 1916 (see page 80). A twenty-first century infantryman is equipped with:

- an automatically loaded assault rifle, with telescopic sight, a laser aim effective up to 400 metres, and also capable of bursts of rapid machine gun fire, and a grenade launcher
- body armour
- personal radio.

▶ A British infantryman's equipment from c.2000

What were the big developments in weapons 1900 to the present?

There have been many new weapons in the modern era, but the five weapons identified below have had a particularly important impact on changing how wars have been fought.

Machine guns

A machine gun is an automatic weapon capable of firing bullets in very quick succession. It was developed in the late nineteenth century and used on a significant scale for the first time in the First World War. Early machine guns were not very mobile, although lighter, more portable machine guns were developed during the First World War. Machine guns have evolved so that, today, lightweight versions are used by infantry and larger guns are mounted on helicopters and tanks.

Tanks

The first tanks were used in 1916. They were armour-plated vehicles, armed with machine guns. Early tanks were slow (7 kmph) and mechanically unreliable (see page 83). Tanks evolved rapidly so that by the Second World War they were stronger, more reliable and capable of speeds of up to 40 km per hour. Tanks changed warfare by enabling infantry to attack even against strong defensive positions. They gave massively increased mobility to infantry, encouraging more mobile warfare. Tanks remain an important part of the Army today. Modern tanks, like the Challenger 2 (in service from 1998) are enormously well protected with Chobham armour that can destroy on impact even armour-piercing missiles. They can travel up to 50 km per hour, and are armed with two large guns and a machine gun.

Nuclear weapons

Nuclear weapons produce massive explosions that are the result of reactions inside the nucleus of an atom. Lethal and harmful radiation is also released by the explosion. Nuclear weapons have only been used twice in war: the two atomic bombs dropped on Hiroshima and Nagasaki in Japan at the end of the Second World War in August 1945. However, at least eight countries now have stocks of nuclear weapons (Britain developed its first nuclear weapon in 1952).

At first nuclear weapons could only be dropped by bomber aircraft (this is how they were dropped on Japan in 1945), but from the 1950s new delivery systems were developed so that nuclear weapons could be deployed in missile warheads, including in extremely long-range intercontinental ballistic missiles (ICBMs), and launched from nuclear submarines. For example, Britain's Trident nuclear programme means Britain's operational nuclear weapons are located aboard four nuclear submarines. The use of these weapons changed warfare by making direct conflict between two countries in possession of these weapons incredibly unlikely as the result would be Mutually Assured Destruction (MAD). Their development was in the era of the Cold War, when there was hostility, but no direct warfare, between the superpowers: the USA and the **USSR**.

Wars were still fought, but these tended to be smaller scale conflicts with the superpowers 'assisting' rival sides, for example in the Korean War (1950–53).

With these weapons as the ultimate deterrents there seemed little point in continuing to build vast armies with conventional weapons, and so armed forces tended to become smaller, but more professional and specialised.

Precision guided missiles (PGMs)

Precision guided missiles do not follow a ballistic trajectory (path of flight) based on the laws of physics, but are guided to their target, and can change direction in flight. The first real precision guided missiles appeared in the late 1960s. They can be guided by a variety of means: radar, heat sensors, Global Positioning Satellites (GPS). GPS technology has made these missiles much cheaper to produce than the previous radar-guided models. They are increasingly becoming the main missiles used in modern warfare.

Unmanned aerial vehicles (UAVs)

UAVs, sometimes known as drones, are pilotless aircraft that can be controlled remotely. First introduced in the 1970s, recent developments in micro electrics have enhanced their capabilities so that they can now be used for **reconnaissance**, **surveillance** and raids. Experiments are being carried out to equip them with missiles. These weapons are changing warfare by removing soldiers from the battlefields.

HOW HAVE WEAPONS CHANGED WARFARE?

1. Describe the impact of each of these weapons on warfare:
   - tanks
   - nuclear weapons
   - unmanned aerial vehicles (UAVs)
   - machine guns
   - precision guided missiles

2. Add information about the weapons on these pages to the first row of your Knowledge Organiser table (see page 87). Make sure you add the detail to the correct date on your table.

3. Write a few sentences to describe the pattern of change in weapons in the final column of your table.

4. Fill in your factor sheet on Science, technology and communications (see page 87). Note the key features of developments in Science, technology and communications, and briefly describe the impact they have had on warfare.

How much did new weapons change warfare?

New weapons are often seen as the driving force behind change in the nature of warfare; they certainly make new tactics *possible*. But the change brought about by new weapons is rarely immediate. It takes time and vast cost to equip entire armies with new weapons and to gain the experience to learn how tactically to make best use of them. Tanks, for example, showed their potential in the First World War, but did not really transform the nature of warfare until the Second World War (1939–45).

There have also been fundamental continuities in warfare during the modern era despite the many changes in weaponry. These continuities include:

- Infantry remain the largest part of the British Army. There are many tasks for which only an infantryman on the ground is capable. For example, defending territory that has been gained and disarming enemy fighters in urban centres.
- Combined arms (see below) remains the main strategy of attack.
- Armies still rely on motorised transport for the movement of troops, equipment and supplies.

COMBINED ARMS TACTICS

Combined arms tactics refers to the close co-ordination of land troops and military aircraft in an attack. From the Second World War, combined arms have been a key strategy in modern warfare. One of the first examples of combined arms was the German Blitzkrieg (Lightning War) tactics in the Second World War. First aircraft would be used to achieve air supremacy by destroying the enemy's aircraft, and then to bomb communications and defence centres. Aircraft would then be used to provide close air support for the army by shooting and bombing enemy land troops as they advanced. Tanks would often advance en masse (often in their thousands) to penetrate enemy defences, cut supply lines and seize key defensive positions. Infantry (usually using motorised transport) consolidated gains by taking up defensive positions to hold the territory. These attacks were fast moving and were only possible because radio enabled the different elements of the attack to co-ordinate. Combined arms have remained a key strategy in modern warfare, being crucial to the Iraq invasion of 2003 (see page 103).

ROLE OF GOVERNMENT ❓

1. Compare the two graphs. Do you notice any relationship between Government spending and the technical sophistication of weapons?

2. Fill in your factor sheet on Governments and individuals (see page 87). Note the key features of developments in Government, and briefly describe the impact they have had on warfare.

The role of Government in the development of weapons

Until 1918 weapons development usually began with individual inventors or was funded by independent industrial companies. This changed after the First World War when the Government took a more active role in funding technical innovations in weapons, having seen how crucial technology could be to winning wars. Radar (see page 92), jet engines and nuclear weapons were all developed under the direct supervision and funding of the Government during the Second World War. Innovations in weapons technologies occurred particularly during periods of war (the First World War, the Second World War and the Cold War) and this is, at least partly, because it was in periods of war that Government expenditure on the military increased (see graph below).

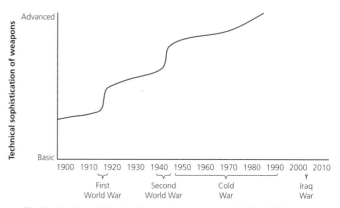

▲ Technical sophistication of weaponry, 1900–2010

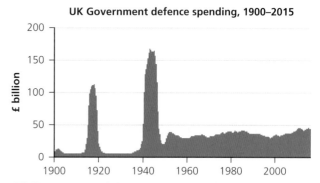

▲ UK Government defence spending, 1900–2005
(£ equivalent to 2005 values)

The investment of Government is vital in equipping modern armies, given the enormous cost of many of these high-tech modern weapons (a single Challenger 2 tank alone costs £4 million). The fact that the UK Government has become increasingly wealthy during the modern era is essential to its ability to afford to equip and maintain a modern army. Britain's Gross Domestic Product (GDP) has increased fivefold between 1900 and 2005, and Government's revenues from direct taxation (one of its main sources of income) has risen from £17 billion in 1900, to £110 billion in 1945, to almost £700 billion in 2005 (relative to 2005 values).

5.5 How significant were changes in transport to warfare?

Developments in transport have had an enormous impact on the nature of warfare. Modern armies require enormous **logistical** support due to the nature of their weapons, which require large amounts of oil, petrol, ammunition and electrics. Armies can only advance as fast as these things can be supplied.

There have been substantial changes in transport since 1900, enabling the more rapid movement of larger quantities of equipment over longer distances. Some historians see developments in transport as more significant than innovations in weapons in changing the nature of warfare.

The importance of logistics is reflected in the growth of the Royal Logistic Corps which is the largest corps in the British Army. It was formed in 1993 by unifying five existing corps.

▲ C-130 Hercules aircraft

Developments in transport that have improved the operation of logistics include:

- **Railways** – were first used on a large scale during the First World War, enabling the mobilisation of mass armies. But they lacked the flexibility to transport troups and equipment to precise locations on the battlefield.

- **Motorised road transport** – by the time of the Second World War, motorised road vehicles, which offered greater flexibility than railway transport, had become the main means of transporting supplies. This has continued into the twenty-first century, with the bulk of supplies in the Iraq War transported by motor vehicles.

- **Air transport** – aircraft have been used since the Second World War to transport troops, equipment and supplies. Most transport aircraft are used to transport troops and supplies within a conflict zone. Aircraft such as the C-130 Hercules are able to transport up to 70 troops with an additional cargo bay suitable for lighter-weight motorised vehicles. In use since 1954, they were also used in the invasion of Iraq in 2003. Helicopters can be used to transport troops and supplies within combat zones.

  However, aircraft have a limited capacity and are very expensive, and it is impossible to transport a mechanised force (especially tanks) by air alone.

- **Sea transport** – ships have always been the method most frequently used to transport large mechanised force, especially tanks, to combat zones overseas. Ships transported more than 90 per cent of the equipment to the Middle East for the Iraq invasion in 2003, which included 15,000 vehicles (including hundreds of tanks) and 9100 shipping containers of supplies. Much of this was transported on roll-on roll-off (ro-ro) vessels, capable of transporting 8000 tonnes (over 200 vehicles).

The vast logistical support required by modern armies is hugely expensive and requires considerable financial expenditure by the Government (one C-130 Hercules transport aircraft costs c.£19 million, for example).

> ## CHANGES IN TRANSPORT ❓
>
> 1. Add the main changes in transport to the relevant column of your Knowledge Organiser table (see page 87).
>
> 2. Add information to your factor sheet on Science, technology and communications. Write about changes in technologies and how this has impacted on warfare.

5.6 How significant were changes in communications to warfare?

Dramatic advances in communications during the modern era had a considerable impact on how battles were fought and in the surveillance of the enemy. Before the 1900s, most battlefield communications continued to rely on traditional voice command, gesture and signalling with flags or similar. Surveillance relied on the work of spies or, during the First World War, small reconnaissance aircraft flying over enemy territory.

> How might the developments in communications technologies described below have changed the ways in which wars could be fought (including surveillance of the enemy)? **?**

Cable telephones

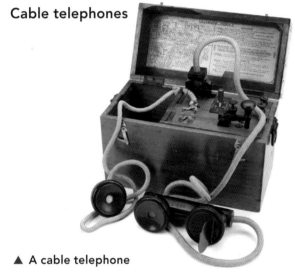

▲ A cable telephone

Available from the late nineteenth century, and used a lot in the First World War, cable telephones were capable of transmitting Morse code and spoken messages down cables. Cables needed to be laid before messages could be transmitted but these cables could be cut by shells (see page 81).

Wireless/radio

▲ A wireless radio

Wireless radios (widely available from the 1920s), could transmit Morse Code and spoken messages without the use of cables. Such radios were first used by pilots in the last years of the First World War. Wireless radio had enormous military application since it enabled troops in the field (and pilots in the air) to communicate with each other and hence to co-ordinate their attacks. Co-ordination between land troops and air support was crucial to the development of **combined arms tactics** from the Second World War onwards (see box below).

Radar

Radar stands for **RA**dio **D**etection **A**nd **R**anging. It uses radion waves to locate the position of objects by detecting when radio waves 'bounce off' solid objects. It was developed during the 1930s and was first used by the British in the Second World War when it was crucial in ensuring the British retained air supremacy over Britain. It is a key surveillance technology and is still used in surveillance and for targeting guided missiles.

Deciphering coded messages

Important military communications, including those sent by spies working in the Special Operations Executive (SOE), were usually sent by Morse Code, having first been enciphered (put into code). But, despite this, it was usually possible for enemy code-breakers to decode enciphered messages sent by radio. In Britain a code-breaking centre was set up during the Second World War at Bletchley Park for the purpose of intercepting and decoding enemy messages. The surveillance work of these code-breakers had an enormous impact in enabling the Allied victory.

High-tech digital technology

The development of digital technologies from the 1970s helped to overcome one of the major weaknesses of wireless radio communication, namely the risk that enemies could intercept messages and learn about military preparations and movements. This is because, in digital technology, messages can be encrypted (codified) in very complex ways which makes deciphering extremely difficult. Messages are converted into electronic impulses which are then sent to the 'receiving' device where they are converted back into their original sound/pictorial form. Enciphering messages (and trying to decipher enemy codes) is now a key area of surveillance in modern warfare.

Digital technologies have enabled the development of a wide variety of high-tech communication devices that include:

- mobile phones (first introduced in the 1970s)
- the internet
- satellite communications (such as Global Positioning Satellites (GPS) which have in turn enabled the development of precision targeted weapons, such as precision guided missiles (PGMs) and Unmanned Aerial Vehicles (UAVs or drones).

▶ **Modern high-tech Unmanned Aerial Vehicles or drones have, since the 1960s, been used in surveillance operations. Their uses include flying reconnaissance missions over enemy territory to gather information about enemy troops movements and gathering data to assist in target acquisition. There was extensive use of surveillance drones such as this one in the Iraq War from 2003**

CHANGES IN COMMUNICATIONS AND SURVEILLANCE

1. Draw a timeline from 1900–2010. Mark on the timeline when the key communications technologies described on pages 91–92 were introduced.

2. Explain how the development of radio changed how wars were fought.

3. Which of the technologies described above are useful in the surveillance of the enemy?

4. Add information about developments in communications to the relevant row of your Knowledge Organiser table (see page 87). Make sure you add the detail to the correct date on your table.

5. Write a few sentences describing the pattern of change in communications to the final column on your table.

6. Fill in your factor sheet on Science, technology and communications (see page 87). Note the key features of developments in communications technologies, and briefly describe the impact they have had on warfare.

5.7 How has the composition of the Army changed in the modern era?

The modern era has seen dramatic variations in the size of the British Army. The graph below outlines the main changes in its size.

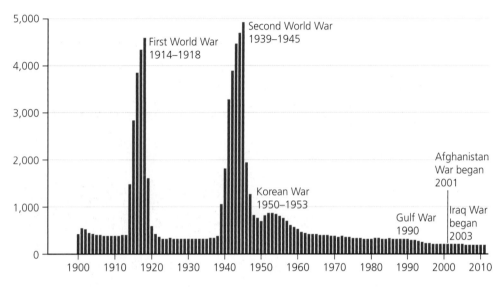

▲ The size of the British armed forces 1900 to the present (thousands). This graph shows the numbers in the British Military (including Army, Navy and Airforce). Army numbers make up about two thirds of the total

The two peaks in army size took place during the two World Wars when conscription was introduced to create mass armies. The period after 1945 has been characterised by shrinkage in the size of armies. This is largely a consequence of the development of nuclear weapons which meant military deterrent lay not with the size of armies, but with the possession of nuclear weapons (see page 89). The development of other high-tech weapons continued to apparently reduce the need for troops on the ground, contributing to further shrinkage.

HOW HAS THE ARMY CHANGED IN SIZE?

1. Add information from the graph above into 'composition of armies' row of your Knowledge Organiser table (see page 87).
2. Write a sentence in the final column of your Knowledge Organiser to describe the main pattern of change in the size of the Army.

Increasing professionalism and specialisation

A trend during the modern era has been for the increased specialisation of roles within the Army. Before 1900 the Army was mainly divided simply into artillery, infantry and cavalry, but now there are many different specialisms. The British Army recruitment website advertises roles for radar surveillance operators, rocket system gunners, tank gunners, infantry, artillery IT systems operators, tank crew, logistical support and many more.

The growth in specialist roles is in large part a consequence of the development of new and numerous high-tech weapons and communications technologies that require more specific training and expertise to use. The trend for increased specialisation was evident from the First World War when the following were established:

■ Specialist schools for the training of snipers
■ An Intelligence Corps (for the gathering of intelligence and aerial photographs – a new possibility due to technical developments in photography and aircraft)
■ Specialised bomb disposal units to dispose safely of unexploded bombs

SPECIALISED BOMB DISPOSAL UNITS

The number of specialised bomb disposal units grew considerably during the Second World War and the mass bombing of British cities during the Blitz (see pages 132–38). An Explosive Ordnance Disposal (EOD) Regiment (part of the Royal Logistics Corps) was established after the Second World War. Its importance continued with the growth in terrorist tactics, such as bomb threats to British cities by the **IRA** during the **Troubles** in Northern Ireland in the 1970s and 1980s, and, more recently, by Islamic extremists.

▲ Royal Navy Bomb Disposal with their robot detonator at Brighton Station

▲ The badge of the Special Air Service (SAS) carrying their motto: Who Dares Wins. The SAS was first established during the Second World War to carry out operations behind enemy lines. It has since developed into an elite, tough regiment specialising in **counterinsurgency operations** against guerrilla forces and in **counterterrorist operations**

Dealing with guerrilla warfare

The increase of **guerrilla warfare** from the 1970s has also created the need for more specialised forces. Guerrilla **insurgents** avoid fighting conventional battles because they lack the high-tech weaponry of modern state armies. Instead they use tactics of ambush that exploit their greater knowledge of the local terrain. For all their sophistication, high-tech modern state armies find it difficult to deal with such threats; even the most modern weapons are of little use against suicide bombers and improvised explosive devices (IEDs) left at the roadside or under trucks. IEDs accounted for approximately 63 per cent of British and American troop deaths in the first four years of the Iraq War (see page 103). The precision guided weapons of modern armies are also of limited use against insurgents, since the attacks tend to be based in cities, where even precision guided weapons will result in unacceptably high civilian casualties.

One response to these challenges has been the development of specialist counter terrorism forces that try to use the tactics of the terrorists themselves. A former soldier in the Special Air Service (SAS), Andy Mcnab wrote: 'Part of learning to fight terrorists was knowing how to be one.'

COMPOSITION OF ARMIES: INCREASED SPECIALISATION AND PROFESSIONALISM

1. Add information about the specialisation of roles in the Army into the 'composition of armies' row of your Knowledge Organiser table (see page 87).

2. Write a sentence in the final column of your Knowledge Organiser to describe the main pattern of change in the specialisation and professionalisation of the Army.

5.8 How has recruitment changed in the modern era?

The recruitment and training of combatants has changed significantly in the modern era.

CHANGING METHODS OF RECRUITMENT

1. Read the information on pages 96–97 and indicate whether a 23-year-old individual serving in the army at each of the dates below is likely to have been a volunteer or conscript (or could have been either).

   a) 1914   b) 1916   c) 1932   d) 1940   e) 1961   f) 2003

Recruitment in the First World War

At the start of the First World War, the British Army was relatively small (250,000 regular soldiers in the standing army; 700,000 including **reserves**). There was therefore an urgent need to recruit more troops. The Government began an enormous recruitment campaign, organised by the Minister for War, Lord Kitchener. This campaign used a variety of means including posters, newspaper and songs to encourage men to enlist. Serving in the Army was presented as a man's glorious patriotic duty, an opportunity for adventure, and necessary to defeat the 'evil' enemy. The public response was enthusiastic, reflecting a society in which **patriotism**, duty and fear of the threat of German militarism was deeply ingrained. Within eight weeks 750,000 men had volunteered. By the end of the war, some 2.67 million men had voluntarily enlisted; most had done so by early 1916. By the end of the war, almost one-quarter of the total male population of England and Ireland had joined up.

Private George Morgan, a volunteer soldier, describes how many people enlisted in the First World War:

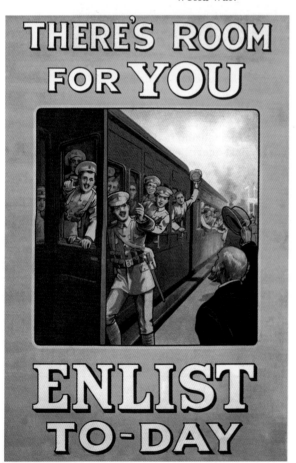

▲ A recruitment poster during the First World War

We had been brought up to believe that Britain was the best country in the world and we wanted to defend her. The history taught to us at school showed that we were better than other people (didn't we always win the last war?) and now all the news was that Germany was the aggressor and we wanted to show the Germans what we could do.

Conscription

The decline in volunteer recruits from 1915 compelled the Government to introduce **conscription** in March 1916 for men aged between 18 and 41. At first only single men were conscripted, but this was broadened to include married men from May 1916. There were exemptions for those with certain medical conditions or for those working in vital war industries such as steel production, munitions and ship building. Eventually 2.77 million British men were conscripted into the Army.

Recruitment between the World Wars

Conscription was ended after the First World War, the size of the Army was reduced considerably and recruitment returned to being voluntary.

Recruitment during the Second World War

The need for enormous numbers of combatants in the Second World War meant that conscription was brought in again, this time from the start of the war in October 1939. It was applied to an increasingly wide age group as the war progressed, eventually with men between the ages of 18 and 51 liable to be called up, although there were exemptions as in the First World War. Over 3.5 million men had been enlisted into the Army by the end of the war (the majority of these were conscripted).

Recruitment after 1945

Conscription continued to a more limited extent in the years after the end of the Second World War, partly due to the needs of maintaining the **British Empire** and partly due to needs of defence in Cold War era (see page 101). This peacetime conscription, known as **National Service**, was introduced in 1948. This stated that men aged between 17 and 21 were expected to serve in the Army for 18 months and to remain on the reserve list for four years. National Service lasted until 1960. Of course, during the period of National Service, men did still volunteer for the Army and became professional soldiers.

▲ A female soldier c.2003

Recruitment after 1960

After 1960 recruitment returned to being entirely voluntary and has remained so to the present day. Recruits are accepted from the age of 16 (although troops have to be 18 before they are allowed on **active service**). The maximum age for recruitment is 33 years. Troops usually serve for about 22 years (the minimum requirement is four years).

A significant recent change has been to the position of women in the Army. Although women did serve in combat operations during the Second World War, this was as part of special missions and not as part of the regular army. Their roles included:

- flying aircraft from factories to airfields
- deciphering coded messages
- working as spies in the Special Operations Executive (SOE).

From 1949 women were recognised as part of the Amy, serving in the Women's Royal Army Corps, although their combat roles remained restricted until 1991 when women first served alongside men in combat. The proportion of women in the Army in 2014 was 9.9 per cent. However, women remain excluded from certain regiments including the SAS (see page 95).

Officers

The majority of officers in the modern era enter the Army at officer level. Most have gained a university degree followed by officer training at military training colleges like Sandhurst Military Academy. As was the case in the past, few officers were promoted from the ranks. This contrasts with the situation during the First World War when as many as 41 per cent of officers were commissioned from the ranks (the figure had been less than 5 per cent before the war). However, this was less due to a change in attitudes about promotions than to necessity because of the extremely high casualty rate among officers (particularly junior officers) in the First World War.

HOW HAD RECRUITMENT CHANGED?

1. Add information about recruitment to the relevant row of your Knowledge Organiser table (see page 87).
2. Add a sentence describing the overall patterns of change in recruitment to the final column of your table.

5.9 How has the civilian experience of warfare changed in the modern era?

Civilian involvement in warfare was at its greatest during the **total wars** of the first half of the twentieth century (First World War and Second World War). One of the features of the modern era has been the blurring of the distinction between civilians and combatants.

The First World War, 1914–18

Some of the ways in which civilians were affected by the war are described in this extract from a letter written by Joe Hollister (living and working in New Cross in south-east London) to his father on 19 March 1917.

> We received Amy's letter and were pleased to hear you were better after being ill … Events seem to be moving more rapidly now on the Western Front, [once we] get the Germans out of their trenches perhaps our cavalry will get a look in and keep them on the run! My [colleague] at the office died of pneumonia in France in January after serving with the Artillery for a year and eight months without having been up to the fighting line, yet you hear of others being out and killed four months after joining up …
>
> It's extraordinary the amount of female labour employed in the City now, in the trains of a morning of ten passengers in a compartment there is generally an average of 8 females … the railway companies have employed them for a long while, [and as] tramcars, lamplighters … in fact in almost every sphere of activity. When 'Tommy' [the nickname given to British infantry] comes home he will be keeping and minding the kids while the women go out to work.
>
> The Zepps [Zeppelins] made another futile attempt to pay us a visit on Friday night, but I don't think they will get as far as London again. I expect, however, they will continue to harass the coast towns where they can drop their bombs … We really need to find means to deal effectively with German submarines to relieve the scarcity of food stuffs … things in London in this respect are beginning to be serious, no potatoes to be had, sugar almost unobtainable, meat and cheese becoming [very expensive]. I tried [to grow] vegetables instead of flowers in the garden last year …

?

1. Does the letter suggest that civilians were very well informed about the reality of the fighting on the Front? Why? The information on pages 85–6 might be useful to answer this question.
2. What did the writer notice about women working during the war?
3. In what way were civilians endangered? Does this threat seem to have affected many people in Britain?
4. What shortages did people experience? Why?

The impact of the First World War on civilians

During the First World War, civilians in Britain were affected to a degree that was previously unknown. It was the first total war, requiring people living in Britain to play a key role in the fight for victory. Indeed, Britain itself was referred to as the **Home Front**. This was because military success depended on mobilising vast resources of manpower, weapons, ammunition and food. Civilians were conscripted into the army or encouraged to work in munitions production and other vital war industries.

Women at work

With so many men enlisted in the Army, women took over many of the jobs formerly done by men, such as in the munitions industries, transport and farming, joining, for example, the Women's Land Army. This was a contrast to before the war where women in paid employment would mainly have worked in domestic service or textile industries. By the end of the war the number of women in paid employment had increased to 7.3 million; a rise of almost 1.5 million since 1914.

Bombing raids

German Zeppelins (airships) dropped bombs on England in a total of 556 raids throughout the war. From May 1917 Germany began using Gotha bomber aircraft in bombing raids over Britain; in one raid in London on 13 June 1917 158 people were killed. Overall, German air raids accounted for 1413 of the 1570 wartime military and civilian deaths in Britain (159 of these were killed in Zeppelin raids). Only in 1917 was an official air-raid warning system introduced, with blackouts and policemen on bicycles issuing warning. Public air raid shelters were informal, such as the London Underground. Since civilians were a vital part of the war effort in 'total war', they were seen in many ways as legitimate targets.

Food shortages

Food shortages were a significant issue, with German U-boats sinking ships importing essential foodstuffs. The Government intervened to manage the situation. Rationing of basic food items such as fats, sugar and meat was introduced from February 1918, and price controls were imposed on essentials like bread.

The increased role of Government

A total war such as the First World War was only possible because the organisational ability of the Government had increased enormously by the twentieth century. It required massive government intervention to manage the economic and manpower resources necessary to sustain war on the scale of the First World War for four years. The Defence of the Realm Act, passed in August 1914, gave the Government emergency powers to issue directives that had the force of law without obtaining consent from all of Parliament. During the war government:

- took control of the railways and requisitioned merchant ships for the transportation of military supplies and troops
- controlled wages in the munitions and mining industries, and forbade strikes in government controlled industries
- set up a Ministry of Food which controlled and subsidised the price of bread (at 9 pence) to ensure even the poorest could afford bread despite food shortages, forbade the feeding of bread to birds (to prevent waste) and, in January 1918, introduced **rationing**
- forbade the flying of kites, purchase of binoculars, lighting of bonfires, talking about military affairs in public places, all of which were attempts to minimise the risks of signalling to or communicating with the enemy.

The importance and impact of Government intervention was demonstrated by the Munitions Crisis of 1915. In 1915 a shortage of shells, particularly high-explosive shells, was blamed for the failure of British offensives on the Western Front. The so-called Munitions Crisis was widely publicised in the media. The Government responded by establishing a Ministry of Munitions which oversaw increased Government investment in, and control and management of, the munitions industries to increase production and efficiency: the Government directly managed 250 factories and supervised a further 20,000. The impact of the Government measures were considerable: in 1914 only half a million shells were produced; in 1917 the figure was 76 million.

CIVILIANS IN THE FIRST WORLD WAR

1.  Add information about how civilians in Britain were affected by the First World War to the final row of your Knowledge Organiser table from page 87.
2. 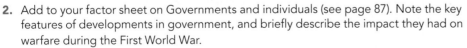 Add to your factor sheet on Governments and individuals (see page 87). Note the key features of developments in government, and briefly describe the impact they had on warfare during the First World War.

The Second World War

British civilians were affected by the Second World War to an even greater degree than they had been by the First World War. The Second World War was also a total war and government again took on emergency powers (through another Defence of the Realm Act) to control and organise the Home Front. New Government controls included compelling factories to shift to war production, introducing conscription, organising the evacuation of children from cities that were being bombed (see page 127), banning strike action in war industries, implementing rationing, and forbidding the use of petrol in private cars.

Shortages

- Rationing of essential foodstuffs, including sugar, butter and meats, was introduced in January 1940.
- Up to half of all industry was devoted to the war effort so there were very few consumer goods.
- Recycling campaigns like 'Make do and mend' encouraged re-using old clothing.

Information about the war: censorship and propaganda

- News about the war was received through newspapers, photographs, cinema and radio (which had become common in homes in the 1930s).
- Reporting about the war was closely censored by the Government.
- Propaganda posters and reports were produced.

British civilian experience in the Second World War

Targeted in air raids

- There were frequent and intense air raids on civilian targets, particularly in London, during what became known as the Blitz in 1940. Approximately 60,000 civilians were killed and 2 million homes destroyed (see page 132).
- In total war, civilians were regarded as legitimate targets and air raids had a strategic significance as it was hoped that intense bombings would weaken civilian morale.

Conscripted

- Conscription was introduced from October 1939 (see page 96).

Workforce

- Millions of women were employed in war industries such as munitions and ship building – 6.5 million women were employed in factories or shipyards.

How did the Government intervene to organise and manage the home front in the First and Second World Wars?

THE TREATMENT OF CONSCIENTIOUS OBJECTORS IN THE WORLD WARS

Conscientious objectors refused to serve in the Army saying that to fight went against their concience or beliefs. Many were religious (often Christian **Quakers**), others were pacifists. In the First World War 16,000 men applied for exemption from military service on the grounds of conscience; in the Second World War this figure was 60,000 men and 1000 women.

In both wars conscientious objectors had to *prove* their beliefs were genuinely held at tribunals. In the First World War these tribunals often did not provide a fair hearing. Panel members, which included miltary personel, were often hostile to conscientious objectors; they tended to be fairer during the Second World War.

If the conscientious objectors' claims were judged to be genuine they would be given conditional exemptions which offered them alternative non-combative war work, such as ambulance drivers, in agriculture or in bomb disposal units. Those who refused this work or who refused to enlist despite their objections not being judged genuine, faced imprisonment. Almost 6000 were imprisoned during the First World War, and 3000 during the Second World War.

Attitudes in society towards conscientious objectors were frequently hostile in both wars, although to a lesser extent in the Second World War. Conscientious objectors were condemned as 'slackers', cowards and sympathisers with the enemy. They and their families were frequently ostracised and sometimes even faced verbal and physical assault.

Attitudes in society

The harsh treatment of many conscientious objectors (see box) was partly a result of the widespread belief in the patriotic duty to defend Britain against the enemy, which meant that the majority of men did enlist when they were conscripted. This was very different to attitudes in society by 2000 which tended to stress individual freedom over duty and loyalty to a particular state.

◀ A badge that could be displayed in the window of a home. It showed the pride felt at having a member of the family serving in the Army

ATTITUDES IN SOCIETY

Add to your factor sheet on Attitudes in society (see page 87). Note the key features of Attitudes in society, and briefly describe the impact they have had on warfare.

The Cold War – fear of nuclear war

Hostilities between the two world superpowers, the USA and the USSR, dominated international politics between 1945 and 1991. This conflict became known as the Cold War since, despite threats and propaganda, the two superpowers never engaged in direct conflict with each other. The greatest fear for civilians in the Cold War (c.1945–91) was the threat of a nuclear strike. In Britain this threat felt very real, especially in the 1980s when US bombers and missiles stationed in the UK made Britain feel like it could be a legitimate target for Soviet missiles. The Government issued public information in leaflets, and broadcasts on radio and television to inform people about what to do in the event of a nuclear attack.

▲ Protect and Survive leaflet (how to protect your home from nuclear strike)

Attitudes towards war appeared to be changing with increasing numbers of civilian opposition groups to war, such as the Campaign for Nuclear Disarmament (CND). But peace campaigners had little effect on policy as escalation of the nuclear arms race continued until 1991 and the collapse of the Soviet Union.

The 'War on terror' – the fear of terrorism

Most recently the threat to civilian populations has come from acts of terrorism. Just how much acts of terrorism could affect civilians was demonstrated in the **militant Islamist** al-Qaeda attacks on 11 September 2001, when hijacked airliners flew into the World Trade Center Towers in New York killing nearly 3000 civilians. A 'war on terror' was subsequently declared by the USA, supported by its allies including Britain. Terrorist organisations and those who supported them have been the targets of military action around the world, particularly in the Middle East.

The threat of terrorism, from organised groups or disaffected individuals, has continued. On 7 July 2005 four Islamist extremist suicide bombers detonated bombs on the London Underground, killing 52 people and injuring 700. The rise of the militant Islamist extremist Islamic State of Iraq and the Levant (ISIL) from 2014, following the breakdown of government in Iraq and Syria, has intensified the terrorist threat. It was members of ISIL that claimed responsibility for the massacre of 130 civilians in the terror attack in Paris on 13 November 2015.

Changing attitudes towards war and their impact

Modern attitudes are likely to be less supportive of Britain going to war than they were in 1900. This is partly a result of changes in education and attitudes, which no longer promote unquestioning patriotism. It is also due to the growth of media reporting (on television and especially on the internet, which is harder for the Governnment to attempt to control or censor) which has presented the public with a more 'real' view of conflict and of its horrors, including civilian casualties and military errors. This increased power of the media to influence attitudes and hence Government policy and military strategy has become known as the CNN effect (named after the 24-hour US news channel).

The increase in civilian concern about casualties has had an impact on government policies. This is because the twentieth century saw a dramatic expansion in the size of the electorate (men and women from the age of 21 were permitted to vote from 1928; this was lowered to 18 in 1969). For governments to stay in power they have to be seen to be sensitive to public opinion. This can have an impact on military strategy because governments are keen to minimise casualties, which means they employ military tactics which minimise their likelihood, such as using drones and surgical air strikes (highly targeted bombing raids), even when it is arguable whether these are the most appropriate military solution. Negative public opinion (heavily influenced by media reporting) also encouraged military withdrawal in 2009 from the Iraq War, before the region was adequately stabilised (see page 103). However, the power of public opinion should not be exaggerated; anti-war demonstrations, however strong and well supported, frequently achieve very little.

HOW DID THE CIVILIAN EXPERIENCE OF WARFARE CHANGE IN THE MODERN ERA?

1. Make a copy of the Venn diagram. Record similarities and differences between the ways in which civilians have been affected by warfare during the modern era. Try to include information about: attitudes to war, impact on daily life, government controls, media reporting, propaganda and censorship.

2. Complete the final row of your Knowledge Organiser table (see page 87) about the civilian experience of warfare.

3. Write a few sentences in the final column of your Knowledge Organiser table describing the pattern of change.

4. Add to your factor sheets on Governments and individuals and Attitudes in society (see page 87). Note the key features, and briefly describe the impact they have had on warfare.

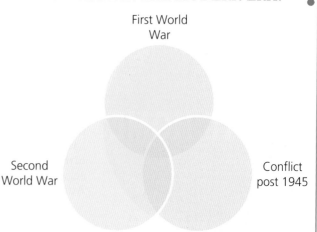

First World War

Second World War

Conflict post 1945

5.10 Case study: The invasion of Iraq, 2003

This chapter has shown that rapid and dramatic changes took place in the nature of warfare during the modern era. Just how different had warfare become by 2000?

- Had modern weaponry completely transformed warfare?
- Were there any continuities in the tactics and problems facing troops at war?

To try to answer such questions we will look at your final case study: the Iraq War that began in 2003.

Who was involved in the 2003 Iraq War?

The invasion of Iraq was led by US troops. Britain sent significant numbers of military personnel (almost 40,000 from the Army, Royal Airforce and Royal Navy), but the US deployed almost four times this number. Troops were equipped with a wide range of modern weapons, giving them enormous firepower and precision targeting. They faced an Iraqi Army of approximately 375,000, but with mostly outdated weaponry dating back to the Cold War era.

WHY THE INVASION OF IRAQ?

The purpose of the invasion (codenamed Operation Iraqi Freedom) was to depose the Iraqi dictator Saddam Hussein, whom it was feared was developing Weapons of Mass Destruction (WMDs), including nuclear, chemical and biological weapons, that might be used to attack neighbouring countries and to support international terrorism against America and its allies. It was part of the US President George Bush's 'war on terror' (see page 102).

What happened during the invasion?

The Allies used 'shock and awe' tactics to invade Iraq, meaning that they used their overwhelming firepower to dominate and make rapid progress against the Iraqi military. The main elements of the invasion were:

- Extensive surveillance of the location and nature of Iraqi territory, particularly of key missile and defence sites. A lot of this surveillance was carried out by UVAs or drones.
- Air strikes (beginning some weeks before the invasion) against key Iraqi defence, missile and communications sites.
- An armoured infantry advance (using tanks and armoured personnel carriers), supported by aircraft, to achieve a rapid advance on key cities, particularly Baghdad (the Iraqi capital) and Basra (the main British objective).

It took only sixteen days for US troops to capture Baghdad, and within 21 days most of the key Iraqi cities had been occupied by Allied troops. Saddam Hussein was finally captured in December 2003 and subsequently tried and executed for war crimes in 2006.

How effective were Allied weapons?

Allied weaponry performed well, although it was not invulnerable. The British Challenger 2 tanks were able to make rapid progress and offered excellent protection to their crews. Only two of these tanks were lost in the invasion (one due to friendly fire). The Americans lost sixteen tanks, with 35 more damaged. Most were damaged by Iraq rocket propelled grenades (RPGs) in close-quarter fighting in urban centres.

But not all infantry were so well protected. Many infantry travelled in armoured personnel vehicles, such as Scimitars, carrying out reconnaissance patrols, but these offered little protection for the crews against rockets and small arms fire or improvised explosive devices (IEDs).

▲ Household Cavalry Regiment take fuel, water and food on board a scimitar tank in Southern Iraq, April 2003

In the invasion the casualties were 139 US and 33 UK dead. Iraqi civilian casualties are estimated at between 3200 and 7200.

THE INVASION OF IRAQ

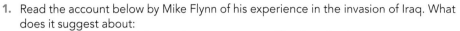

1. Read the account below by Mike Flynn of his experience in the invasion of Iraq. What does it suggest about:
   a) the effectiveness of the modern weapons used by the Allies?
   b) how good communications help infantry in battle?
   c) the problems still faced by infantry in battle, and the reasons for these problems?

B An account of the invasion of Iraq by Mick Flynn taken from his book *Bullet Magnet,* published in 2010. Flynn was traveling in a scimitar in a group of four vehicles that were part of an armoured reconnaissance patrol on 28 March 2003.

A mortar bomb exploded about 200m to our rear with an almighty bang! We'd run right up onto the Iraqi position and we were under direct enemy fire [from an armoured personnel carrier armed with machine gun and anti-tank missiles]. The metal rain was creeping ever-closer to our vehicle. But [our] scimitar's new laser aiming and ranging system was deadly accurate: I gave him the order. 'Fire!' … I could see our rounds [successfully] exploding on and around the Iraqis.

… I wanted some air support … [but only specific forward air controllers can call in air support so as to minimise the risk of friendly fire incidents] When our forward air controller was happy the target was a safe distance from all friendly forces, and that it was confirmed as hostile, he called in the [aircraft by radio]. A few minutes later, a pair of aircraft came screaming up. Popping out a constant stream of brilliant orange infra-red decoy flares, they wheeled around ready to run in on the [enemy] rocket launcher. The only problem being, they couldn't actually see it among the trees [after several attempts the aircraft missed their targets and returned to base].

[The scimitars were then confronted by an Iraqi tank.] At the same time as I saw the tank, it saw us: the turret slewed round, and the gun laid on our position … the tank opened fire and the explosion shook the scimitar to its metal bones … we radioed for assistance. Then there was a deep roar of jets from the sky. I looked up to see the unmistakable silhouette of an A-10 [aircraft] looming up … it carried antitank missiles, rockets, bombs and … rotary cannon … that fires a concentrated storm of depleted uranium rounds that can mince armour at more than 60 rounds per second. … [But] what were the A-10 pilots aiming at? As that thought struck home, the pit of my stomach dropped away. I heard someone [over the radio] shout on the net 'we're being engaged by A-10s! Check fire! Check fire! Check fire!' The check fire command tells every unit and call sign on your side to cease fire immediately … anyone can make the call, but you have to make it in a dire emergency. With a terrible sinking feeling, I realised the A-10 pilots weren't patched into the assault brigade radio net. They were unable to hear. [Two of the Scimitars in the group were hit and three British troops were seriously injured and one was killed.]

… I [had to] switch my attention back onto the enemy armour … I had three Armour Piercing Sabot rounds loaded ready to fire. 'Sabot' is extremely effective when it comes to destroying enemy armour. A sabot round is a long thin dart of extremely dense, heavy metal or depleted uranium … travelling at hypersonic speed, the metal arrow strikes a tiny area of the enemy armour, vapourises in on contact and punches through. We'd fired at least 20 rounds and I still hadn't seen a hit … then I saw one of our rounds strike home … the tank stopped dead in its tracks and I watched the crew dismount and run away. What about the second tank … after a slight pause it started to roll forward again.

From invasion to insurgency

Although the invasion of Iraq was rapid and successful in defeating the Iraqi military, gaining control of the cities proved much more difficult. Violent attacks on Allied troops by anti-American **insurgents** quickly escalated, as did conflict between rival Iraqi militant groups who sought to establish control. This type of warfare against small militant groups, rather than against a country's legitimate armed forces, is known as insurgency.

Much of the violence took the form of **guerrilla** or terrorist activities against US and British troops. They included ambushes by hit and run gunmen, car bombs, roadside improvised explosive devices (IEDs) and **suicide bombers**. The insurgents usually fought in the cities, making good use of their knowledge of the local environment and blending in with civilians. All this made it particularly difficult for the Allies to defeat the insurgents (see page 95).

The insurgency became unmanageable, and Allied military casualties steadily rose far higher than the numbers killed in the invasion of Iraq. Public opinion in Britain became increasingly hostile to the continuation of the war. After some, but not complete, success in reducing the insurgency, and transferring power to the new Iraqi military, British troops withdrew from Iraq in 2009 (the US withdrew in 2010). The casualties from 2003 to the final withdrawal numbered 179 British dead and 4400 US dead and 32,000 wounded.

The difficulty in dealing with Iraq insurgency highlighted that for all their effectiveness there is a limit to what modern high-tech weapons can achieve. It has led to further calls for an increase in the role of specialist counterinsurgency troops and tactics.

▲ Fighting insurgents in urban centres proved a difficult task for the Allied militaries

HOW FAR HAD WAR CHANGED BY 2003? ?

1. What evidence is there from the Iraq War that modern high-tech weaponry had changed the nature of warfare? Think about:
   - the strength of the weapons used
   - precision targeting
   - drones.

2. Did the Iraq War show any fundamental continuities with previous wars? Think about:
   - use of combined arms tactics
   - need for infantry on the ground
   - problems with communications.

3. Write a paragraph with your thoughts on how far modern weaponry had transformed the nature of warfare by 2003.

5.11 Reaching a judgement

Let's now return to the big Enquiry Question for this chapter:

'Developments in science, technology and communications were the main reason for rapid changes to the nature of warfare in the modern era.' How far do you agree? Explain your answer.

This question asks you to reach a judgement on **how far** science, technology and communications were the most important factor in explaining changes in warfare. The table and activities below will help you do this.

Main changes	Evidence of the role of science, technology and communications in explaining the changes in warfare	Evidence of the role of other factors in explaining the changes in warfare
• a huge number of new types of weapons • weapons increasingly more powerful and accurate • substantial advances in communications enabling more rapid and reliable communications on the battlefield		
• significant variations in the size of British armies – from the largest ever (in the two world wars) to declining numbers from the 1980s • increased specialisation and professionalisation of troops		
• conscription in the two world wars • increased specialised training		
• greatest intensity of civilian involvement and experience of war in the two world wars • fear of nuclear war in Cold War and terrorist threat from 1970s • increased media coverage of wars		

1. Draw a large copy of the table above.

2. Fill in the second column of the table by adding evidence where appropriate to show how science, technology and communications explain the changes in warfare. Use the factor sheet you created for 'Science, technology and communications' on page 87 to help you.

3. Fill in the third column of the table by adding evidence where appropriate to show how the other factors explain the changes in warfare. Use the factor sheets you created on page 87 to help you.

4. The factors often work together to bring about changes. Suggest some explanations of where the factors worked together to bring about changes? You can draw a factor map and label arrows to show this if you wish.

5. Place the three factors in order from the most to the least important in explaining the changes which took place in each of the following topics:
   – weapons
   – composition of armies
   – recruitment and training of combatants
   – experience of civilians

6. Explain how important each of the factors was in creating changes in warfare.
   This brief answer is now your overall answer to the question.

Communicating your answer

Remember that it is important to think carefully about how you are going to organise your answer before you begin to write.

As a **how far** question you will need to show that you can evaluate the evidence **for** and **against** the statement that science, technology and communications were the most important cause of change in warfare in the modern era. You could write your answer with a **for** and **against** structure with a conclusion in which you evaluate and present your own judgement. Alternatively you could organise your answer by topics, evaluating the relative importance of the different factors in explaining change in each. You will find further guidance in the writing guide on pages 162–76.

Now write your answer to the enquiry question.

Practice question

1. Explain **one** way in which communications on the battlefield during the Battle of the Somme (1916) were similar to those at the Battle of Waterloo (1815).
2. Explain why the methods of recruitment to the British Army changed so much between 1900 and 2000.
3. 'The impact of war on civilians' lives has been enormous in the modern era.' How far do you agree with this statement? Explain your answer.

Visible learning: Revise and remember

Test yourself

Now have a go at testing yourself to help make all that knowledge stick! Have a go at these questions. Remember there will be some questions from previous chapters too – see how much you remember.

1 What two main formations did the infantry use at the Battle of Waterloo?	2 Explain two ways in which the Crimean War suggested a new type of warfare and two ways in which it showed continuities with previous wars.	3 Explain two innovations in weapons that took place between 1850 and 1900.	4 In what year did the Battle of the Somme take place?
5 Explain three reasons why the British casualties were so high on the first day of the Battle of the Somme.	6 Explain three similarities between the civilian experience of war in Britain during the First and Second World Wars.	7 In what war was radar first used? For what?	8 List four weapons used by the Allies during the Iraq invasion in 2003.

Now, set some questions yourself.

The Big Story

Now it's time to return for a final time to your big chart summarising the main points of the Big Story. Fill in the remaining columns for the period 1900 to the present day. Remember you don't need lots of detail, just summarise the main points.

	1250–1500	1500–1700	1700–1900	1900–present
Weapons				
Composition of armies (number, type and tactics of combatants)				
Recruitment and training of combatants				
Experience of civilians				

6 Conclusion: identifying patterns of change and continuity

Congratulations – you have finished your study of almost 800 years of history! That's a lot of history. You now have a good understanding of the changes (and continuities) that took place in warfare between c.1250 and the present.

The table below gives a very basic summary of the main developments in the nature and experience of warfare. You probably have a similar, even more detailed table that you created as part of your 'revise and remember' work throughout in the book.

Topic	1250–1500	1500–1700
Weapons	<ul><li>swords</li><li>lances</li><li>spears</li><li>longbow</li><li>crossbows</li><li>cannon (from c.1320)</li></ul>	<ul><li>muskets (matchlock and flintlock)</li><li>artillery (cannon)</li><li>pistols</li><li>pikes</li><li>swords</li></ul>
Composition of armies (number, type and tactics of combatants)	<ul><li>knights</li><li>infantry the major proportion of the army (increasingly longbow men)</li><li>no permanent army</li></ul>	<ul><li>cavalry</li><li>infantry the major proportion of the army (musketeers and pike men)</li><li>artillery (very small in number)</li><li>permanent army from 1660</li></ul>
Recruitment and training of combatants	<ul><li>knights from social elites: feudal summons, voluntary service, contracts (indentures)</li><li>infantry initially compulsion (Commissions of Array) but later contracts (indentures) especially longbow men</li><li>no official training but encouragement to archery practice</li><li>elite chivalric culture emphasised the importance of military prowess through tournaments and jousts</li></ul>	<ul><li>cavalry from social elites</li><li>infantry: Commissions of Array and conscription in Civil Wars</li><li>after 1660 permanent army, made up of professional paid soldiers</li><li>increased emphasis on drill training, particularly for infantry</li></ul>
Experience of civilians	<ul><li>could be compelled to serve in armies</li><li>food requisitioned (purveyance)</li><li>provided shelter for troops</li><li>taxes paid to fund wars</li><li>victims of raid and pillage (mainly border and coastal areas)</li><li>received little news about wars</li></ul>	<ul><li>could be compelled to serve in armies</li><li>food requisitioned</li><li>provided shelter to troops</li><li>taxes directly imposed to fund wars</li><li>victims of raid and pillage, especially during Civil Wars</li><li>received some news about wars through propaganda (printed news pamphlets)</li></ul>

Identifying patterns of change and continuity

Now you have a broad view of the entire period from c.1250 to the present, it becomes easier to identify patterns of change across the time periods. Trends become more apparent, as do possible turning points.

Look back to page 6 to remind yourselves of the patterns of change you might find. It is worth thinking a little bit about what these terms mean.

■ a **turning point** is a decisive or very significant change (usually a change in the direction of a development) that often has long-lasting results.

■ a **trend** is usually a gradual, predictable change in the same direction. For example, it might be a weapon that continues to be used, but by an increased number of troops, or gradual technical improvements of a weapon.

■ a **continuity** describes something that stays the same.

Now, using the chart below (or your own version) have a go at identifying different patterns of change in the nature and experience of warfare.

1700–1900	1900–present
• muskets (flintlock) • artillery • rifles • swords • pistols • machine guns	• rifles • tanks • machine guns • nuclear weapons • artillery • Precision guided missiles • aircraft • Unmanned aerial vehicles (drones) • chemical weapons (gas)
• cavalry • infantry the major proportion of the army (musketeers and riflemen) • artillery (an increasing number)	• infantry the major proportion of the army • artillery • logistics increasingly important • growth of specialised troops
• cavalry from social elites – purchase system • infantry professional paid soldiers (service period typically 21 years), but low pay • drill training important for infantry	• conscription during First and Second World Wars and National Service, 1948–60 • professional, paid volunteer troops for most of the period • specialised training has become increasingly important.
• provided shelter and food to troops, but less so as barracks were built • taxes increased to fund wars, e.g. income tax • received news (and photographs) of foreign wars more quickly due to improvements in communications (telegraph)	• conscripts in First and Second World Wars • victims of aerial bombings in First and Second World Wars • women into factories and other essential war work in First and Second World Wars • food shortages in First and Second World Wars • propaganda and censorship in reporting in First and Second World War, but in more recent conflicts increased media coverage and less censorship due to improvements in communications • fear of nuclear war (during Cold War) • fear of terrorism

IDENTIFYING PATTERNS OF CHANGE

1. Identify two continuities and two trends across at least two periods in the nature or experience of warfare. Write a few sentences to support your view.

2. Identify two possible turning points in the nature or experience of warfare. Write a few sentences to support your view. You will need to refer backwards to show why it was a big change and forwards to show evidence of lasting change.

3. In what period/periods does the greatest amount of change appear to have taken place? Give reasons for your view.

4. Explain one way in which the experience of civilians was:
   a) similar in the 1400s and the 1600s
   b) different in the 1700s and the 1900s

6. Explain one way in which the recruitment and training of combatants was:
   a) similar in the 1700s and the 1900s
   b) different in the 1400s and the 1700s.

A bit more on turning points

You might get asked in the exam to explain if or why something was an important turning point in a particular topic. Let's have a look at a few changes that might be considered to have been significant turning points in the nature and experience of warfare (the page numbers indicate where you will find relevant information in the rest of the book):

- the introduction of gunpowder weapons (particularly matchlock muskets) from the late fifteenth century (page 34)
- the establishment of the New Model Army in 1645 (page 41)
- the invention and use of railways from the nineteenth century (page 64)
- the introduction of machine guns from the late nineteenth/early twentieth centuries (page 88)
- the development of radio (enabling communication with and between troops in the field from the Second World War) (page 92)
- the development of nuclear weapons (from 1945) (page 89).

To make a case for something being a turning point you will need to:

- explain how it led to a decisive change in weapons / composition of armies / recruitment and training of combatants / experience of civilians. You will need to refer back to *before* to show how it changed things.
- provide evidence that the change was long lasting.

TURNING POINTS ❓

1. Divide the class into groups. Each group should take one of the developments above and make a case for that development being an important turning point.

2. Think of arguments as to why each of the developments above might *not* be seen as a turning point. Clues:
   - Did anything stay the same despite these developments?
   - How long did it take to bring about significant change? Can something that takes a very long time to change things be called a turning point? This is probably a matter of opinion, but worth considering.

3. Which of the developments above do you think brought about the most important changes? Explain your answer.

Science, technology and communications: a driver for change?

You may have noticed that all the turning points you looked at on the previous page were related to the factor of **Science, technology and communications**. This seems to have been a particularly important factor in driving changes in warfare. Here are just a few examples:

- The shift in tactics during the sixteenth and seventeenth centuries when infantry came to be deployed in squares, rather than the linear formations of the Middle Ages, was largely a result of the new dominance of the musket (page 38).
- The decline in the role of cavalry on the battlefield, which had become obsolete by the early twentieth century, was mainly a result of developments in science and technology which increased the power, range and numbers of artillery on the battlefield (page 72).
- The increased use of radio from the 1920s made possible new tactics of combined arms (the co-ordinated use of infantry, motorised and air power) that have remained central to the tactics of modern armies up to the present (page 90).
- The development of motorised road transport transformed the logistical supply of armies from the 1930s, making possible large, mobile campaigns since the Second World War (see page 91).
- The increased specialisation of modern military personnel was a direct consequence of the growth of specialised weaponry that required particular knowledge to operate (page 94).
- The shrinkage in the size of the army after 1945 was a consequence of the development of nuclear weapons, as nuclear power, not mass armies, became the main military deterrent; it was no longer worth the expense of maintaining very large armies (page 89).

Does this mean that Science, technology and communications should be seen as the most important factor in driving change in warfare? Certainly it was a very important factor. But, there have been significant changes that have not depended on developments in Science, technology and communications. Here are some examples:

- The dominance of longbow men in the armies of the later Middle Ages was a change that did not depend on technological innovations in weaponry since the longbow had been in existence even in the early Middle Ages.
- The establishment of permanent standing armies from the 1660s owed more to developments in government than science and technology.
- Changes to the recruitment of officers in the nineteenth century with Cardwell's reforms were not a consequence of Science, technology and communications.

Science, technology and communications: not sufficient alone

Most major changes do appear to be connected to Science, technology and communications. But this does not mean that on its own, the factor was enough to explain these changes. Other factors also played an important role. We can visualise how the factors often worked together in a factor map.

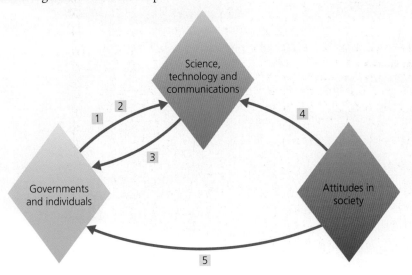

LINKING SCIENCE, TECHNOLOGY AND COMMUNICATIONS

Can you think of explanations that might explain the links between Science, technology and communications and each of the other factors?

Science, technology and communications often worked with the other factors to bring about changes in warfare. For example:

1. **Government** was often responsible for funding the development or adoption of new weapons, communications or transport systems. There is a strong correlation between increased government investment in the military in wartime and an increase in innovations in weapons technologies (see page 90).

2. **Government** might also act as a block on the use of particular weapons, for example, chemical and nuclear weapons – fearing the political, social and economic consequences of their use.

3. **Science, technology and communications** produced new weapons which *enabled* new tactical possibilities, encouraging **individuals** to develop new tactics. There was often a time lag between the invention of a new weapon and the development of tactics that made best use of the weapon's capabilities, as with the deployment of tanks in the First World War (see page 83).

4 and 5. **Attitudes in society** have impacted on the use of weapons as much as their technological capabilities. Knights of the Middle Ages disparaged missile weapons as unchivalrous, contributing to their continued use of sword and lance rather than arrows. More recently, civilian discontent at military personnel and civilian casualties have increased the likelihood of the government prioritising the use of precision air strikes and drones as a way to minimise casualties (although this is not always the most effective way to counter guerrilla tactics).

We can therefore conclude that Science, technology and communications was a particularly important factor in explaining changes in warfare. But, it rarely brought about immediate dramatic change as new weapons tended to be introduced gradually (often due to the costs involved), and it took time for their best tactic uses to be realised. Ultimately, Science, technology and communications were rarely sufficient on their own, without the other factors, to explain the changes that have taken place in the nature and experience of warfare between c.1250 and the present.

Practice questions

1. 'The introduction of cannon in the fourteenth century was the most important change in the nature of warfare in the Middle Ages.' How far do you agree? Explain your answer.

2. 'The widespread adoption of muskets in the sixteenth century was a significant turning point in the nature of warfare.' How far do you agree? Explain your answer.

3. 'Developments in air transport and aerial support transformed the nature of warfare in the twentieth century.' How far do you agree? Explain your answer.

4. 'Science, technology and communications was the most important factor in explaining changes in the nature and experience of warfare.' How far do you agree? Explain your answer.

Part 2: The historic environment: London and the Second World War, 1939–45

What is this historic environment unit about?

This unit counts for 10 per cent of your GCSE course. It is linked to the thematic unit on Warfare and British Society in this book in two ways:

1. You will use your knowledge of warfare in the early twentieth century in this unit.
2. The enquiry approach you used to study 'Warfare' will help considerably because this unit is designed to develop your skills in historical enquiry – from asking questions to communicating your answer. We spent a lot of time on enquiry in 'Warfare' to prepare you for this.

There are also three major differences with your work on the thematic unit on Warfare:

1. This unit focuses on a single place, a historic site – London.
2. It focuses on a very short period, the years 1939–45.
3. It looks much more closely at the contemporary sources and how we use them in an enquiry.

> This book does not provide all the material you will use for this unit. This is deliberate! We have given you the structure for your enquiry and plenty of information and sources but your teacher will add more sources, perhaps relating to people's experiences in London during the war.

ENQUIRY ?

Describe in your own words the enquiry process you use to investigate a new historical topic.

1.1 War children – questions and sources

When I was researching this part of the book, I came across the phrase 'dead end kids' on a website dedicated to local history in the East End of London (www.whitechapelsociety. com). The website explained that during the **Blitz**, the large-scale air raids on London carried out by the German **Luftwaffe** in 1940–41, groups of children and teenagers had banded together and worked as unofficial firefighters and air-raid wardens. I wondered if there were any pictures. So, I used an internet images search to look for 'dead end kids'. This first search was a red herring, as this was the name given to a group of child-actors in Hollywood in the 1930s – I later discovered that the Wapping 'Dead End Kids' had copied the name of the gang of young film stars. My second search term: 'Wapping dead end kids Blitz' brought up the picture you see here, with the caption 'Ten-year-old Shamus O'Brien, mascot of the 'Dead End Kids'. I found this picture really moving – the way that this boy is grinning, the hat that is far too big for his head, and the man's coat that is too big for his shoulders. I wanted to know why these young people were taking on the wartime roles that we would expect adults to have. All of a sudden I was hooked on their story, I wanted to know more – this was my starting point for exploring life in London during the Second World War.

▲ A photo of Shamus O'Brien from the *Picture Post*, 1941

This is the sort of thing that happens when you start to investigate history for yourself. Sometimes it's a note in a book or diary. Sometimes it happens when you find something that doesn't fit in with what you thought you already knew, and sometimes it is a face in a picture that grabs your attention, and makes you ask questions. I wanted to know more about this boy Shamus, and the Dead End Kids. I was surprised to read his story because I had thought that children were evacuated from London early in the war.

Developing your enquiry – names

When we are studying historical sources, even those from the age of digitisation and electronic records, we need to remember that it is humans who are making most of the records – writing or typing names and data onto pieces of paper or into databases. This means that names of people, places, dates and times of events are sometimes recorded in one way in one source, and in a different way in another source.

Where can I start? Well, an internet search can only get me so far. The image of Shamus had a caption which told me that it was taken for a photographic newspaper called the *Picture Post* in April 1941, but also that it was never published. I was able to find some more names of the other young people involved, and some more pictures, but these could not answer the many questions that I had about the Dead End Kids.

ASKING QUESTIONS

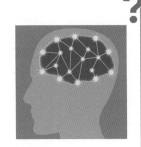

One of the skills you practised in the thematic unit on Warfare was asking good historical questions. Asking questions is an important part of this unit because it plays a part in your GCSE examination. So, we'll pause here, and ask you to ask some questions.

Make a list of questions you want to ask about London during the Second World War. They could be about the Dead End Kids, or about the experience of others living in London. Use the question starters below to help you.

When ...?   What ...?   Why ...?   How ...?   What happened ...?   Where ...?
What effects ...?   How significant ...?   Did it really ...?   Who ...?   Did they ...?

Asking questions, identifying sources

This page shows you some of the questions you could ask about life in London during the Second World War, together with some of the sources you might use to answer those questions. Both questions and sources are here because one aim of this unit is to work out which sources might be most helpful in answering individual questions. You know by now that sources are not 'useful' or 'useless' in themselves – their usefulness depends on what question you are trying to answer. For example, one source may be very useful for learning about the techniques used to raise morale, but completely unhelpful if you want to find out about how many shelters were built in back gardens.

QUESTIONS AND SOURCES ?

Choose two of the questions below or from your list of questions from page 113. Which of the sources below do you think might be most useful for answering each of your two questions? Explain why you think each source might be useful.

We do not expect you to know the 'right' answers at this stage. This task is to get you thinking about what kinds of information *might* be in the sources and which questions they *may* help with. In the rest of this unit you will get to know most of these sources and find out which questions they are most useful for answering.

Some questions

- Why was London under attack?
- What had happened to the evacuated children?
- Were there enough 'proper' firefighters and volunteers?
- What was the effect of the bombing on the people of London?
- How did the Government try to protect people?

- Who were the Dead End Kids?
- Why did they choose that name for their gang?
- Why hadn't these children been evacuated?
- What happened to the Dead End Kids? Did they survive?
- Why did they get their pictures taken?

Sources

- Official records of individuals, e.g. birth certificates
- National newspaper reports
- Newsreels
- Local Council Records
- Posters and information pamphlets printed by the Government

- National census documents and records
- Photographs
- Reports on morale sent to the Government by 'Mass Observation'
- Diaries written at the time
- Memoirs by those who lived through the Blitz

Organising your understanding of the sources

Why did we set up the activities on the opposite page? It is because this unit is about how you undertake a historical enquiry and about the kinds of sources we use as well as being about London during the Second World War. Therefore you are going to use a variety of sources and learn different things from them. The first thing you will learn is the most obvious – the sources will:

■ Increase your knowledge and understanding of the Second World War and London's part in it.

However, other things you learn about the sources are just as important and will be tested in your examination. You will find out:

■ What kinds of sources help us investigate London during the Second World War 1939–45.
■ Which sources are most useful for investigating individual aspects of life in London at that time, and for answering particular questions.

To keep track of the sources and what we can learn from them we suggest you use a Knowledge Organiser such as the table below, perhaps on A3 paper or as a Word document. You may wish to keep additional, detailed notes to support the summary in your table. Completing the table is an important reminder that this unit is about enquiry and sources as well as about London during the Second World War.

Here is a guide to completing your table over the next few weeks:

1. After you have worked on a section of this unit identify which sources you have used and fill in a row of this table for each source. Decide which type of source each items is, e.g. is it a personal account, photograph, etc.? The text will remind you to do this.
2. Put the category in column 1 and the example (e.g. a newspaper article about the Dead End Kids) in column 2.
3. Then complete columns 3–6 for the source.

You may use sources that fit more than one category of source or you may use other kinds of sources not listed below. Don't worry if sources do not fit neatly – historical research is unpredictable and you often find things that you don't expect. That's one of the reasons why it's enjoyable!

It is also important to remember that one source will not tell us everything we want to know. We should always try to use a combination of sources. This is because each source may add different information, perhaps because different people created them at different times, or because they are different types of source – a photograph and a diary perhaps. Using a variety of sources also allows us to check what each is saying as we always need to ask whether the evidence in a source is typical of the evidence as a whole.

Types of sources N – National L – Local	Examples of this type of source you have used	Which questions can this source help answer?	What information does it provide to help with those questions?	Which questions does this source NOT help with or why do we have to use it cautiously?	Which other kind of source might you use in combination with this source?

Dead ends and new directions

I'd like to know more about the lad in the picture on page 113, and the Dead End Kids. Usually I'd look at the census. The census is a survey of the population that the government has carried out every ten years since 1801. The census is designed to help the Government collect taxes and plan the services that it needs to provide. It gives us a record of who was living in each house on every street, and what they did for work. However, census material is not released for 100 years. I therefore would not expect the 1931 census to be released until 2031. However, in fact, the 1931 census will never be released.

The story of the 1931 census teaches historians an important lesson – documents do not always survive. Censuses are collected on paper, and before computerisation they were collected and written onto lists, record books and maps. In 1942 a fire started in the warehouse where the records were stored. It was probably started by a cigarette smoked by one of the people employed to watch out for fires. The entire census was destroyed. The 1941 census never happened, because of the war. There was a national survey in 1939 so that the government could create the records it needed for a national identity card scheme – to combat German espionage, and to help organise rations and conscription. This led to further frustration for me. The 1939 survey is being digitised, and was only released just as I finished writing this section. However, you might be able to use it in your enquiries.

Though I could use an online search of deaths and births to trace the Dead End Kids, all I would get is a place and date of birth and death for each – these pieces of information are useful for checking other documents, but they wouldn't tell me anything about their wartime experiences.

Instead I turned to newspapers. Public libraries often have access to these, electronically or on paper. I found a reference to the Dead End Kids of Wapping in the *Reading Eagle* newspaper from June 1941. This is the earliest reference to the Kids that I can find – and it has in it many of the features that are found in later re-tellings – rescues and tragic deaths, and a reference to Patsie Duggan, the 'young truck driver' who led the gang. Patsy is also mentioned in a report from 1945 entitled 'The Duggans of Wapping', written by Mollie Panter-Downes, an American reporter for the *New Yorker* magazine. Panter-Downes tells the wider story of the Duggans' war. The article filled in some details that I was able to use to find out some more of the story.

Names and places – spellings in newspaper articles

Sometimes, and especially in news reports when things were written down by journalists for typing up later, names have different spellings in different reports or different records. The news stories about Patsy Duggan spell his name in two ways, but this doesn't mean that these are necessarily two different people – though sometimes it could!

Source A: An extract from an interview with Eileen Duggan, Patsy's sister, in 1945. From a newspaper article 'The Duggans of Wapping', written by American Journalist Mollie Panter-Downes, published in March 1945

The nights was awful in 1940 because the Jerries was trying to knock out the poor old East End because of the docks being so important, see. My brother Patsy wasn't in the Army then; 'e was at 'ome, working down at the docks, and 'e got together a bunch of the boys round 'Ermatige Wall and started training them for fire spotting. They was all ages, from nineteen to thirteen – all boys except Maureen, and they let 'er in because she's always round with their gang, and as nippy as any of them. They called themselves the Dead End Kids, and pretty soon they wasn't only spotting fires, they was fighting them. They clubbed together and bought 'atchets and 'oses, and the A.R.P. people give them tin 'ats, and when an incendiary drops anywhere in our district, off they go to it with all their fireman's stuff piled up on a barrow.

Later in the report the reporter goes on to describe in detail some of the Kids' adventures, and tells us that Patsy's cousin Leslie was one of the Kids who died while fighting fires, along with two others, Ronnie Ayres and Bert Eden. Panter-Downes also tells us the names of Patsy's brothers and his father. These details enabled me to use the online databases of births and deaths to find out that Patsy survived the war, and died in 1990 in Kent. Though I knew that Patsy had a long life, I seemed to have reached the end in my research about the 'Dead End Kids' of Wapping.

Source B

▲ A picture of the Dead End Kids 'rushing to the scene of a fire' in the East End in April 1941. All these pictures of 'the Kids' were taken by Bert Hardy, a talented photographer of ordinary life during and after the War

But sometimes in history one question leads to others. As I read through the other news reports which had the phrase 'dead end kids' in them, an interesting picture and a new direction in my research started to appear. It seemed that the name 'dead end kids' was often used to describe children very negatively. In fact, the newspaper headlines about these children much more often went like this:

GREAT ARMY OF LEFT BEHIND CHILDREN
Daily Mail, 5 November 1940

DEAD END KIDS SPEND LIVES UNDERGROUND
Daily Mail, 6 November 1940

LONDON'S DEAD END KIDS MUST GO BACK TO SCHOOL – BY ORDER
Daily Mail, 4 December 1940

FLOOD OF CHILD CRIME [...] SWEEPING THE COUNTRY
Daily Mail, 11 September 1941

So, for the editor of the *Daily Mail* at least, children in London were a problem, and were thought of as 'left behind' and criminals. I had thought that all the children in London were evacuated out of London in the first weeks of the war in 1939, but it seems that perhaps large numbers were 'left behind'. Why did so many stay? What problems did this cause? Why didn't the *Daily Mail* pick up the heroic story of the Dead End Kids that so interested the photographer Bert Hardy?

THE DUGGANS OF WAPPING

1. Why do you think the story of the Duggans was so interesting to readers in England and America?
2. Why has Panter-Downes left off the 'h' from the front of so many words?
3. Find out what the following terms mean.

   firewatching   ARP   Jerries   incendiaries
4. Why did the Dead End Kids choose this name for their gang?
5. What can you learn from the extract about the ways in which the Government and people tried to cope with the bombings that it faced in 1941?
6. What other questions would this kind of document be useful for? Explain why it would be useful.

117

Visible learning: Planning my enquiry

I know a little about some of the Dead End Kids, but I have a lot of questions. How do I plan my way from knowing a little and having lots of questions to finding the answers and knowing a lot more?

Stage 1 What do I know?

This is a summary of my main starting points:

- During the Second World War some children were 'left behind'.
- Some people were worried about the 'left behind' children.
- Bombing raids on London in 1940 were terrible.
- People were killed during the bombing raids.
- The Germans dropped incendiary bombs on London.

Stage 2 What do I want to find out?

I need a set of questions as targets when I do my research so I know when I've completed my enquiry:

- What made London an important target?
- What did the Government do to prepare for the bombing and to protect people?
- Why had the evacuation left so many children behind?
- What kinds of weapons and defences were used?
- Which places faced the worst bombing? Why?
- What effects did the bombing have on everyday life and on the buildings of London?

But I must be flexible and add to my questions if I find unexpected information.

Visible learning

Tackling new topics with confidence

I use this plan to help me explore any historical topic that is new to me. Starting to investigate a new topic can feel worrying, like starting completely from scratch, because dates, names and events are different *but* it's important to remember that *how* we study every topic is very similar. We use this same plan whether we're exploring Roman history or the Second World War. We have shown you this approach very visibly so you feel more confident whenever you start to tackle a new topic. Look back to pages 114–15 for more detail on how to carry out an enquiry.

Letting you into a secret

I have written a few history books, and I was a history teacher for more than ten years. You might think I must know everything there is to know about history, but that's not true. The 'secret' is that there are quite a few historical topics I don't know much about at all because I have never had to study or write about them. Though I know quite a lot about the international situation during the Second World War, I am not an expert in every aspect of what happened to London during the war. I therefore need to find out a lot more about the war, and about London in order to start to find the answers for my questions about the 'Dead End Kids' and the other 'left behind' children.

Stage 3 Where will I research and find the answers?

There are two kinds of sources I can use.

1. Books, articles and websites written by experts on the war

 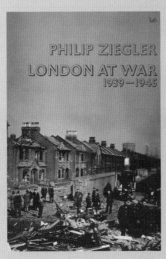

2. Sources from the war – photographs; accounts written by citizens, Government officials, ARP wardens and others

Stage 4 How will I do this research?

I need to:

- Have my questions in mind so I always read with a purpose – to answer those questions.
- Keep careful notes, using my own Knowledge Organisers, so that I don't end up with a heap of disorganised information.
- Make sure the books I read and websites I use are really by experts. This means checking who wrote them and how they know what they're telling me.
- Ask questions about the sources I use. For example, is a photograph typical of conditions in London at that time, was the author present at the events he or she is describing, which are the most useful sources for each question?
- Remember that I may not be able to find exact and complete answers to all my questions so I need to use words such as 'probably',' in all likelihood', 'possibly'.
- There may be questions I can't answer at all!

- **Most of all I need to keep thinking! I might find unexpected information which prompts new questions or suggests I look in other books or records. I can't predict exactly what I'll find at the beginning of an enquiry. I need to remember that I'm allowed to change my mind about my answer to a question as I find out more.**

1.2 The context of London and the Second World War, 1939–45

Let's begin by exploring the location – London during the Second World War.

A QUICK HISTORY OF THE SECOND WORLD WAR

1. Read through the timeline on pages 120–21 once.
   a) Produce a living graph of the war like the one opposite to record the hopes and fears of Britons during the war.
   b) Then focus in on Londoners in particular and make a living graph for them. When would their hopes have peaked? When would they have felt most scared?

2. Discuss with a friend and see if you can divide the Second World War into different phases, or times when things seemed to be going better or worse.

3. Why might the bombing in 1940 stand out as being so terrible in Eileen Duggan's memory?

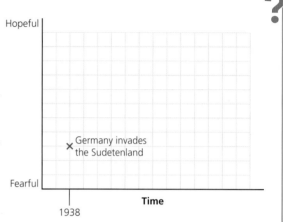

1938

German forces marched into Austria, then threatened the Sudetenland in Czechoslovakia. In London gas masks were given out to the population and mock gas attacks were carried out. Trenches were dug in parks and squares, to give some shelter in the case of air raids. British Prime Minister Neville Chamberlain travelled to Munich to meet Hitler. He agreed to Germany's take-over of the Sudetenland.

Information highlighted in blue refers to events that directly affect Londoners.

1939

In March Germany invaded the rest of Czechoslovakia. London's authorities hastily recruited wardens and volunteer firefighters in preparation for attack, and imposed a blackout, as well as organising the evacuation of thousands of children out of the city. Two million Anderson Shelters were distributed. On 1 September Germany invaded Poland. Britain and France declared war on 3 September.

September 1939–April 1940

The long period of Phoney War. For the eight months immediately after Britain and France entered the war, there were no major military land operations on the Western Front. Germany then quickly conquered Norway, Belgium, Holland and France. They used new tactics of armoured units moving quickly with air support, called Blitzkrieg or lightning-war.

Summer–Autumn 1940

Germany planned a sea-borne invasion of Britain but first tried to destroy Britain's air defences. The Battle of Britain was fought by British fighter planes against German bombers and fighters to stop this destruction.

Autumn–Winter 1940

As the weather changed, the window for a sea invasion closed and German tactics shifted to bombing towns and cities, a campaign which became known as the Blitz. Councils, Fire Authorities and the ARP wardens were close to being overwhelmed. Shelters were crowded, insanitary and often unsafe.

Spring 1941

A lull in the bombing in London ended on 10 May 1941 when the largest raid of the war took place. Almost 1500 people died, and 11,000 homes were destroyed.

Summer 1941

There were a few small raids in June and July, but when Germany attacked Russia in June 1941 it became clear that her attention had shifted away from Britain.

Autumn–Winter 1941

The Japanese attacked the American naval base at Pearl Harbor, and then took over American and British territory in Asia. Food shortages eased as supplies from America arrived. Diaries suggest that people in London turned their attention to the wider war, rather than just their own circumstances.

Spring 1942

Bad news continued. Defeats in North Africa and across Asia led to low morale, and a further shortage of material and food such as tin, rice, spices and rubber. ARP wardens and firefighters continued to train and to carry out mock gas attacks and bombings, but only scattered attacks occurred.

Autumn–Winter 1942

There was news of victories in North Africa, then celebrations when the German Army was defeated at El Alamein in Egypt.

1943

Sporadic small air raids continued. Enemy forces were slowly pushed back after a series of victories in North Africa, Russia and the Pacific. In the summer blackout restrictions were relaxed – lights in trains stayed on, as did traffic lights, and people were allowed to carry torches.

Spring 1944

Smaller-scale air attacks which Londoners called 'Little Blitz' faded as the Luftwaffe losses mounted up.

Summer–Autumn 1944

The **D-Day** landings in June and the fall of Rome to American troops made Londoners fear a large revenge attack. V1 and V2 'pilotless' weapons began falling in September 1944.

Spring 1945

By March the threat of air attack vanished as German airbases and **V-weapon** launch sites in Northern France were captured.

Summer 1945

On 8 May 1945 Germany surrendered. Crowds flocked to central landmarks like Trafalgar Square and Buckingham Palace to celebrate VE Day. VJ (Victory over Japan) followed in August.

WHY WASN'T LONDON A TARGET BEFORE SEPTEMBER 1940?

The long Phoney War ended with the attacks on Belgium, Holland and Luxembourg on 10 May 1940. For the rest of the summer of 1940 German fighters and bombers attacked RAF ground bases and aircraft. It wasn't until September that the first targeted raids on London took place. Why did the Luftwaffe take so long to target London? The answer isn't clear, but there are two possible reasons:

- Firstly, it seems that German military planners did not think that a 'knock out blow' to a capital city could quickly defeat a country. Their Blitzkrieg tactics actually meant using bombers as support for infantry and mechanised armies as they took enemy territory. Therefore, they did not see any military reason to target large cities unless these were also under attack from their infantry.

- Secondly, the historian George Quester has also suggested that both sides wanted to avoid bombing cities in the early days of the war as they were afraid of 'retaliation bombing' that would damage their own population and morale. Quester argues that Hitler only ordered attacks on London after Churchill ordered an attack on Berlin on 25 August to divert the Luftwaffe's attention from its attacks on British airfields and radar stations. If this was the case, it was effective. Three weeks after the British attack on Berlin, the Blitz started.

We need to know about the important places that made London a target, the places where the bombs usually fell, as well as the names of the **boroughs** that made up London. We should also look out for the parks and buildings where shelters and deep shelters were built, and the underground rail stations where thousands sheltered from the bombing raids.

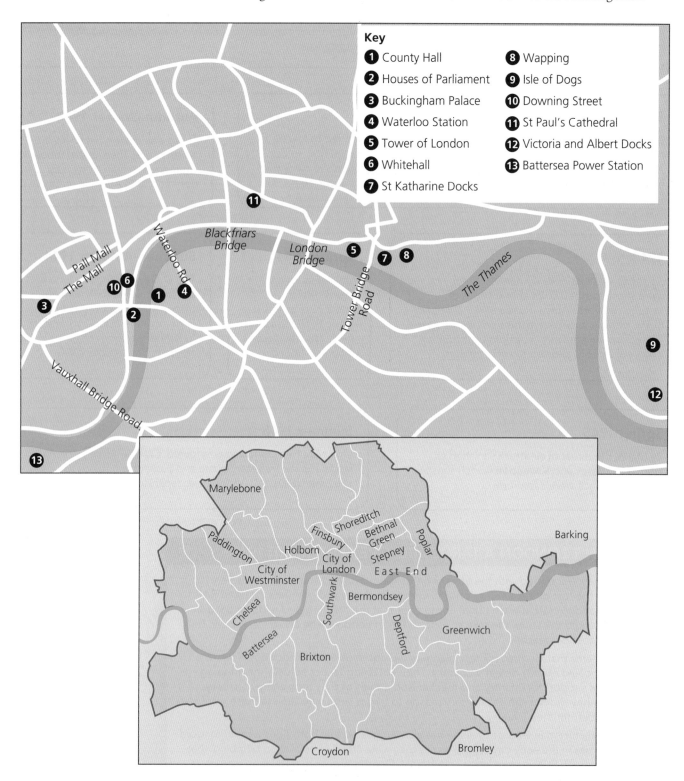

Key
1 County Hall
2 Houses of Parliament
3 Buckingham Palace
4 Waterloo Station
5 Tower of London
6 Whitehall
7 St Katharine Docks
8 Wapping
9 Isle of Dogs
10 Downing Street
11 St Paul's Cathedral
12 Victoria and Albert Docks
13 Battersea Power Station

▲ London and Central London in 1939 (since 1945 the boundaries and names of some of these boroughs have changed)

Four key places London during the Second World War

London is a very large place, and there are many areas that I could have chosen to write about. Investigating and writing your own history means that you sometimes have to decide not to follow up certain routes or opportunities. Sometimes this is because of space or time; sometimes because you can't find the information you need. In this case I have decided to focus on those areas that will give you a good idea of the variety of experiences in the war, as well as helping you understand why London was a target.

RECORDING YOUR KNOWLEDGE ABOUT THE DIFFERENT PARTS OF LONDON

Make a Knowledge Organiser to record the different reasons why each part of London was a target. Use a table like the one below. Write in any evidence that suggests each reason was important in those areas being targeted.

Place	Reason 1: To damage London's economy	Reason 2: To damage the population's morale	Reason 3: To damage the Government	Reason 4: To damage Britain's military
The East End				
Westminster				
The City of London				
The suburbs				

The East End

The East End (see the map on page 122) is the area on the north of the River Thames, to the east of the Tower of London, which is marked on the map. In 1939 it was a mixed area of dense housing, often in terraces or **tenement flats**; cinemas; theatres; pubs; shops; gas works; warehouses and factories. However, the most important targets were the docks, where food, raw materials and weaponry were loaded and unloaded. Wapping, where the Dead End Kids lived, was the riverside part of the borough of Stepney, which was one of the biggest boroughs of the East End, and is on a slight curving bend of the river just to the west of the famous loop which makes up the Isle of Dogs. The East End was the first part of London hit, during a mis-targeted raid in August 1940, and was then actively targeted during the first Blitz in 1940–41.

The East End was a focus of the attacks throughout the Blitz of the winter of 1940–41, and into the spring of 1941 because of the port of London, and because of its eastern position nearer the German air bases in northern France. In the 'Little Blitz' of January to April 1944, and the V1 and V2 rocket attacks of summer 1944 into the spring of 1945, the East End of London was hit badly again. Sources A and B are two people's recollections of the Blitz in the East End.

THE EAST END

1. What does Source A tell us about:
   a) Why this part of London was a target?
   b) What conditions were like in the shelters?
2. What does Source B tell us about the effects of the first attacks on ordinary Londoners?

Source A Gerry Michaels remembering how he and his family would shelter in a warehouse in Tilbury in Stepney during the raids, from the archive of the Museum of London

At eight years of age I, with my sister who was twelve, would gradually work our way to the front so that when the doors opened in we would rush to claim our bed spaces by spreading our blankets if possible against the wall in one of the empty loading bays. People who came late would have to spend the night sleeping on the rolls of unyielding newsprint or stacks of boxes of margarine. The latter wasn't so bad as gradually during the night the heat of their bodies would seep through the cartons softening the margarine which would gradually assume the shape of their bodies.

Source B Len Jones an East End resident, member of the Home Guard, and survivor of the war, from John Marriot's book *Beyond the Tower: A History of East London*, published in 2011

I went out to see how our house was, and when I got there the front door was lying back, and the glass of the windows had fallen in, and I could see the house had virtually disappeared. Inside, everything was blown to pieces, you could see it all by the red glow reflecting from the fires that were raging outside. Then I looked out the back and suddenly I realised that where my father's shed and workshop used to be, was just a pile of rubble, bricks. Then I saw two bodies, two heads sticking up and I recognised one head in particular; it was a Chinese man, Mr Say, he had one eye closed, and then I began to realise that he was dead.

Westminster

Westminster is home to Buckingham Palace, which was the residence of King George VI. The centre of national government was also at Whitehall, by the river in Westminster, and therefore the place where the war effort was organised. Downing Street, where the Prime Minister and Chancellor of the Exchequer still work, is also in this area and the Palace of Westminster nearby is where the Houses of Parliament sat during the war. Westminster wasn't directly targeted in the first few days of the Blitz. Buckingham Palace was hit on 13 September, but it wasn't until May 1941 that this part of London was heavily hit. On 10 May 1941, the last of the large raids of the Blitz, the House of Common's chamber was destroyed by a fire started by an **incendiary bomb** on the roof of the Palace of Westminster.

Source C

▲ Reporters inspecting the damage to the House of Commons chamber on the morning of 11 May 1941

Visible learning

Warning! Generalisations can be bad for your marks

Generalisations are big statements that, for example, can make conditions everywhere in London during the war sound the same. When we think of London during the Second World War several pictures might spring into our minds – perhaps the fires of the Blitz or hundreds of people bedding down for the night in a tube station. These things did happen at some times, but, as we have seen, not everywhere fitted into that generalisation. Some parts of London saw terrible damage during the Blitz, but were quiet afterwards. Others were affected much less. These pages tell you about variety as well as telling you what was unusual about some of the events in London during the war. Generalisations give us a 'general' picture, but we must always ask of any description or photograph, **'Was this really typical of experiences and conditions all over London during the War?'**

The City

The City of London is the area to the east of Westminster and covers the area that was the original walled Roman city. It is the financial centre of England, and contains important buildings such as the Bank of England, the Stock Exchange and important rail and telephone links, such as the Faraday Building which contained London's telephone exchange. You couldn't just dial a phone number in the 1940s; you had to talk to an operator to connect you with the person you needed to talk to, so this building was vital for communications. During the war these institutions kept the economy working, and the Bank raised money through **war bonds** to enable the Government to spend money on the war effort. The City was the target of intensive bombing on 29 December 1940. The fires that threatened St Paul's Cathedral in the centre of the City became known as the Second Great Fire of London. St Paul's was saved, but large areas of the City were destroyed as a result of the 1500 fires started by more than 100,000 incendiary bombs.

Suburban London

Most of London's population lived in the suburbs surrounding the centre, in places that were technically part of Essex, Kent, Middlesex or Surrey. Some of these places were towns in their own right, such as Croydon. Many suburbs had been built since the early twentieth century, so there were regulations which set out minimum sizes for each house, and houses often had good sized gardens with room for Anderson Shelters (see page 129).

However, we should not assume that all these places were the same or had the same experiences during the war. Those to the east such as Croydon, Greenwich, Barking and Bromley seem to have suffered a larger tonnage of bombs than those to the west of London. When we take into account the size of each borough, the central and eastern boroughs definitely suffered the greater density of bombs. Those suburbs to the west were not on the flight path from German bases in northern France, and tended to have fewer bombs dropped on them, though even some of these western boroughs did see terrible bombings and casualties.

LONDON AS A TARGET

1. What made the East End a particular target throughout the different bombing campaigns?
2. Explain why the Luftwaffe targeted:
   a) Westminster
   b) the City
   c) the suburbs
3. Explain why the Dead End Kids' experiences during the war might have been different from those of many children living in the suburbs.
4. Read the timeline on pages 120–21 and the description of the different parts of London again and make a list of the different kinds of weapons that the Luftwaffe used.

USING ONLINE SOURCES OF DATA IN YOUR ENQUIRY

I wanted to know which parts of London were hardest hit. I used a website created by the University of Plymouth, www.bombsight.org, which gives an estimated total for the number of bombs dropped in each borough of London between October 1940 and June 1941. Their data is collected from the reports made by the London Fire Brigade during the Blitz. I decided to take the totals for each borough and place them in a spreadsheet, so that I could compare them by the number of high explosive bombs dropped. I then added a column for the area of each borough, and used a formula to calculate the bombs per square mile. When I'd done this I started to think that each part of London would have had a very different population density – the number of people living per square mile. Using data from the Greater London Authority's 'London Datastore', at http://data.london.gov.uk/dataset/population-change-1939-2015, I was able to add another 'population' column and work out, with another formula, the number of bombs that had fallen in each area for each 1000 people living there. The differences are remarkable, even as we remember that these are estimates. The data was collected using modern boroughs, which were re-organised after the war. The old borough of Stepney, where the Dead End Kids worked, is now part of Tower Hamlets.

Worst affected area by *number* of bombs dropped

Borough	High-explosive bombs dropped
Bromley	2,228
Southwark	1,651
Westminster	1,436
Greenwich	1,396
Croydon	1,338
Bexley	1,296
Tower Hamlets	1,259
Newham	1,240
Lambeth	1,215

Worst affected area by *density* of bombs dropped

Borough	Bombs per square mile
City	242
Westminster	173
Tower Hamlets	165
Southwark	148
Islington	119
Lambeth	117
Hackney	100
Kensington and Chelsea	100
Camden	97

Borough	Bombs per resident
City	30
Bromley	9
Bexley	7
Greenwich	5
Richmond-upon-Thames	5
Croydon	4
Westminster	4
Hillingdon	3
Southwark	3

Look carefully at the map on page 122, and use a modern map of London to work out where the places in these tables are. Look at the descriptions of the different places in London (pages 123–25) and see if you can understand why these places might have been a particular target for the Luftwaffe.

So the Duggans and the Dead End Kids were living right in the eye of the storm in 1940 when the bombs started falling. Not only did they live in a heavily populated area, which meant that attacks there could affect morale, the same area was filled with businesses, warehouses and ports which meant that attacks here could affect the economy and affect supplies for the military. Finally Stepney and the East End were on the flight path from the German bases in France to the rest of London, where there were other economic, military and government targets.

Explain each of the reasons why London was a target in September 1940. Use what you have read and the map below to help you.

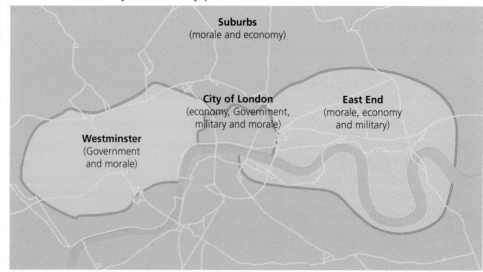

▲ Areas of London targeted during the Blitz and reasons they were targeted

1.3 Preparations for war

I now know that the Duggans and the Dead End Kids were living Wapping, in Stepney and that this was part of London that was especially heavily affected by the Second World War. The factories, docks and number of people crowded together made this area a high-priority target for the Luftwaffe. What I don't understand is why there were so many children left in Wapping, and why they were all together during air raids. I had thought that children had been evacuated from London. Why were they still there, in danger?

WERE THE PREPARATIONS FOR WAR SUCCESSFUL? **?**

Look at the information on pages 127–30. You are going to use them to weigh up the evidence and make a judgement about whether the preparations for war were successful.

First make a Knowledge Organiser like the one below to record your thinking and fill it in as you read pages 127–30. Then, using the evidence you have collected, explain whether you think the preparations for war were successful or not.

Preparation	Successes	Failures	Sources – and why they are useful in helping me decide	Further questions I need to ask
Evacuation				
Shelters				
Gas masks				
Blackout				

Preparations for war: evacuation

Before the war, military planners had feared that bombing raids would destroy whole cities. London, with its industries, the centre of government and a large proportion of the country's population, was an obvious target. A committee set up to estimate Germany's air power feared that up to 3500 tons of bombs would be dropped in the first attack on London, killing 58,000 people in the first 24 hours.

It was also feared that millions of people would flee from London and other cities, so the government planned an orderly evacuation. In 1938 an Air Raid Precautions (ARP) committee led by Sir John Anderson, a civil servant and later Home Secretary, split the country into three types of area. Danger areas were those thought likely to be attacked, neutral areas were those thought to be not direct targets but which might be attacked, and reception areas were those thought to be safe. The idea was to give free transport to 1,400,000 people (schoolchildren under the care of their teachers, young infants and their mothers, pregnant women

and the blind or disabled), and to ask for those who could afford it to pay towards their 'billeting' – their food and shelter in reception areas.

War was declared on 3 September but two days earlier, evacuation from London began. A total of 1.3 million people, mostly children, were evacuated on special trains, and 600,000 on red London double decker buses. They had a mixed welcome in the towns and countryside of the reception areas. Some found good homes, a few staying in their evacuation billets for the duration of the war. Some found it difficult to fit in with their new families and neighbours, and some were cruelly treated. During the Phoney War, when the threat of air raids seemed to diminish, the majority of the evacuees returned. By January 1940, 300,000 had already done so, and by March there were only 300,000 evacuees still in the reception areas. The sources on page 128 give some newspaper accounts of the evacuation.

How could I find out more about evacuation? These three extracts seem to provide valuable evidence about the process of evacuation, but before I can decide how useful they are as evidence, I have to think about the questions below them.

Source A From *The Times* newspaper, 5 September 1939

Evacuation from London

Up to Sunday night about 600,000 children and adults had been evacuated from the London area, and yesterday probably another 50,000 were added to that total. The children went away in high spirits. ... from the reception areas mothers have already received news of their children, for each child was provided with a postcard which was dispatched on arrival.

Source B From *The Times* newspaper, 20 October 1939, reporting on a broadcast by Lord De La Warr, the minister for Education

... children, Lord De La Warr said, had been left behind in London, with little or no control or supervision and with even less education. Many of them are running wild, and all sorts of stories were heard about what was happening. He would like to open the schools, but he did not feel justified, as yet, in assuming that there would be no air raids.

Source C From The *Daily Mail* newspaper, 27 December 1940

20,000 Children Go Home

At least 20,000 children, it is estimated, returned to their homes from evacuation areas during the Christmas holiday. Parents eager to have their sons and daughters round them again ignored the appeals of the Ministry of Health to leave their children. Already 50 percent of the children evacuated from London have returned.

1. What **valuable information** does each report give me?

For example, Source A tells me that the Government wanted to present the evacuation as a complete success.

What do Sources B and C tell me? What else does A tell me?

2. Does Lord De La Warr (Source B) **seem well informed** and does his evidence agree with other sources?

For example, De La Warr seems to be repeating 'stories' with little detail, possibly those reported under headlines like the ones on page 117. What do we already know about what some of these 'left behind' children were doing?

3. Does my **knowledge of evacuation** suggest these sources are useful evidence?

For example, Source A tells us about the way the Government tried to present evacuation.

What else are these sources useful for?

Thinking carefully about sources

When you use a source there are three stages to think about:

a) What is it telling you about the subject of the enquiry – either directly or through what you can infer?

b) What does the information about the author or speaker and details such as the date suggest about how reliable or useful the source is for the enquiry?

c) How does your knowledge of the topic help you decide how useful the source is? For example, from your knowledge, does an account seem typical of other accounts of the same topic?

EVACUATION ?

1. Explain why the government created an evacuation plan.
2. What does the timing of the evacuation tell us about the fear of bombing?
3. What evidence is there that evacuation was a complex and difficult task?
4. Why did people start to return to London?
5. How can we use the information in Sources B and C to explain the attitude of the *Daily Mail* headlines on page 117?
6. Do the *Daily Mail* headlines tell us more about why the Dead End Kids chose this name?
7. How useful are Sources A, B and C for explaining why the Dead End Kids were still in London?

Source D

▲ Families putting up their Anderson Shelters at the start of the war

Preparations for war: shelters

Anderson's committee also ordered the design of a shelter which could be built in back gardens. This 'Anderson Shelter', shown in Source D, was made out of corrugated iron sheets, which were used to line and roof over a pit dug in the ground. Earth was piled on top of the roof to protect against the blast of nearby bombs or shrapnel that flew around in an explosion. However, these shelters could not provide protection against a direct hit from a bomb. In 1938 these shelters were given out free to many people. Those who earned more than £250 a year (which was quite a good wage) had to pay £7 and pay for the cost of the shelter being dug and built. One and a half million shelters were put up. However, some people preferred to stay in their homes, so in 1941 the Morrison Shelter (named after Herbert Morrison, the Home Secretary) was introduced. This was a large steel table, the sides of which were covered with wire netting which could be lifted so that up to three people could shelter inside. The Morrison Shelter was effective because it stopped people from being crushed by collapsing buildings.

As we'll see, the Government did not want to build deep shelters. It was afraid that once people were underground, it would be impossible to get them back to the surface again. Some borough councils ordered the digging of trenches in parks such as Clapham Common and Hyde Park. Surface shelters were also used; these had brick walls, sometimes protected by earth or sandbag banks with concrete roofs. They became known as 'Morrison Sandwiches' because an explosion nearby would blow out the walls, causing the roof to collapse on whoever was inside. The government also printed leaflets and made information films which advised people how to 'shelter in their own homes'. These tips included boarding up the bottom of windows with old doors or creating blast barriers using piles of dirt. Millions of windows were covered with crosses of parcel tape or strips of curtain lace to stop shards of glass from injuring people.

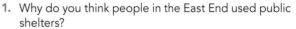

> **SHELTERS**
>
> 1. Why do you think people in the East End used public shelters?
> 2. Explain why there were not many underground shelters during the Phoney War.

Preparations for war: gas masks

The use of chemical gasses as weapons had been banned in agreements signed by Britain, France and Germany in the 1920s and 1930s, but many thought these promises would be broken. In 1938 the Government issued gas masks to all adults and, in 1938 and 1939, smaller ones to children, and even gas proof cradles for putting babies in. Posters and leaflets encouraged people to carry their gas masks, and in the very first days of the war most people did. A survey carried out by Mass Observation, a research group recording people's lives and attitudes before and during the war, found that during the Phoney War, fewer and fewer people carried their masks. By March 1940 perhaps as few as 5 per cent of the population took their gas masks out with them. Even at the height of the Blitz, only about one third of people carried theirs.

Preparations for war: blackout

In July 1939, more than a month before war was actually declared, the government sent round a leaflet explaining the need for a blackout to make it harder for German bombers to find cities during night raids. The leaflet explained how to use dye and chemicals to make paint for soaking old curtains and bed sheets so that they could be used to block light emerging from windows. Volunteer ARP Wardens were appointed in the run-up to September. Most manned observation posts and sounded air raid sirens to warn of a raid. They also told the fire services when fires broke out, led people to shelters in air raids, used first aid to help the injured and kept people away from dangerous damaged buildings or unexploded bombs. One of their main tasks was to patrol and make sure that the blackout was effective. During the Phoney War they were often thought of as 'busybodies', as they ordered people to put out lights and fix blackout covers that had slipped.

Source E

"From down here I can see a chink of light through your dining-room curtains quite distinctly."

▲ *Punch* cartoon 'From down here I can see a chink of light through your dining room curtains...'. This cartoon from late October 1939 shows that during the Phoney War some people thought that ARP wardens were busybodies who took their roles too seriously. Punch magazine was a satirical news magazine that used political cartoons

SHELTERS, BLACKOUT AND GAS MASKS ?

1. Look at Source D (page 129) and Source E and F. What effect did the Phoney War have on London's preparations for war?

2. How useful are these sources in explaining why the Dead End Kids weren't sheltering with their families when the attacks did come?

Source F Maggie Joy Blunt recorded an entry in her diary about a visit to London in January 1940, from *We Are At War: The Diaries of Five Ordinary People in Extraordinary Times*, by Simon Garfield, published in 2006

Less than 50 per cent of the population seemed to be carrying gas masks now. June and I decided to take ours when we went, on principle, but it was an effort and an irritation. The blackout has slackened considerably. I noticed streaks of light from doors and windows which would never have been allowed at the beginning of the war, but I hear that regulations are still strictly enforced in all coastal towns.

1. What valuable information does Maggie Blunt give me?

2. Is Blunt convincing, and does her evidence agree with other sources?

3. Does my knowledge of London during the war suggest this is useful evidence?

EXPLORING THE SOURCES – PREPARATIONS FOR WAR

1. Describe two features of:
   a) An Anderson Shelter
   b) A Morrison Shelter
   c) The evacuation made in 1940
   d) The blackout

2. How useful are Sources D and E for an enquiry into what was done to prepare Londoners for air raid attacks? Explain your answer using Sources D and E and your knowledge of the historical context.

3. How useful are Source F and G for an enquiry into the fears that many Londoners had at the start of the Second World War? Explain your answers using Sources F and G and your knowledge of the historical context.

4. How could you follow up Source E to find out more about how the blackout worked? Use the following headings:
   a) Detail in Source E that I would follow up
   b) Question I would ask
   c) What type of source I could use
   d) How this might help answer my question

Source G Cyril Demarne, a fireman, reflects in an interview for an oral history project on the preparations for attack, from *The War on Our Doorstep* by Harriet Salisbury, published in 2012

The whole of the population had been issued with gas masks, the firemen who'd be on the streets during the air raids were given service respirators, the same as what the armed forced were given, and the ordinary civilians were given the civilian type. Mothers with small babies were given a pouch-like thing to put the infant in. She was expected to put the baby in there and sit and pump to put air into the baby during an air raid. Can you imagine?

Source H A young woman's diary, written in September and then November 1939 for the Mass Observation organisation, from *Love and War in London: the Mass Observation Wartime Diary of Olivia Crockett*, published in 2008

Put up black curtains. Noticed that house next door, inhabited by refugee Jews is brilliantly lit. ... went out after supper with Father to work out where local ARP post is. Walked through black streets, pouring rain, mostly eery ... Felt more cheerful trying on gas mask with sisters in front mirror. Momentarily forgetful ribald laughter. I shall think gas masks are incredibly funny until I have to use one in earnest.

Blacking out has been an almost un-solvable problem in a house with stone surrounds to the window. The ... use of nails and drawing pins is defeated and the problem has been attacked in so many ways that the visit of a young constable last night declaring the blackout was unsatisfactory reduced the more highly-strung members of the household to an impotent hysterical outburst.

Source J

HELP THE CITY CHILDREN

making a new home for Evacuees is a National Service.

ISSUED BY THE MINISTRY OF HEALTH

▲ 'Help the City Children' – A poster published by the Ministry of Health

---

Source I A woman recalls the Anderson Shelter arriving at her house during an interview for an oral history project from *The War on Our Doorstep* by Harriet Salisbury, published in 2012

And dad was caring, sensible, looked after his bits and pieces, loved his garden. It broke his heart when he had to tear it all up and put an air raid shelter down there when the war came. They said 'you've got a shelter, you have to put it in your back garden.' But he said 'it's me garden' and they said 'well you know we've issued it out to you, you do it'. Anyhow he must have thought, this is – he'd been through the First World War. He must have thought 'this is something I've got to do'.

I could not find the exact date when this poster was made. Can you make an informed guess, using the timeline on pages 120–21?

1.4 The nature of the attacks on London

Now I want to find out a little more about the detail of the attacks on London, and to fit the story of the Duggans and the Dead End Kids into this big picture. The first proper attack of the Blitz was the day and night of 7 September 1940. Before then only a few brief attacks had taken place, such as the attack on Croydon and its airport on 15 August when over 60 people were killed in half an hour's bombing. There were three phases of bombing on London and I'd like to find out more about each – including some of the key events of each phase.

1. The Blitz, which ended on 11 May 1941
2. The 'Little Blitz' from 21 January to late May 1944
3. The V1 and V2 rocket attacks from mid-June 1944 to 27 March 1945

We have split the attacks into three phases. You need to understand the nature of each different phase and to record a list of key words to help you remember each of them. You could make a table like this:

The Blitz	The Little Blitz	V1 and V2 attacks
Key words:	Key words:	Key words:

1 The Blitz

The East End was the main target of the first night of the attack, 7 September 1940, which became known as 'Black Saturday'. There was bombing throughout the day, and the evening brought the start of 57 consecutive nights on which London was bombed. The bombs fell first in South East London, in Bermondsey, just across the river from Wapping where the Duggans lived, and the focus of the attacks remained on the East End:

- St Katharine Docks – hit by more than 160 high-explosive bombs in the first week of the Blitz
- Woolwich Arsenal – which contained artillery and ammunition factories
- the Victoria and Albert Docks, and nearby Silvertown, the Isle of Dogs and its docks were all badly hit and damaged.

TYPES OF INCENDIARIES USED DURING THE ATTACKS

Brandbombe

These were 1-kilogram bombs designed to be dropped in large numbers over buildings and houses. They were heavy enough to break through roofs into loft spaces and building interiors where they would burn and start fires. They were filled with a mixture of magnesium and metal oxides which burns very well and with great heat. As the Blitz went on, firewatchers became better at dealing with them by covering them with wet sand or by moving them off roofs. The German designers therefore started fitting Brandbombe with small explosive charges, often on long timers to so that ARP wardens and firefighters were reluctant to get too near to them.

Flammenbombe

These bombs were barrels filled with oil and set with a detonator that would go off on impact, splashing burning oil around and starting more fires. Though these bombs were terrifying, they often failed to explode on landing.

Sprengbrandbombe C 50

This bomb was first used in 1942. It was in a 50-kg bomb case, but instead of explosives it was filled with smaller bombs. Each of these was filled with magnesium and six fire-starting bombs. A small TNT explosive charge was designed to spray these over a 100-metre radius to start as many fires as possible.

However, the west of London was also hit on the night of 7 September 1940. Battersea Power station was damaged, and the gas supply system was also disrupted across the east and west of London. All in all, 350 bombers and 600 fighter escorts dropped more than 330 tons of explosive bombs in a raid that lasted 24 hours, with one brief lull. The high-explosive bombs and **parachute mines** damaged buildings and were an important cause of the 430 people killed and the 1600 people wounded. However, it was the incendiaries that stretched the ARP and firefighters to their limits on that first night, and during the other intense Blitz attacks.

During that raid on 7 September 440 canisters of incendiaries were dropped on London, each holding around 250 1-kilogram Brandbombe. The records of the London Fire Brigade from that raid have been compiled by the *Guardian* newspaper. Combing through them tells us about the kinds of places that were damaged. Bakers, grocers, wine-merchants, armouries, houses, tobacconists, timber yards, flour stores, warehouses, an electrical cable factory, musical instrument makers, engineering works, metalworks, coal merchants, sweet factories, rope makers and other industrial sites were damaged or destroyed.

Firefighting in the Blitz

How dangerous was it to be a firefighter? The answer is – very dangerous. Walter Turley (see Source A) was one of the first firefighters to be killed in the Blitz. The first raid on 7 September saw 1000 fire hoses and pumps being used to fight 17 major fires and 19 smaller ones. Damaged water mains hampered the effort so emergency pumps took water directly from the Thames.

Walter was leading an eleven-man fire crew. They were all killed when a building collapsed on them. Walter's team was mostly made up of civilian 'Auxiliary Firemen'. On that first night, 25,000 of these auxiliaries fought fires using hand pumps, portable ladders, sandbags and buckets as well as mobile fire pumps and hoses. Along with Walter, 327 men and women from the Fire Service or the Auxiliary Fire service were killed in London during the war.

On 29 December, another huge raid targeted the City of London, the business and finance district. Incendiaries left 1600 fires burning. The job of the firefighters was made very difficult by a shortage of water. Explosive bombs had damaged the water mains, and the Thames was at low ebb; water was pumped from boats in the middle of the river, and also from trucks driven into the city.

Source A Details from the Commonwealth War Graves Commission record of civilians killed in the Second World War. Many records are not as detailed as this one, which even gives a place of death

> TURLEY, WALTER JAMES, age 39; Fireman, West Ham Fire Brigade. Son of Mr. W. Turley, of 51 Deerfield Cottages, The Hyde, Hendon, Middlesex; husband of A. E. Turley, of 3 Cranley Road, Plaistow. 7 September 1940, at Corporation Depot, Abbey Road.

Source B From *In Case of Fire: The Illustrated History and Modern Role of the London Fire Brigade*, by Neil Wallington, published in 2005

Once again, the AFS (Auxiliary Fire Service) firewomen played an invaluable role during the raid. They drove petrol carriers loaded with jerrycans into the heart of the danger zones taking precious fuel supplies to keep the roaring pumps at work. They also manned canteen vans, brewing hundreds of gallons of tea and cocoa.

FIREFIGHTING

1. Why were incendiaries more destructive than explosive bombs?
2. Explain why firefighting in the Blitz was so dangerous.
3. Explain why firefighting was so difficult during the Blitz.

Firefighting: the Dead End Kids

On page 133 we saw the record of William Turley's death in the lists of civilians killed during the war. Further down these lists I came across two more names that were familiar.

Mollie Panter-Downes' piece for the *New Yorker* contains a reference to 'two of the [Dead End] Kids, Ronnie Ayres and Bert Eden [who] were killed during the raids while tackling blazes with the gang'. So, these official records support Panter-Downes' article. A quick look at the map tells me that they died on opposite sides of St Katharine Docks, about 250 metres from the shelter at Watson's Wharf. I felt very sad when I read these names and matched them up with the newspaper piece and the map. I have written other books and taught countless lessons in which we discuss how certain people have died, without feeling like this. I wonder if, having seen photographs, having read these accounts and traced the different places on the map, I have made myself feel differently about the Dead End Kids than I had before.

> **Source C** Details from the records of Commonwealth War Graves Commission of civilians killed in the Second World War
>
> EADON, Albert Francis, age 16. Son of A. G. and A. Eadon, of 47 Matilda House, Thomas Moore Street, Wapping. 29 December 1940, at St Katharine's Way.
> EYRES, Ronald Leslie, age 18. Son of Frederick George and Emily Eyres, of 6 Colville House, Lark Row, Bethnal Green. 29 December 1940, at Thomas Moore Street.

SPELLINGS ?

Notice how Panter-Downes spells Bert and Ronnie's names differently than the records of the War Graves Commission. Which do you think is the right one? How might this affect our enquiries?

Firewatching

The raid on 29 December killed only a very few people compared with other Blitz attacks – the estimate is 160. However, the new tactics of focusing wave after wave of incendiaries on a limited area threatened some of London's most important buildings, such as the Bank of England, and, more symbolically, St Paul's Cathedral, which had been built after the Great Fire of London in 1666. The fires of 29 December 1940 became known as the Second Great Fire of London, and St Paul's was only saved because of the teams of volunteer firewatchers who put out fires on the roof as 28 incendiaries hit it. This and other incidents made the Government realise the value of firewatchers and, by the end of 1940, streets, offices, factories and other workplaces were required to draw up rosters for compulsory fire watching.

Though St Paul's survived, other important historic buildings did not. Many other churches burnt down that night, some of which had been designed by Sir Christopher Wren, an architect employed by Charles II to help rebuild London after the Great Fire of 1666.

> **Source D** An extract from the diary of Mrs Constance Mile, written as the Blitz was going on, and published in 2013
>
> Kenneth tells me that … all the bridges are intact. This is pretty wonderful considering the enemy use the river as a guide. He said that when he hears bombs dropping he at once becomes anxious about certain factories and power-stations. … It appears that the raid over London was perfectly devastating. They sent thousands of incendiary bombs hurtling over the City and dozens of fires were blazing for hours. More Wren churches and the Guildhall are gutted.

The end of the first Blitz

In the early months of 1941 London had some quieter nights, as the Luftwaffe targeted other towns and cities. However, on the night of 10 and 11 May 1941, the Germans launched the war's most destructive raid on London. A total of 1436 people were killed and 1792 were injured. After this, London was free from air raids until the Little Blitz of 1944, as Germany focused on its attack on Russia. Approximately 20,000 people were killed in this first phase of the Blitz and 1,150,000 houses were damaged or destroyed. One in six people in the London area suffered at least one day of homelessness – around 1.4 million people.

WHAT STORY DOES AN IMAGE TELL?

The survival of St Paul's gave the Blitz its most iconic image – the dome of the cathedral rising over the smouldering city on the night of 29 December 1940.

Source E St Paul's Cathedral, 29 December 1940, taken by *Daily Mail* photographer Herbert Mason

The image was used and read in two ways. On the front page of the *Daily Mail* on 31 December the headline was 'St Paul's stands Unharmed in the Midst of the Burning City', and the image became a symbol of Britain's' resistance. Almost a month later the German newspaper *Berliner Illustrierte Zeitung* used the same picture with the headline 'Die City von London brennt!' – the City of London burns! The same picture seems to give different information with a different headline, and as historians we must take a step back and think about how the 'information' is being used to encourage us to think in a certain way.

29 DECEMBER 1940

1. On page 126 we read that London was a target because of the impact bombing would have on the economy, Government, morale and the military. Read Source E and explain how useful it is in helping us to work out why the City of London was a target.

2. How significant was this raid for Londoners living in the different parts of the city that we mentioned on page 126?

3. How significant was it for the Dead End Kids?

2 The Little Blitz

This phase, between 21 January 1944 and April 1944 was much less intensive than the Blitz of 1940–41. Germany could only assemble 475 aircraft to make these attacks, and her best pilots had been killed in missions over Russia, leaving only inexperienced crews who often missed their targets. Even so, these raids killed over 1500 people. The inexperienced German crews were easy targets for fighters and ground **anti-aircraft** crews, and the Germans lost about 70 aircraft a month between January and April, when the attacks fizzled out.

EXPLOSIVE BOMBS

High explosive

High-explosive bombs came in many different shapes and sizes, and had different code names. They could weigh between 50 kg and 1800 kg. The largest bomb was known as a 'Satan'. Some created a blast that destroyed buildings, others with heavier cases shattered and caused maximum shrapnel damage.

Parachute mines

These mines weighed 1000 kilograms and were designed to sink ships at sea. They had contact or magnetic triggers (which were set off by the iron in ships' hulls). They were also sometimes dropped by parachute onto important targets on land. When they exploded above the ground the damage was worse because none of its force was soaked up by the earth. Sometimes the parachute would become entangled in cables or buildings and the mine would be left hanging, often to explode later.

Anti-personnel bombs

Butterfly bombs were types of **cluster bombs** that would open up (and look like butterflies) when they hit the ground, scattering **bomblets** that could be fitted with detonators which went off after a certain time, or if they were picked up.

---

3 V1 attacks

The D-Day landings on 6 June 1944 and the gradual liberation of Northern France meant that Britain was further out of range of Germany's dwindling bomber fleet. However, a new threat emerged on 13 June when an explosion in a Gravesend vegetable garden was taken for a crashing enemy plane. In fact, this was the first recorded impact of a V1 flying bomb (see diagram opposite). These 'pilotless planes' had a jet engine, and carried a 1-ton explosive **payload** at 400 miles an hour. They had very crude guidance systems and were designed to travel along in one direction, for a certain distance, then dive into the ground and explode. Their engines made a loud buzzing sound and became known as 'buzz bombs' or 'doodlebugs'.

Doodlebugs were a terrifying weapon because there was often no warning, or the warnings were meaningless as the constant flight of these 'pilotless planes' meant that people were always on high alert. The noise added to the fear. The buzz of the engines would stop as the V1 descended sharply, so it was the quiet before the explosion that Londoners learned to listen out for.

Many of the V1s never reached their target. After the first week of attacks, the anti-aircraft crews were told not to try to shoot them down, as this often led to them landing in the areas where more people lived on the outskirts of London. Croydon was directly under the flight path from Holland where the V1s were launched and suffered the worst in the V1 campaign. Just over 140 V1s hit this area, destroying 1000 houses and badly damaging nearly 60,000. Eventually the anti-aircraft guns and **barrage balloons** were moved to the area between the south coast and London, where shooting down the V1s would cause less damage.

A total of 9000 V1 rockets were launched from ground launch sites. When the Allies overran these launch sites the Germans then launched 1200 further V1s from bombers specially adapted to carry them. Of the 10,200 weapons fired, around 6900 reached Britain, of which 3800 were shot down by British defences, which got more and more effective at bringing them down. By August 1944 it was thought that only around 17 per cent of V1s launched were hitting London. Over the whole V1 campaign 5475 people were killed, but these statistics hide terrible stories. One 'bug' might not injure anyone, but another could kill tens of civilians.

New Cross in Deptford saw the damage that V1 rockets could bring. In July 1944 a V1 exploded on the Marks and Spencer store, killing 60 people. The destroyed buildings can be clearly seen on the right-hand side of this official bomb damage map (the darker the colour, the more damage). The V1 blast is shown by a circle on the right-hand side of the picture. In November a Woolworths store, the black-coloured building on the left at the centre of another smaller circle, was hit by a different but no less dreadful weapon – the V2 rocket.

▲ Cutaway of a flying bomb V1 rocket

Labels: Jet engine, Compressed air, Fuel, Warhead, Auto-pilot, Compass

Source F

▲ A section of one of the official 'Bomb Damage Maps' produced by the London County Council after the war. Black indicates areas that were totally destroyed; purple those that were damaged beyond repair; red areas seriously damaged; orange general blast damage; yellow means minor blast damage; green indicates areas that had been cleared; small circles indicate damage from a V-2 rocket and large circles a V-1 rocket

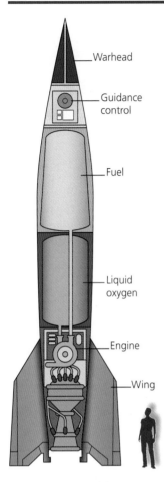

▲ Cutaway of a V2 rocket. The V2 was a liquid oxygen and ethanol-fuelled rocket with a 1-ton warhead. It had a range of 200 miles and could fly at 55 miles altitude

- Warhead
- Guidance control
- Fuel
- Liquid oxygen
- Engine
- Wing

3 V2 attacks

V2 rockets were launched from mobile sites, which made them harder to find and attack. They were an early form of **ballistic missile** which meant that they launched upwards and travelled through the upper atmosphere before coming more or less straight down on their target. This made it nearly impossible for anti-aircraft gunners to target them, and brought little chance of warning or reaching shelter.

The government was worried about the effect of this new weapon on morale, so after the first rockets fell in early September 1944 they tried to prevent the story from being printed in newspapers, and instead told the public that gas lines had exploded. By November people were sceptical of this story, especially as the numbers of rockets hitting London was increasing rapidly – from 12 in the first week of November to 27 in the third week. The government only admitted the existence of the V2 rockets after the German government itself announced them in a radio broadcast on 8 November. The government still restricted the kinds of information that the press could report about the V2 attacks – they didn't want the Germans to find out how many of their rockets had got through, or how accurate their targeting was.

Then, on Saturday 25 November, the Woolworths on New Cross Road in Deptford was hit by a V2 rocket. The store was full because people had heard there was a delivery of new cooking pans, which had been very hard to buy since the start of the war. There was a long queue of people waiting for a chance to buy one. The building collapsed, killing 168 people, and injuring 122 people on the street. Despite the efforts of the fire services and passers-by who attempted to dig people out with their hands, only one person inside the building survived.

> **Source G June Gaida, who was thirteen years old at the time remembers the Deptford disaster**
>
> I was going shopping that morning for my mother and suddenly there was a blinding flash and a roaring, rushing sound. I was thrown into the air. There was noise all around me, a deafening terrible noise that beat against my eardrums and, when I fell to the ground, I curled myself up into a ball to protect myself …
>
> When the noise had faded I picked myself up and I was coated with brick dust, with slivers of glass in my hair. Then I walked towards Woolworths. Things were still falling out of the sky, there were bricks, masonry, and bits of people …
>
> Outside the pub there was a bus and it had been concertinaed, with rows of people sitting inside, all covered in dust and dead. I looked towards where Woolworths had been and there was nothing. There was just an enormous gap covered by a cloud of dust … No building, just piles of rubble and bricks, and from underneath it all I could hear people screaming.

LONDON AT WAR

Now you know in more detail what Londoners had to go through during the war, re-visit your timeline from pages 120–21 and improve your second living graph so that it better shows how Londoners might have felt using the information on pages 138–39.

Source H A fireman recalls the effect of the first attack on 7 September 1940 in an interview for an oral history project, from *The War on Our Doorstep* by Harriet Salisbury, published in 2012

We knew the docks would be a number one target so we put five fire stations in there and they were housed in warehouses. We'd got the docks to work from our water supply, [but were told] that if food warehouses were involved we had to use clean water from the mains. But the fires that occurred in the first Blitz – we had to order five hundred fire pumps for the docks. There was eleven miles of quays there, all lined with warehouses filled with combustibles, fifty ships in there, all combustible. So you can see how five hundred pumps wouldn't go very far.

Source I Extract from Mass Observation record '12-12-E Air Raids on London', June 1944. An extract from documents in a file marked 'raid feelings' – which contained conversations overheard by observers working for Mass Observation on 21 June 1944

Oh! It's terrible, – it's all going to have a bad effect on the factories – when they hear those planes [V1 doodlebugs] come over all the girls stop work. We've lost a shop girl, a very nice girl she was, over in the Battersea branch – lived at Deptford. Well, she popped into her own place, just to have a sluice [wash] before starting off to work, and that bloody plane landed right outside her door. There were old women grumbling outside the Battersea office: "where's that bloody girl?". And the manageress – she told me herself – she said, "Don't you speak like that. That girl's dead".

Source J A newspaper article from the *Daily Mail* 30 August 1944

V1 Battle Ending

Sir Earnest Gowers, Senior Civil Defence Regional Commissioner for London, forecast yesterday that the V1 battle will soon be over. He said: 'We are not yet finished with this battle this long drawn-out attempt to break the Spirit of London, although we may now hope ... that this final phase is nearing its end.'

AA guns were in action again yesterday when flying bombs were launched across the Channel at intervals. The gunners met with quick successes, and a fair proportion of the robots was hit and destroyed over the sea off one part of Southern England.

EXPLORING THE SOURCES: THE ATTACKS ON LONDON

1. Describe two features of:
   a) explosive bombs
   b) incendiary bombs
   c) the V1 and V2 attacks.

2. How useful are Sources H and I for an enquiry into the weapons that were used in the attacks on London during the Second World War? Explain your answer using Sources H and I and your knowledge of the historical context.

3. How useful are Sources I and J for an enquiry into the different phases of the attack on London during Second World War? Explain your answer using Sources I and J and your knowledge of the historical context.

4. How could you follow up Source J to find out more about the V1 and V2 rocket attacks? Use the following headings:
   a) Detail in Source J that I would follow up
   b) Question I would ask
   c) The type of source I could use
   d) How this might help answer my question

1.5 The impact of the Blitz: were shelters safe?

We have found some answers to many of the big questions that we had at the start of our enquiry. We've learned about the preparations that the Government put in place, and the attacks that the people of London faced. In this section we will find out whether the preparations were effective – did they protect the Londoners? Were people able to carry on with their lives and their work? Could they even find ways of enjoying themselves?

We might think that this picture of the Dead End Kids, the electric lighting and brick walls, helps us to get a sense of what it was like hiding in a shelter. We might imagine being underground, perhaps the walls are damp and bombs falling might sound like dull thuds on the surface above our heads. Life in underground shelters is often the first image we bring to mind when we think about the Blitz.

Source A

▲ This 1941 picture of the Dead End Kids in their HQ shelter, at Watson's Wharf in Stepney, shows Patsy Duggan at the back of the picture, wearing an armband

However, many people didn't shelter underground, and in the East End many of the largest shelters were surface level shelters – Watson's Wharf included. These gave protection against blast damage from bombs, but did not protect them from direct hits.

The government did build deep shelters, but nowhere near enough to protect all Londoners. The few deep tunnels built as shelters were used to shelter civil servants. Only in 1944 were four opened to the public during the Little Blitz and V weapon attacks (see page 136). At first, the Government even tried to prevent people sheltering in the Underground. They worried that once safe underground, people would refuse to come up, or that a bomb landing in the Thames might breach the underground tunnels and flood stations, drowning those in them.

Visible learning

Asking good questions

One of the problems with a question like 'Did people feel safe in shelters' is that we really need to ask other questions before we can answer this one. For instance, we could ask 'Which type of shelter' or 'When in the war?' or 'Which type of people?' or 'Who was in charge of the shelter?'. Otherwise we could be falling into the trap of generalising – see page 124.

Life in the shelters

However, during the first days of the Blitz people ignored the ban on using tube stations. Many bought tickets and refused to leave, others pushed past the barriers and went down to the platforms. Thousands also crowded into surface shelters. As the Blitz went on, long queues formed at shelters as early as mid morning. Children were sent to hold a place in the line and bag a good pitch for the rest of the family.

Shelters could be crowded and very insanitary – buckets used as temporary toilets were easily spilled, and over-crowding meant that people often had to stand through the night. Some lacked lighting or ventilation for fresh air. One famously terrible shelter was in the basement of the Tilbury Depot near Fenchurch Street Station. Ritchie Calder, a *Daily Herald* journalist described it in his book *Carry On London*, published in 1941:

> [Tilbury was] not only the most unhygienic place I have ever seen, it was definitely unsafe. Yet numbers as high, on some estimates, as 14,000 to 16,000 people crowded into it on those dreadful nights when hell was let loose on East London — people of every type and condition, every colour and creed found their way there.
>
> When ships docked, seamen would come to roister for a few hours. Scotland Yard knew where to look for bombed-out criminals. Prostitutes paraded there. Hawkers peddled greasy, cold fried fish which cloyed the already foul atmosphere and fights had to be broken up by the police.

Aldwych – a better shelter

Many tube stations were also unhealthy in the early days of the Blitz. However, a shelter was built at the un-used Aldwych station. Walls were whitewashed to improve lighting, toilets were fitted instead of buckets, bunk beds were fitted and wardens were appointed to run the shelter. A medical clinic and first aid, canteen, library and even educational lectures were provided. There was a ticket system so that people didn't have to queue to get in. However, Aldwych only held some of the 120,000 people seeking shelter in the Underground each night.

Private shelters

People also sheltered in the basements of their houses, in crypts beneath churches and in private underground shelters. Businesses used their own basements; John Lewis sold tea and Penguin chocolate biscuits to customers sheltering in the basement of its Oxford Street store. The Savoy Hotel offered overnight shelters in its basement for dinner guests. On 14 September 1940 there was a famous invasion of the Savoy's shelter by 77 Stepney residents led by **Communist** activist Phil Piratin. Eventually the hotel agreed to let them stay, and Piratin bought cups of tea for his followers. The newspapers' coverage of this event further raised the issue of conditions in public shelters.

Some shelters were not as safe as we might think. We could argue that life in the shelters was dangerous and unhealthy. Divide a paper in two, and on one side collect evidence that shelters were safe, and on the other collect evidence that they were dangerous or unhealthy.

SHELTERS

1. Describe two features of the Tilbury shelter that made it an unpleasant place.

2. Read the extract from Ritchie Calder's book above.
   a) Why might the government have been concerned to read reports like this?
   b) Why might this this extract help to explain why the Dead End Kids did not stay in their shelters when the bombs were falling?

LIFE IN THE SHELTERS

1. Describe two features of shelter life in the first weeks of the Blitz.
2. Describe two reasons why some people thought that shelter provision was unfair.

Government investigations into shelter conditions

Concern about conditions in shelters led the Government to set up a committee under Lord Horder to investigate. The Ministry of Health also sent investigators around the shelters – their reports contain interesting information about the conditions (see Source B). As a result the improvements made at Aldwych were made in other shelters – and eventually many large shelters had medical services, libraries and even entertainment.

Mickey's Shelter

Some people did not wait for the council or the government to improve things. One example is the Fruit and Wool Exchange, a huge warehouse in Stepney in East London where up to 5000 people had been sheltering in a basement. Mickey Davis (who was very short and nicknamed 'The Midget') and his wife Doris took matters into their own hands. They collected money from wealthy donors to pay for medicines, organised volunteer doctors to set up a clinic and stretcher bearers to make first aid stations. They brought in bunks and even set up a canteen. The example of what could be done at Aldwych and at Mickey's Shelter convinced the government to make new rules about shelters. They appointed shelter marshals and invested money in installing toilets, and in other places they also set up bunks and brought in ticketing so that people didn't have to queue.

> **Source B** From a Progress Report drafted by the Ministry of Health investigation into improvements of shelters in Poplar, from *Sources for History of London 1939–45* by Heather Creaton published in 1998
>
> The policy in Poplar is to concentrate on the smaller shelters and make them more attractive.
>
> Ventilation. In most of them this is very deficient.
>
> Overcrowding. The large basement shelters are grossly overcrowded, the trench shelters almost empty
>
> Medical Aid Posts. Nil The [council] will now consider introducing these and has arranged to meet the local Doctors to start a group system. There are no nurses available.

Source C

▲ A meeting of the Shelter Committee at Mickey's Shelter. Mickey Davis can be seen on the left

CHANGES TO SHELTERS ?

1. Describe two features of the Aldwych shelter and Mickey's Shelter that made them better places to hide from the Blitz.

2. Explain why the Government was reluctant at first to build more shelters like these.

3. 'Anger by ordinary people had more effect on the development of shelters than government policy.' How much evidence is there to support this statement? What statement could you come up with that better describes the reasons why shelters changed?

Shelter disasters

Being underground did not make you safe. A direct hit from an explosive bomb could penetrate to where people were sheltering, as we can see from this newspaper report from 11 September 1940 (Source D).

Source D A Scottish newspaper report of the effects of a bomb hitting a school, from the *Daily Record and Sunday Mail*, 11 September 1940

School Bombed – Many Dead

Many bodies have so far been recovered from the school in East London which was wrecked by a direct hit during Monday night's raids.

Some of the persons extricated from beneath the mass of twisted girders and debris were still alive, but it is understood that they died while being conveyed in ambulances to the hospital. It is feared that there will be only a few survivors. The rescue squads found two babies one aged nine months and the other six months, alive. They were rushed to hospital, and it is thought that they might recover.

A tragic feature is that arrangements were made for these refugees to be transferred to the country today. It is expected that the rescue work will go on for at least 24 hours.

---

1 Read Source D carefully. What information can you find out about this disaster?

2 What information is missing from this source that you would expect to find in a newspaper report?

Actually there is little concrete information here. Other newspapers that reported on this disaster claimed that 500 people were sheltering in the school, and also emphasised that doctors and nurses had rushed to the scene, working overnight by torchlight to rescue survivors. But other than this, there was little detail in these reports either.

South Hallsville

The parachute mine that caused this destruction fell on South Hallsville School north of the Royal Victoria Docks in the East End. By 11 September 1940 there were actually more than 600 people sheltering in the school, many were children waiting for evacuation after their own homes had been destroyed in the raids of 7 September onwards. Only 77 bodies were recovered. The details were hidden from the public because the Government feared the effect on morale.

DEVELOPING YOUR ENQUIRY

How could you follow up the *Daily Record and Sunday Mail* report in Source D?

1. Which details in the report could you follow up?

2. What questions could you ask?

3. What types of source could you use?

4. How might these help to answer your questions?

Source E

▲ A volunteer helps children do their homework in Mickey's Shelter

South Hallsville showed that, despite official fears about high death rates, and the psychological impact of air raids, the Government and some local governments were not well prepared for looking after the victims of the Blitz who had survived the early raids. In a book written during the Blitz, Ritchie Calder, a journalist, describes attitudes to the homeless:

> [the homeless were] treated, not as casualties, as they certainly were, but as casuals [tramps or travellers] … strict limitations were placed by the Ministry of Health on the extent to which the Council might provide either food or bedding [with] a disgraceful minimum of blankets [and only] a hot drink and a dry bully-beef sandwich to the victims.

By the end of October most areas in London had much better-run centres for those made homeless by the Blitz, with hot food, medical care and, most importantly, information that would help the homeless to start to recover. As the historian Juliet Gardiner points out, they needed a great deal of information.

Source F A historian's view of what bombed out Londoners would have needed help with (from *Wartime Britain 1939–1945* by Juliette Gardiner, published in 2005)

emergency cash grants, … where they could replace their identity cards, ration and pension books and gas masks, where they could get clothes, who would help them salvage any furniture, … and how they were to find somewhere to live.

Bethnal Green

As we have seen, news of disasters like that at Hallsville School was often hidden from the public. Another example is the Bethnal Green Tube disaster. By March 1943 underground shelters were much better organised than in the first days of the Blitz, but the station entrances at Bethnal Green had not been designed to allow thousands of people to quickly get down to safety.

During the Blitz, attacks had been regular and mostly at night. However, by early 1943 there were often small lightning raids in which one or two bombers would sneak past defences. This meant that there was much less warning. On 7 March 1943 an air raid siren sounded in Bethnal Green and people began to go down into the Tube. Nearby a new rocket anti-aircraft defence battery was fired. The sound startled people at the entrance who started to crowd down the steps. At the bottom, a woman had fallen over because there was only a rope hand rail. Others fell too, but those at the top, panicking, continued to push down the stairs. In a very short time hundreds had fallen over; 173 people died from suffocation.

The impact of the shelter disasters

As with the events at South Hallsville School, the newspapers did not properly report the Bethnal Green disaster, because they had agreed not to print stories that might affect morale. The Government was worried about admitting that panic had played a part in the disaster. The impact seems to have been that instead of relying on news reports, people started to listen to and spread rumours about the disasters.

Source G From a Mass Observation report into morale, gathered on 23 March 1943 by their observers overhearing conversations.

F45 [means a female aged 45] says Bethnal Green Tube accident was caused by ARP [wardens] turning a hose on young hooligans annoying people at the entrance to the shelter, which started a panic

---

Ritchie Calder, the campaigning journalist, wrote a book published in 1941 called *The Lesson of London*. In it he highlighted the lack of preparation the Government had made for dealing with those made homeless by bombing. Calder's campaign meant that improving this provision was one positive impact of the South Hallsville disaster.

SHELTER SAFETY ?

1. 'Shelters were dangerous and unhealthy.' To what extent do you agree with this statement based on what you have read so far? What evidence best supports your view.

2. What important questions might you need to ask to help you improve your answer to Question 1?

1.6 The impact of the Blitz: government and the morale of Londoners

The government was very worried about how the **morale** of Londoners would be affected by bombing. The Ministry of Information set up a Home Intelligence Department (HID) to collect information about how well morale was holding up. Every week Home Intelligence Reports were collated by this department, and given to the government. In his book *The Myth of the Blitz*, Angus Calder lists nine sources of information that the HID used, including:

> **Source A An extract from Angus Calder's book *The Myth of the Blitz*, published in 2012**
>
> 1 Summaries of the Press
> 2 Reports from Postal Censorship ... also Telephone Censorship
> 3 Reports from police stations
> 4 Reports from Mass Observation [see below]
> 5 BBC Listener Research reports
> 6 Reports from W H Smiths newsagents
> 7 Reports from managers of Granada Cinemas
> 8 Reports from various charities such as the Citizens Advice Bureau
> 9 Reports from Scottish MPs

HOME INTELLIGENCE REPORTS

1. What does the list in Source A tell you about the sources of information that the government had access to?
2. What kinds of ideas and opinions might the government struggle to get hold of using only the items on this list?

Mass Observation

One of the key groups sending information to the Home Intelligence Service was Mass Observation (MO). MO, a group created before the war, collected diary entries from 'ordinary people' to try and make a record about life in Britain. It is still working today – you can find it at www.massobs.org.uk. They collected letters, diaries and papers sent in by people living all over the country. The London entries are a very interesting record of the Blitz and its impact, written as the attacks were going on. They tell you how people felt during the Blitz and what they feared – but they also tell you about rumours and stories that they heard, which might not be true but do tell us a great deal about how the war made people feel.

Summaries of these reports were read by three people who then wrote the weekly report, which started with a general description then went into more detail about particular areas (see Sources B and C).

> **Source B From the Home Intelligence Report of the week following 7 and 8 September 1940**
>
> In the areas which have been most heavily raided there has been little sign of panic and none of defeatism, but rather of bitterness and increased determination to 'see it through'. There is widespread and deeply felt apprehension [fear], which is apparent mostly in the London Dock area, of a continuation of raids ...
>
> As far as the East End is concerned, this is beginning to show itself in an aimless evacuation to what are believed to be safer places, e.g. the St. James's Park shelters and Paddington Station ...
>
> Men working in factories in the East End are encouraging their wives and families in this haphazard escape, but express their own willingness to stay and face further raids if they can be sure that their relations are in comparative safety.

> **Source C From the 'regional reports' section of the report, and written by a regional officer of the Home Intelligence Department**
>
> London Region:
>
> In Dockside areas the population is showing visible signs of nerve cracking from constant ordeal. Old women and mothers are undermining morale of young women and men by their extreme nervousness and lack of resilience. Men state they cannot sleep because they must keep up the morale of their families and express strong desire to get their families away from danger areas.

MORALE IN THE EAST END

1. What is the overall message about morale in these reports (Sources B and C)?
2. Why have the authors focused on the East End?
3. Why might reports like these not be able to show lots of details about how people were feeling?
4. What other sources might you need to look at to find out how people felt after the Blitz first started?
5. What questions might these reports inspire?

Government propaganda

The government took steps to keep morale as high as possible. As we have seen, newspapers were reluctant to print too many details of accidents. The **official censor** also stepped in to stop too much information being published about where V1 and V2 bombs were falling. Some propaganda was used to persuade people to behave in certain ways. For example, the government was keen to encourage Londoners to see themselves as being able to 'take it', that a 'Blitz spirit' would see them through the attacks and the war.

One important way in which the government did this was through posters on street corners and at underground stations. They were helped by people who worked in advertising before the war and now worked for the government, creating propaganda.

> **Source D** Extract from a document called 'Principles and Objectives of Wartime propaganda', which was issued to the BBC by the Ministry of Information at the outbreak of the War in 1939
>
> 1. What is at stake is the ideal of a good life which free men have created through two thousand years. A life based on equal justice, on respect for the individual, family affections and the love of truth.
> 2. Nazi Germany boasts the justice of the Gestapo, the break up of the family and truth distorted to serve ruthless party ends.
> 3. Defeat means the end of life as we understand it in Western Europe.

Source E

LEAVE HITLER TO ME SONNY — <u>YOU</u> OUGHT TO BE OUT OF LONDON

ISSUED BY THE MINISTRY OF HEALTH

Source F

LOOKOUT IN THE BLACKOUT

THINK BEFORE YOU CROSS THE ROAD

PRINCIPLES AND OBJECTIVES OF WARTIME PROPAGANDA

Visit www.bbc.co.uk/archive/hawhaw/8928.shtml and read the 'Principles and Objectives of Wartime propaganda'.

1. Discuss with a partner what you think were the four key aims for propaganda, as set out in those 'Principles and Objectives'. When you've agreed them, write them as separate headings on a piece of paper.

2. Now look closely at the propaganda posters on page 146 and this page (Sources E–H) and work out which of the key aims seem to have influenced these posters.

3. Do some more research of your own and find some other posters. Do they also suggest that these key aims were important? What other aims did the government have in making these posters?

In addition to these posters, the government also used newsreels and cinema to sell to the public the idea that Londoners could take it. *London Can Take It!* was a film about the Blitz set in October 1940. It was designed to be shown in cinemas in America, as part of the effort by the British government to persuade Americans that they should help Britain in the struggle against Nazi Germany. It was made shorter and retitled *Britain Can Take It* and also shown in British cinemas.

If you search YouTube for 'Britain Can Take It' you will find this version for British viewers. The opening title is shown over a picture of St Paul's, which was becoming a symbol of resistance. However, the real focus of the film is the people of London, and it had a clear message to get across:

> **Source I From the voiceover script of *Britain Can Take It* made in 1940.**
>
> Many of the people at whom you are looking now are members of the greatest civilian army ever to be assembled. These men and women who have worked all day in offices or in markets are now hurrying home to change into the uniform of their particular service. ... These civilians are good soldiers.

Source G

Source H

1.7 The impact of the Blitz: disruption to work and leisure

Where was this photograph taken?

The photo was taken in the City of London. Page 125 will remind me why this area might have been a target, and might give me a clue about what was going on here.

When was this photograph taken?

The photograph was taken on 9 January 1941. If I look back at my notes from earlier in the chapter I might be able to work out what had been happening in London in the weeks before this was taken (see page 120).

Source A

Who are the people in it?

This is where the caption can help a little, but I have to make an educated guess about this. The City was the business district of London, which perhaps means that these people are city workers. Most of them have notebooks and pens or pencils in their hands – they want to remember what's on the notices tied to the post – so they're writing them down.

Which of your questions are answered by the caption?

I found this photograph in a picture library. It had a caption: '9 January 1941: A group of people checking the addresses attached to a traffic light, a novel "change of address bureaux" for many bombed out businesses in the City of London during the Blitz'.

When I look at a photo like the one on page 148 I have to think for a while, look carefully and ask questions about it before I understand what is going on. Look closely, not only at the people and figures in the foreground, but also what is behind them. What questions might you need answers to before you can start to make a more informed guess about what is going on? Write your questions down. I wonder if your questions are like those in the boxes around the photo.

What was going on?

The caption helps here, but so does the historical context – our existing knowledge about the raids on London. On 29 December 1940 there was a huge raid which hit the city very badly. We know that incendiaries burned down many buildings in which businesses were based. It looks like these people are looking for notices about changes of address for businesses that they work with. Perhaps they are employees trying to find out where they should go to work? Perhaps they are customers or suppliers of these businesses?

Why was this photograph taken?

We have to use all the information we have to make some educated guesses. As we know, the Government was concerned about morale – how confident and happy the people living in London were, and how well they were coping with the Blitz. Newspapers were under lots of pressure to print only optimistic pictures, those that showed bravery, or which suggested that life was carrying on despite the bombs. This picture seems to do at least some of these things. You could see it as an attempt to show that for Londoners it was 'business as usual' – even if they did have to work around some problems brought by the destruction of the Blitz.

> ### Developing your enquiry
>
> What other questions might you ask about Source A to help us to understand the impact of the Blitz on daily life, work and leisure?
>
> 1. Was this a typical scene?
> 2. What else did businesses do to protect themselves?

Disruption and danger at work

Some businesses and even some Government departments had avoided the risk of being bombed out by evacuating their workers and offices at the start of the war, only returning from 1943 onwards as the risk of air raids diminished. Some of the offices of the Bank of England were evacuated to Hampshire, and a large part of its **gold reserves** were sent to Canada. Other businesses adapted to the Blitz by closing early, so that their staff and customers could get home or to shelters before the nightly bombing raids started.

> **Source B** A man recalls his days as an office boy in the City of London during the Blitz.
> Adapted from *How We Lived Then* by N. Longmate, published in 1971
>
> [I had to] collect each department manager's and director's papers when the sirens sounded, put them in his special steel box, and convey the lot to the basement strong room. I soon worked this down to a five-minute limit – ten boxes from the fourth floor via the lift to the basement. [Often] no sooner had I got everything in the strong room the 'all clear' sounded.

Difficulties in carrying on as normal

As we have seen from the picture on page 148, and from looking at the V2 attack on the Woolworths on Deptford High Street in 1944 (see page 137), businesses could be themselves badly disrupted or damaged by bombs. Mickey Davis of Mickey's Shelter (see page 142) was an optician whose shop had been destroyed. The raid on 29 December, which caused the Second Great Fire of London (see page 134), destroyed thousands of buildings and left businesses without premises. For many people, the disruption that the Blitz brought to transport meant that even getting in and out of work was often very difficult, even if their own premises had not been affected.

> **Source C** A woman recalls trying to get to work in London on Monday 9 September 1940. Adapted from *How We Lived Then* by N. Longmate, published in 1971
>
> The Tube was closed at Balham. I hitchhiked a lift from a lorry driver [then] walked over Southwark Bridge, as we were not allowed to cross London Bridge, and when I got to the office I understood why. Rubble and glass were all over the place, and there was a gas main still belching flames at the end of the bridge. Firemen, who had been up all night were standing round. They looked so tired.

More generally, many businesses found that they were affected by rules which rationed the amount of food, or clothes that their customers could buy. Many also found that they had to cut their hours so that their employees could get to their shelters before the raids started. Many businesses noticed that their turnover and profits fell as their customers evacuated or moved out of London in the early days of the Blitz. As the war went on and shortages carried on the many big brands continued to advertise, even though they could not make the goods that they had sold before the war, in the hope that they would be able to sell again quickly after the war ended.

The Duggans at work

Mollie Panter-Downes' newspaper piece about the Duggans and the Dead End Kids (see page 116) also gives us lots of information about the kind of work that people did in the East End – Mr Duggan Senior (Patsy's father) was a dustman collecting waste food to feed to pigs, Eileen worked as a **land girl** – replacing men who had left their work on farms when they were called up to the Army. Patsy had joined the Army and Maureen, the only girl in the Kids, was working packing tea leaves into boxes. One of the things that I'm learning is that even during the most difficult periods, life has to go on, and people made great efforts to keep working, and living, as normally as possible.

Leisure activities and enjoying yourself

Londoners still found ways of enjoying themselves. Most people had access to a radio, which they used for listening to the news, but also to comedies. The cinemas and theatres were closed for a very short time at the start of the war, and though both were allowed to open again by 12 September 1939, cinema recovered much more quickly than theatre.

People went to the cinema to see rousing films such as *In Which We Serve*, about the survival of the crew of a sinking warship. Cinemas not only showed films, but also helped keep people informed, to an extent, through **newsreels**. These newsreels were censored by the Government, though usually this worked through a system of 'self censorship' which meant that producers would put things in the best possible light. Often the producers had difficulty in getting footage of important events, because these happened somewhere remote. One Mass Observation report noted that Londoners were becoming more and more positive about the propaganda in newsreels – perhaps because they wanted their morale to be lifted (see Source D).

> **Source D From a Mass Observation Report on Newsreels, 7 October 1940**
> In August 1940, ... nobody objected to the newsreels on the ground that they were propaganda, but 7 per cent said that they were good propaganda. These were not enthusiastic over the point and nobody said that they liked the reels because they were propaganda; but this does seem to indicate a changing attitude towards the word.

Theatre

The slow recovery of the theatres may have been because people didn't want to travel into the centre of London during the Blitz. Many London theatres closed for the whole war, and the theatre companies instead worked in larger towns and cities in the rest of the country. Perhaps because people wanted to have their minds taken off the dangers and difficulties of their lives, the most successful plays of the early war in London were comedies and Agatha Christie murder mysteries. The most successful play of the war was Noel Coward's *Blythe Spirit*, a short comedy play about a novelist researching ghosts and psychics who accidentally summons the disruptive spirit of his first wife.

The Government began to support the theatres as the war went on, by subsidising plays which could be used to encourage national pride. There was a revival of Shakespeare's plays, for instance. As the threat from bombing got less, more theatres reopened and more serious plays about the effort on the home front became popular, such as Esther McCracken's *No Medals*.

> **Source E From the *Observer* newspaper's 'Theatre News' column, 6 November 1941**
> London is to have at least one full sized pantomime at Christmas. Jack will climb the beanstalk at the Coliseum in search of ... adventures, seasonable, heroic and spectacular .... Donald Wolfit has planned a Christmas season of Shakespeare at the Garrick Theatre. This will open with ... *A Midsummer Night's Dream* ... . On Wednesday, the Hippodrome, restored and redecorated, will re-open with George Black's new show *Get a Load of This*, described as a 'surprise musical'.

Pubs

Many people also went to the pub. There is some evidence that more women, at a younger age, started to visit pubs as the number of women in employment increased, and as there was less to spend their wages on in the shops. Pubs did suffer shortages of beer and spirits and even of glasses at some points in the war, and many regulars took their own glasses to the pub with them. Singing in the pub, as well as in the shelter, was just one of the ways in which people tried to keep their spirits up. According to Mollie Panter-Downes, Patsy Duggan was back in Wapping in July 1944 on leave and playing the piano to entertain his friends in his local pub when it was badly damaged in a V1 blast which also destroyed the Duggan's home.

> ## IMPACT OF THE BLITZ ?
>
> 1. Make two lists of the ways in which the bombing disrupted work and leisure.
> 2. Make notes for each disruption about how Londoners tried to carry on as normal.
> 3. What kinds of sources (see page 114 for some ideas) could be useful in finding out more about these difficulties, or the things that people did to carry on?

Dance halls

The National Gallery held lunchtime classical concerts in its basement, but far the most popular musical entertainment for young people was the dance hall. Dance halls were popular across the country, and church halls, canteens in factories and other public spaces would be cleared for Friday and Saturday night dances. In London the biggest dance halls, such as the Astoria, could have more than 10,000 visitors a week. The dancing became much less formal than before the war; one of the biggest crazes was 'the jitterbug'. One Mass Observation observer attempted to describe 'truckin' – one of the steps in this dance, which he saw at the Paramount Dance Hall on the Tottenham Court Road, just after the war started in 1939.

Dancing became even more popular in dance halls near bases full of soldiers from France, Canada and, after December 1941, from America. American soldiers were well paid, and had access to food rations that others didn't – even being able to get hold of luxuries such as ice-cream, which meant that they were sought after as boyfriends and as dancing partners. Women and men from all over the world danced in dance halls across London during the Second World War.

Source F

▲ Jitterbug dancers before the start of the war, in a dance hall in 1938

Source G

1. Right foot on stroking the floor for four beats, whilst the left beats on the floor in rhythm (looks like a cat walking in the wet).
2. Hopping on right leg and raising left leg kick foot in double time for one bar.
3. In the middle of usual truckin' steps the chap does a split and draws himself up slowly taking about three bars to do it.
4. Leaning forward from the waist hands held in front of body in a clasp, partner about 3 feet away in same position facing. Then progress sideways by wriggling feet on the ground – the toe and heel both being kept on the ground in some cases, in others heel on ground to pointing upwards.

Exploring the sources: the impact of the attacks

1. How useful are Sources A and B for an enquiry into the impact of the Blitz on morale? Explain your answer using Sources A and B and your knowledge of the historical context.

2. How useful are Sources C and D for an enquiry into the conditions in the Air Raid Shelters in London? Explain your answer using Sources C and D and your knowledge of the historical context.

3. How could you follow up Source C to find out more about life in the shelters in London? Use the following headings:
   - Detail in Source C that I would follow up
   - Question I would ask
   - The type of source I could use
   - How this might help answer my question

Source A Mollie Panter-Downes, an American journalist writing for the *New Yorker* news magazine described the effect of the Blitz for her readers in the USA, 17 September 1940

For Londoners there are no longer such things as good nights; there are only bad nights, worse nights and better nights. Hardly anyone has slept at all in the past weeks. The sirens go off at approximately the same time every evening, and in the poorer districts, queues of people carrying blankets, thermos flasks, and babies begin to form quite early outside the air raid shelters ... after a few of these nights, sleep of a kind comes from complete exhaustion.

Source B From a young woman's diary written on 11 September 1940, from *Love and War in London: the Mass Observation Wartime Diary of Olivia Crockett*, published in 2008

Sunday night I put out an incendiary beside the coal cellar. Monday night a high explosive at the end of the Garden brought all the walls down and made a crater ten feet deep and thirty in diameter. The Ministry of Information local boards have a notice: 'Local Damage, two houses hit, no casualties'. Bloody Farce. There are literally hundreds of houses down in this borough of Deptford.

Every night we have been in the cellar. I cannot sleep, especially since I was the only one awake to hear the incendiary bomb and was able to put it out within two minutes of landing. I daren't sleep now. I roam about the house and garden and keep going back to the cellar when the lights are overhead and report progress to the others.

Source C

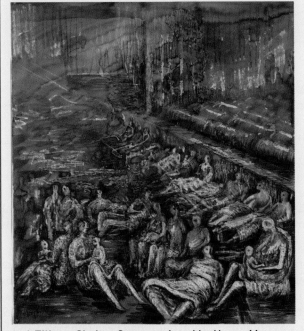

▲ A Tilbury Shelter Scene, painted by Henry Moore

Source D

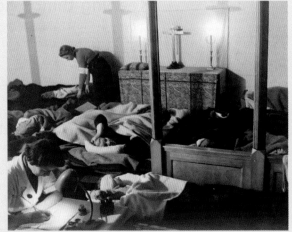

▲ Air raid shelter in John Keble Church, Mill Hill, London, England, 1940

1.8 London's response to the war: Keeping things going

The Dead End Kids gang separated as each of them was sent off to different parts of the war effort. Some, like Maureen, went to work in factories. Others took roles in the military. But where were the decisions being made about where they went, and how the country should be run in wartime? Who decided where the military effort was focused and what to do about shelters and civil defence? And how did they do this in wartime? How did the government keep things going?

CORNELL NOTES

You need to record the information in this section so that you remember how the government kept things going in London during the war. You can use a 'Cornell Notes' Knowledge Organiser to help you do this. Split your page into three as shown in the diagram below. As you read through pages 154–59 you should make notes, as you might do normally. When you have done this read through your notes, and in the wider margin on the left write some questions that are answered by your notes. For instance, you might write 'Eros Statue covered with sandbags for protection' when you are first making notes, and then 'How was public art protected?' when you come back to review these notes. In the bottom box you write further questions that you'd like to find out the answers to, or make a note of anything that confuses you.

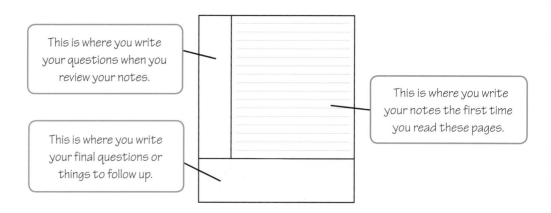

This is where you write your questions when you review your notes.

This is where you write your notes the first time you read these pages.

This is where you write your final questions or things to follow up.

Keeping things going: the government

Shortly before the war the government decided to create an underground headquarters for the Cabinet and for the Military Chiefs of Staff and their supporting departments, so that the country could still be run while bombing was going on.

The New Public Offices building in Whitehall were eventually chosen for this HQ (see map page 120), because the building had a steel frame and a basement which could be reinforced. A layer of concrete was placed on top of the reinforced basement to act as a shield. The basement was also gas-proofed and protected against flooding in case bombs should cause the river or the nearby Serpentine lake to flood into underground tunnels.

The Cabinet War Rooms, as they became known, eventually became very crowded. The Chiefs of the Army, Navy and Airforce worked there – operations for the whole war were co-ordinated from the Map Room. Churchill, the Prime Minister from 1940, spent most of the war sleeping in the specially prepared annexe of the building above the War Rooms, after Number 10 Downing Street was declared too vulnerable to attack in December 1940. The flat at the New Public Office was not bomb-proof, but it had been reinforced and had steel shutters that could be fitted over the windows to protect against bomb blasts. Churchill continued to hold most of his Cabinet meetings at Number 10.

The Rooms were designed to give the prime minister and key members of his staff a place to work and sleep when the raids were at their worst. However, the War Rooms themselves were not bomb-proof, partly because the concrete slab was not thick enough, and partly because the War Rooms kept expanding into other rooms of the basement of the New Public Office.

THE CABINET WAR ROOMS 1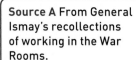

1. Explain why the War Rooms became so busy.
2. Describe the measures taken to protect key members of the government at the New Public Offices.
3. Before you read the next paragraph see if you can predict the facilities and technology that needed to be installed at the War Rooms to make it work properly.

The War Rooms kept growing, with rooms and facilities being added. The Map Room was the most important and busiest room – senior government officials and military officers would meet and discuss the war, as well as eat meals in this room. There was a tiny telephone room with connections to the USA. In the Map Room more telephone connections to the headquarters of the Army, Navy and Airforce were used to update maps on the wall which showed the situation in Africa, Russia, the Middle East and the Far East, and, after 1944, in Western Europe. Broadcasting equipment and a connection to the BBC meant that official broadcasts could be made if needed. There were also bedrooms and offices, a kitchen and mess rooms in which other officers and the guards (who were paratroopers) ate meals. The site was so secret that soldiers in the Army were detailed to clean the rooms, so that civilian cleaners would not see the secrets displayed on the walls and on papers.

Source A From General Ismay's recollections of working in the War Rooms.

Whenever a big battle or critical movement was in progress, it was a temptation to find pretexts for going to the War Room at all hours of the day or night, in order to get the very latest information. The sensation was not unlike visiting a friend in hospital. One entered the room hoping for the best, but fearing the worst.

THE CABINET WAR ROOMS 2

1. How accurate was your list of things that the War Rooms would need?
2. Explain why the War Rooms needed:
   a) maps
   b) telephones
   c) bedrooms and kitchens
3. What follow-up questions might you ask about the evidence in Source A from General Ismay?
4. What sources, or kinds of sources might help you to answer these questions?

Though the slab was thickened and extended several times in 1943, the decision was made that if large raids re-started then the Cabinet Rooms would be moved elsewhere. Alternative centres of government had already been built, but, in practice, though Churchill moved around London, often spending a night in one place, and the next elsewhere, he most often ran the government's affairs from the Cabinet Rooms.

Developing your enquiry

You could investigate the other places that were prepared as underground shelters for parts of the government:

- Dollis Hill – code name 'Paddock'
- Monck Street – code name 'the Rotundas'

Keeping things going: the royal family

> **Source B** From the memoirs of Sir John Colville, a senior civil servant who worked in the Cabinet War Rooms
>
> It was widely believed that London would be reduced to rubble within minutes of war being declared, as recently depicted to an alarmed populace in the film of H.G. Well's book called *The Shape of Things to Come* and it seemed as if this was indeed about to happen.

These same fears expressed in Source B led civil servants to draw up plans to evacuate the royal family and important people and sections of the Civil Service. The plans were abandoned after a test run in 1938 led to chaos and lack of communication between these important parts of government. While King George VI and his wife Queen Elizabeth decided to stay in London, they did send their daughters, Elizabeth (later Queen Elizabeth II) and Margaret, to Windsor Castle in Berkshire, which was thought to be safer than central London. There had been plans to send the whole family to Canada, but these were abandoned.

Buckingham Palace was hit and damaged on the sixth night of the Blitz. In response, Queen Elizabeth said 'it makes me feel that I can look the East End in the face'.

Keeping things going: Dig For Victory

THE GOVERNMENT AND THE ROYAL FAMILY **?**

1. What were the decisions taken about whether the government and royal family should leave London?

2. Explain why the government did not move away.

3. Why do you think the royal family decided to stay?

Source C Vegetable allotments in the moat of the Tower of London in June 1940

Source D Painting by Adrian Allinson, 1942

Source E A photograph taken in 2010 of the same place as Source D

Look closely at Sources D and E. What differences can you see between the pictures?
Write a list of them, and see if you can explain each one.

The photo (Source E) was taken in 2010, and shows a large square in a wealthy part of London. The painting (Source D), by an artist called Adrian Allinson, is of a group of Auxiliary Fire Service volunteers who are working on an allotment garden in the same square in 1942. Frustrations over shortages of vegetables, along with the fear that Britain needed to do more to feed itself, led the Ministry of Agriculture to announce a campaign which became known as 'Dig For Victory'. The ministry wanted people to turn their gardens into vegetable plots in which they could grow their own food. The campaign was a success. Before the war there were around 700,000 plots, which doubled to almost 2 million by its end. Schools taught vegetable gardening as part of their lessons, and parks and city squares were dug over to make way for potatoes, onions and carrots. Many of these plots were in public parks, such as Hyde Park and around the Albert memorial in Kensington Gardens. Part of Victoria Park in Bethnal Green became a pig farm, as well as providing space for allotments. Even the moat of the Tower of London was given over to vegetable gardening.

Growing vegetables in bomb sites

In the East End, where the Dead End Kids lived, we have already seen that people were less likely to have a garden in which they could grow food. Though some East End gardens were turned into vegetable plots, other gardeners took advantage of the space created by the bombing to create new plots. The Bethnal Green Bombed Sites Producers Association produced their second 'Annual Report' in 1943, which tells us quite a lot about how the bombed sites were prepared, and the kind of 'production' that took place.

Source F

▲ This photograph from 1942 shows boys in London clearing a bomb site to create an allotment. They were going to grow beans from seeds sent from America. This photograph was published by the government's Ministry of Information. In what ways did it provide good propaganda to encourage the war effort?

The leaflet discusses how the War Debris Survey lorries were used to take away rubble, and that poultry and rabbits had been bought by the Association and sold on to the members. One item also shows just how important the effort to grow food was to the Government. On 17 June 1943 the Queen visited six sites run by the Association and after a few weeks one of her ladies in waiting wrote to the committee to say:

> The Queen will be grateful if you will thank all those who joined in making her visit so delightful and congratulate the Allotment Holders and Farmers on the success of the National work they are doing.

There was lots of other advice available for those wanting to Dig for Victory and grow their own food. In January 1941 the government issued 'Dig For Victory Leaflet No.1' and afterwards printed other guides about what to plant and when, and how to tackle pests and diseases. Demonstration gardens were set up in public parks, and every Sunday afternoon a radio programme called *In your Garden* gave more tips. One of the people recording their war diaries for Mass Observation went to one of these demonstration gardens.

Source G A Mass Observation diarist records a visit to a vegetable garden in Hyde Park (adapted from www.massobservation.amdigital.co.uk/Documents/Images/Diarist-5098/1258)

I went along to the demonstration allotment in Hyde Park to see how the crops were coming on. There was no-one in attendance this morning, so I could not get any tips on growing crops on poor soil without spending a fortune on manure. The broad beans are doing well, and I noticed some small lettuces the last time I was there have grown into enormous plants like cabbages. [When back home] I noticed a picture in the Evening Standard of Mary Gray and sheep sheering in Hyde Park. Mary was tying up the fleeces when I was there.

Developing your enquiry

1. How useful is Source G in explaining how people learned to grow more food for themselves?
2. What questions could you ask to follow up this source?
3. What other sources might help you to answer these questions? Why would you use these sources?

Keeping things going: safeguarding art and important buildings

Take another look at the pictures on page 157 which you compared. You might have noticed the difference between the plinth in each picture. The statue of King William III on horseback has been removed in the painting. This and many other statues, such as Eros in Piccadilly, were removed and stored in safer places, or otherwise protected in order to avoid damage from bombs.

Source H

▲ The statue of Eros, protected by a pyramid-shaped shield made of sandbags and covered in wood

London was home to many art galleries and museums, such as the National Gallery and the Victoria and Albert (V&A) Museum, which had thousands of pieces of important art in their collections. The V&A was open throughout the war, but many of its important pieces had been moved to a large country house in Somerset. Its ceramic art (pottery) was stored at the same Aldwych tube station that was used as an air raid shelter.

The museum was hit by bombs several times during the Blitz. It continued to hold exhibitions, encouraged by the Government, as part of the efforts to keep Londoners' morale at a high level but, as the originals had been sent into safe storage, most of the paintings were copies. Churchill himself stepped in to stop the National Gallery from sending its paintings abroad. The museum had planned to ship them to Canada, but instead they were sent to a quarry in Blaenau Ffestiniog in Wales for the duration of the War. At the gallery itself lunchtime concerts were held when Myra Hess, a famous pianist, suggested them. She had hoped that up to 500 people would come, but thousands of people queued to see musicians play more than a thousand concerts at the gallery during the war.

'MUSEUMS' AND THE ARTS

1. Describe the measures taken to protect important public art and statues.

2. What did art venues like the V&A and the National Gallery do to keep morale high during the war?

1.9 Conclusions: What have I learned about London in the Second World War?

I began this enquiry with a face – that of Shamus O'Brien, and some questions: Why was a young teenager like Shamus acting as a hero in bombed-out London? Why hadn't he been evacuated? Why didn't the officials send him and his friends into the underground shelters? These questions came out of the general knowledge I had about life in London during the Second World War, that there was an evacuation, that the East End was badly hit, and that many people spent months in the shelters. Writing this book has given me a chance to find out lots more, and given me access to sources that have helped me better understand how people lived.

So, what have I learned?

1. Many people expected London to be heavily attacked within days of the outbreak of the Second World War. Millions were evacuated, and this evacuation started even before war was declared. The Phoney War that lasted between September 1939 and May 1940 was one reason why many of these evacuees came back.

2. Shelter provision where it wasn't possible to install Anderson Shelters was inadequate in the early days of the Blitz. Many people were hiding in surface shelters, which did not feel safe. This might explain why some, like the Dead End Kids, preferred to be outside, taking part in the defence of their houses.

3. The government did take action to improve shelter provision, but to a great extent they were led by many ordinary people taking matters into their own hands – at Underground stations, at the Savoy and at shelters like Mickey's Shelter.

4. Though the war took a great toll on people's lives, they had to find ways of carrying on with the business of living. Most people continued to make their way into work, to pick up the pieces, literally, when they were bombed out, and even to find ways of enjoying themselves when they got the chance.

> **?** What three things have you learnt about life in London during the Second World War?

What did I learn about the Dead End Kids?

What really interested me about the Dead End Kids was not just the bravery (and possibly their foolish bravery) in setting out to help fight fires, and deal with bombs. I wanted to know how this was *possible*. I have two children of my own, and my eldest is not much younger than Shamus O'Brien. I wondered how our family would react in the same circumstances. What I learned was that people don't always act in the safest ways. I also found out that these same ordinary people can do extraordinary things when they are faced with danger. The Kids were astoundingly brave, but they fitted into a larger picture in which volunteers, many of whom were children, worked hard to help other people throughout the war in London. Finally I found out that the official plans of the Government would not have been enough, on their own, to keep London working in the face of the Blitz.

What next?

One of the reasons I chose to study and to teach history is that it is never 'done'. There are always new questions that can be followed up, and often there are new books, or new pieces of research to read, or even more sources to consider and fit into the jigsaw. The questions I would like to explore next are:

1. Did all Londoners decide that they 'could take it' – that they would raise a 'Blitz Spirit' and carry on?
2. What happened to the homeless – how were they re-housed?
3. What about after the war – how did London cope with the soldiers who returned from the fighting?
4. What happened to the Duggans, and the surviving Dead End Kids?

To find out the answers I need to think about what kinds of sources I could use. Which of the sources in the box might help me answer these questions?

> Diaries
>
> Local government maps of damaged property
>
> Registers of births, deaths and marriages
>
> Guidance printed to help bombed-out families
>
> Newspaper articles
>
> Newsreels
>
> Government statistics
>
> Records of Cabinet Meetings

Visible learning: Review and Revise

This activity will help you practise asking questions and choosing sources. This is a good activity to do with a partner, so that you can share ideas.

1 Choose one of the topics in the pink box below. Write down at least two questions you want to ask about it to deepen your knowledge.

2 Look at the sources in the *blue box*. Select one source that might help you answer your questions, and then explain how it might do this. You could choose different sources for each question.

3 Repeat these steps for at least one more topic.

Topics to find out more about

1 The targets of the attack	**2** Family life	**3** Evacuation – why so many returned
4 Life for the 'left behind' kids	**5** Life during the blackout	**6** Saving St Pauls
7 Shelter disasters	**8** The Tilbury shelter	**9** Bomb disposal
10 How morale changed during the war	**11** Dance halls and cinema	**12** Damage to schools and education
13 Working in the Cabinet War rooms	**14** How the lives of women changed	**15** How businesses coped with the war

Sources you could use

A Memoirs and autobiographies **B** Photographs **C** Local newspapers **D** Local council records **E** Central government records **F** Newspapers	**G** Mass Observation reports to the Cabinet **H** Newsreels **I** Reports and diaries from individual Mass Observation volunteers **J** Cinema posters	**K** Government propaganda posters **L** Maps of bomb damage **M** Business accounts

1 Test yourself

The more you identify what you're not sure about, the more chance you have of filling those gaps and doing well in the exam. How many of these can you get right?

1 What was an ARP warden?	**2** Why is the census not yet much use for historians investigating the Second World War?	**3** What was an incendiary?
4 Explain 'fire spotting'.	**5** What different meanings did the phrase 'dead end kids' have?	**6** Why was the East End a particular target for the Luftwaffe?
7 Which areas were more like to have Anderson Shelters?	**8** Explain three different ways in which Londoners prepared for attack.	**9** Explain the three phases of the attacks on London.
10 Why did the government come under pressure to improve shelters?	**11** List three ways in which the government tried to a) measure and b) improve morale.	**12** What did 'Dig for Victory' mean?

Part 3: Writing better history

Introducing the exam

Simply knowing a lot of content is not enough to achieve a good grade in your GCSE History exam. You need to know how to write effective answers to the questions. Pages 165–76 give you an insight into the exam and provide guidance on how to approach the different questions. This page and page 163 introduce the structure of Paper 1 of your exam. The guidance on page 163 and on page 164 helps you approach your exam with confidence.

Paper 1 is divided into two sections. Section A covers the **study of a historic environment** on London and the Second World War, 1939–45. Section B covers the **thematic study** of Warfare and British society c.1250–present.

Paper 1: Thematic study and historic environment

Option 11: Warfare and British society, c.1250–present and London and the Second World War, 1939–45

Time: 1 hour 15 minutes
You must have:

① ➤ Source Booklet (enclosed)

Instructions

② ➤ • Answer Questions 1 and 2 from Section A.

③ ➤ • From Section B, answer Questions 3 and 4 and then **EITHER** Question 5 **OR** Question 6.

Information

• The total mark for this paper is 52.

④ ➤ • The marks for each question are shown in brackets.

SECTION A: London and the Second World War, 1939–45

Answer Questions 1 and 2.

⑤ ➤ 1. Describe **two** features of shelters which could make them dangerous or unhealthy places to shelter from bombing during the Blitz.

Feature 1

Feature 2   **(Total for Question 1 = 4 marks)**

⑥ ➤ 2. (a) Study Sources A and B in the Source Booklet.
How useful are Sources A and B (from page 167) for an enquiry into the fears that many Londoners had at the start of the Second World War?

Explain your answer, using Sources A and B and your knowledge of the historical context.

(8 marks)

⑦ ➤ (b) Study Source B.

How could you follow up Source B to find out more about how people prepared their houses for the blackout?

In your answer, you must give the question you would ask and the type of source you could use.

Complete the table below: (4 marks)

Detail in Source B that I would follow up: _____
Question I would ask: _____
What type of source I could use: _____
How this might help answer my question: _____

(Total for Question 2 = 12 marks)
TOTAL FOR SECTION A = 16 MARKS

SECTION B: Warfare and British society, c.1250–present

Answer Questions 3 and 4. Then answer EITHER Question 5 OR 6.

8 → 3. Explain **one** way in which civilians' experiences of warfare in England during the Hundred Years' War (1337–1453) were similar to civilians' experience of the Civil Wars in England (1642–49). (4 marks)

9 → 4. Explain why recruitment to the Army in Britain changed between 1700 and 1900. (12 marks)

10 →
> You may use the following in your answer:
> - Napoleonic Wars (1803–15) • Cardwell's Army reforms
>
> You **must** also use information of your own.

Answer EITHER Question 5 OR Question 6.

Spelling, punctuation, grammar and the use of specialist terminology will be assessed in this question.

EITHER

11 → 5. 'The use of muskets was the main reason for changes in the nature of warfare during the period 1500 to 1700.'

How far do you agree? Explain your answer. (16 marks)

> You may use the following in your answer:
> - the use of musket and pike squares in the English Civil Wars
> - the establishment of the New Model Army (1645)
>
> You **must** also use information of your own.

OR

6. 'The First World War represented a major change in the way that Government recruited soldiers between c.1800–c.2000.'

How far do you agree? Explain your answer. (16 marks)

> You may use the following in your answer:
> - conscription
> - propaganda and financial incentives for recruits
>
> You **must** also use information of your own.

12 →
(Total for spelling, punctuation, grammar and the use of specialist terminology = 4 marks)

(Total for Question 5 or 6 = 20 marks)

Timing tip

It is important to time yourself carefully. One hour and fifteen minutes sounds a long time but it goes very quickly! Some students run out of time because they spend too long on Section A, thinking that it is worth spending half their time on this Section. However, Section A is worth 16 marks whereas Section B is worth 36 marks. The final two questions of Section B are worth more marks than all the other questions put together. This shows the importance of having a time plan and sticking to it.

Look at the plan to the right. You could use this plan or develop your own and check it with your teacher.

Questions 1 and 2 approx. 25 minutes

Questions 3 and 4 approx. 25 minutes

Either Question 5 or 6 approx. 25 minutes

Planning for success

① THE SOURCE BOOKLET

The exam paper on pages 162 and 163 gives you an idea what your exam will look like. We have not included the Source Booklet. For practice use the sources and activities in Part 2 of this book (pages 112–61). Make sure you spend time reading and annotating the sources before you attempt Question 2 in the exam.

② FOLLOW INSTRUCTIONS CAREFULLY

Read the instructions very carefully. Some students miss questions they need to answer while others waste time answering more questions than they need to answer. Remember to answer **both** parts of Question 2 and to choose between EITHER Question 5 OR 6. You will also see that for Question 1 you need to describe **two** key features whereas with Question 3 you only need to explain **one** way in which people's reactions were similar.

③ THINK CAREFULLY ABOUT WHICH QUESTION YOU CHOOSE

After Questions 1, 2, 3 and 4, you need to decide whether to answer Question 5 or Question 6. Do not rush your decision. Think carefully about which question you will perform best on. Plan your answer – it is worth 16 marks, nearly a third of the total marks for the paper.

④ SPEND TIME DE-CODING QUESTIONS

The marks for each question are shown in brackets. This gives you an idea of how much you need to write, as does the space for your answer on the exam paper. However, do not panic if you do not fill all the space. There will probably be more space than you need and the quality of your answer is more important than how much you write. The most important thing is to keep focused on the question. If you include information that is not relevant to the question you will not gain any marks, no matter how much you write!

Read each question carefully before you to start to answer it. Use the advice on de-coding questions on page 165 to make sure you focus on the question.

⑤ DESCRIBING KEY FEATURES

The first question asks you to describe two features of an aspect of the historic environment you have studied. Headings on the exam paper help you write about each feature separately. Advice on how to gain high marks is on pages 174–176.

⑥ EVALUATING THE USEFULNESS OF A SOURCE

This question asks you to evaluate how useful two sources are for a specific enquiry. Use the Source Booklet to annotate the sources. Make sure you use your own knowledge to place the source in its historical context. This is a challenging task. Page 167 explains how to approach this question.

⑦ FOLLOWING UP A SOURCE

This question has four parts. You need to fill in the table on the exam paper. Page 168 provides advice on this question.

⑧ EXPLORING SIMILARITIES OR DIFFERENCES BETWEEN TWO PERIODS

This is the first question that tests you on your knowledge and understanding of Warfare from c.1250 to the present. It will usually ask you to explain a similarity or a difference between the key features of two different periods. Page 169 explains how to answer this question.

⑨ EXPLAINING WHY WARFARE CHANGED (OR STAYED THE SAME)

Questions such as this test your ability to write effective explanations. You may be asked to explain why warfare progressed so quickly or why there was little change during a period. Pages 170–71 help you write a good answer to this question.

⑩ USING THE STIMULUS MATERIAL

When you attempt Question 4 and either Question 5 or 6 you will have bullet points as stimulus material to help plan your answer. You do not have to include them but try to use them to get you thinking and to support your arguments. You must bring in your own knowledge too. If you only use the stimulus material you will not gain high marks for your answer.

⑪ MAKING JUDGEMENTS

This question carries the most marks and requires a longer answer that needs careful planning. You will be provided with a statement. It may be about the pace of change in a period (for example Question 5) or the significance of an individual or a discovery (for example Question 6). Pages 172–73 provides advice on answering this question.

⑫ CHECKING THE QUALITY OF YOUR WRITING

Make sure you leave five minutes at the end of the exam to check your answers. If you are short of time check your answer to the final question first as spelling, punctuation, grammar and use of specialist terminology are assessed in this question. You can gain 4 additional marks on this question – page 173 provides advice on what to focus on. However, remember that the accuracy of your spelling, punctuation and grammar is important in all questions as it affects the clarity of your answer.

De-coding exam questions

The examiners are not trying to catch you out: they are giving you a chance to show what you know – and what you can do with what you know. However, you must stick to the question on the exam paper. Staying focused on the question is crucial. Including information that is not relevant or misreading a question and writing about the wrong topic wastes time and gains you no marks.

To stay focused on the question you will need to practise how to 'de-code' questions. This is particularly important for Section B of the exam paper. Follow these **five steps to success**:

Step 1 Read the question a couple of times. Then look at **how many marks** the question is worth. This tells you how much you are expected to write. Do not spend too long on questions only worth a few marks. Remember it is worth planning the 12- and 16-mark questions.

Step 2 Identify the **conceptual focus** of the question. What is the key concept that the question focuses on? Is it asking you to look at:

- the **significance** of a discovery or individual
- **causation** – the reasons why an event or development happened
- **similarities** – between the key features of different periods
- **change** – the extent of change or continuity, progress or stagnation during a period?

Step 3 Spot the **question type**. Are you being asked to:

- **describe** the key features of a period
- **explain** similarities between periods or why something happened
- **evaluate** how useful a source or collection of sources is
- reach a **judgement** as to how far you agree with a particular statement.

Each question type requires a different approach. Look for key words or phrases that help you work out which approach is needed. The phrase 'How far do you agree?' means you need to weigh the evidence for and against a statement before reaching a balanced judgement. 'Explain why' means that you need to explore a range of reasons why an event happened or why the pace of change during a period was fast or slow.

Step 4 Identify the **content focus**. What is the area of content or topic the examiner wants you to focus on?

Step 5 Look carefully at the **date boundaries** of the question. What time period should you cover in your answer? Stick to this carefully or you will waste time writing about events that are not relevant to the question.

Look at the exam question below. At first glance it appears this question is just about the cavalry charge. This shows the danger of not de-coding a question carefully. If you simply describe what nuclear weapons were you will not get many marks as you are still not focusing on the actual question.

The date boundaries for the question are 1800–2000. If you include references to events in the eighteenth century you will waste time and not pick up any additional marks.

The conceptual focus is significance – you need to reach a judgement on how far the First World War represented a 'major change' in recruitment.

6. 'The First World War represented a major change in the way that Government recruited soldiers between c.1800–c.2000.' How far do you agree? Explain your answer.

(16 marks)

16 marks are available – this means the question requires an extended answer. It is definitely worth planning this answer!

The content focus is more than just the First World War. It is exploring a wider theme – the nature of recruitment.

The phrase 'How far do you agree?' means that this question requires you to reach a judgement about the statement in quotation marks. This means analysing the impact of the First World War on recruitment. It also means weighing its significance against other important developments in recruitment such as Cardwell's reforms.

Practice questions

Look at the other questions in Section B of the exam paper on page 163.

Break each question down into the five steps and check you have de-coded the question effectively.

Describing key features of a period

'Describe' questions only carry 4 marks so it is important to get to the point quickly so you do not waste precious time that is needed for questions that carry 12 or 16 marks.

Look at the question below.

> 1. Describe **two** features of the shelters which could make them dangerous or unhealthy places to shelter from bombing during the Blitz. (4 marks)
>
> Feature 1: _____
>
> Feature 2: _____

Tip 1: Stay relevant to the question

One major problem with 'Describe' questions is that students write too much! They include details that are not relevant to the question. Make sure you stick to the question – describe two key features of the shelters which could make them dangerous or unhealthy places to shelter from bombing during the Blitz.

You do not need to:

- include more than two features (extra features will gain you no more marks)
- evaluate and reach a judgement as to how unhealthy or dangerous the shelters were during the Blitz.

If you write too much you could run out of time later in the exam when you are answering questions that are worth a lot more marks and need longer answers.

Tip 2: Keep it short and simple

You can get 2 marks by simply identifying two features of the shelters that made them dangerous.

For each feature you identify add a sentence that adds further detail and develops your answer.

Look at the example below. Then practise your technique by tackling the examples in the practice question box.

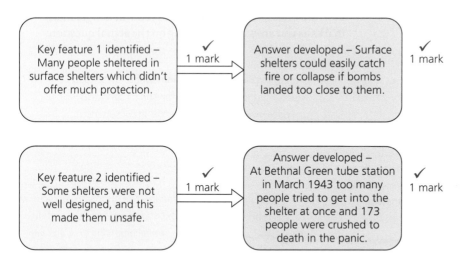

Key feature 1 identified – Many people sheltered in surface shelters which didn't offer much protection. → ✓ 1 mark → Answer developed – Surface shelters could easily catch fire or collapse if bombs landed too close to them. ✓ 1 mark

Key feature 2 identified – Some shelters were not well designed, and this made them unsafe. → ✓ 1 mark → Answer developed – At Bethnal Green tube station in March 1943 too many people tried to get into the shelter at once and 173 people were crushed to death in the panic. ✓ 1 mark

Practice questions

1. Describe two features of Anderson Shelters that meant not all Londoners had one.
2. Describe two features of V2 bombs that made them very dangerous.
3. Describe two features of Mickey's Shelter which made it a better place to shelter.
4. Describe two features of London that made it a target for attack during the Blitz.
5. Describe two features of how dance halls helped improve morale in London during the Second World War.
6. Describe two features of the Cabinet War Rooms that made them important during the Second World War.
7. Describe two features of propaganda used to improve Londoners' morale.

> **REMEMBER**
>
> Stay focused and keep it short and simple. Four sentences are enough for four marks.

Evaluating the usefulness of sources

In Section A of the exam you will be asked to evaluate the value of a source for a specific enquiry. Look at the example below.

> **2. a)** Study Sources A and B. How useful are Sources A and B for an enquiry into the fears that many Londoners had at the start of the Second World War? Explain your answer, using Sources A and B and your own knowledge of the historical context. **(8 marks)**

You should annotate the sources in the booklet before you start to write your answer. Also, to evaluate effectively we need to use criteria. Use the criteria opposite to help you.

> **Source A** From a young woman's diary, written in September and then November 1939 for the Mass Observation organisation, from *Love and War in London: the Mass Observation Wartime Diary of Olivia Crockett,* published in 2008
>
> Put up black curtains. Noticed that house next door, inhabited by refugee Jews is brilliantly lit. [...] went out after supper with Father to work out where local ARP post is. Walked through black streets, pouring rain, mostly eery [...] Felt more cheerful trying on gas mask with sisters in front mirror. Momentarily forgetful ribald laughter. I shall think gas masks are incredibly funny until I have to use one in earnest. Blacking out has been an almost un-solvable problem in a house with stone surrounds to the window. The [...] use of nails and drawing pins is defeated and the problem has been attacked in so many ways that the visit of a young constable last night declaring the blackout was unsatisfactory reduced the more highly-strung members of the household to an impotent hysterical outburst.

> **Source B** A woman recalls the Anderson Shelter arriving at her house during an interview for an oral history project from *The War on Our Doorstep* by Harriet Salisbury, published in 2012.
>
> And dad was caring, sensible, looked after his bits and pieces, loved his garden. It broke his heart when he had to tear it all up and put an air raid shelter down there when the war came. They said 'you've got a shelter, you have to put it in your back garden.' But he said 'it's me garden' and they said 'well you know we've issued it out to you, you do it'. Anyhow he must have thought, this is – he'd been through the First World War. He must have thought this is something I've got to do.

REMEMBER

The question is asking you how useful the sources are, not how useless they are. There will not be any sources that are completely useless. Try not to get bogged down telling the examiner just what is wrong with a source. Look at the strengths of each source as well as considering any limitations. Try to begin and end your answer positively. Start your answer by highlighting how each source *helps* us with this enquiry.

☐ Criteria 1: Consider the content of the source

Highlight or underline useful information for the enquiry in both sources. Make sure you judge how useful it is for the enquiry specified in the question. For this question the sources need to help us understand the fears that many Londoners had at the start of the Second World War. Start your answer by highlighting how each source helps us with this enquiry.

☐ Criteria 2: Consider the provenance of each source

Look at the captions provided above the sources. Think carefully about the following key questions and the impact that this might have on how useful the source is.

■ **What is the nature of the source?**

What type of source is it? How does this affect its utility? For example, a private letter or diary can be useful because the person usually gives his or her honest view.

■ **What are the origins of the source?**

Who produced it? Are they likely to have a good knowledge of the events they talk about? Are they likely to give a one-sided view?

■ **What is the purpose of the source?**

Why was it produced? How might this affect the reliability of the source? For example, a politician's speech or a newspaper report might be produced for propaganda purposes – to encourage people to keep going or to down-play the fears that people had.

☐ Criteria 3: Use your own knowledge of the historical context to evaluate the source

Compare the information and key messages contained in the source with your own knowledge of the enquiry topic. Do the **CAT test**. Ask yourself these three key questions:

■ How **comprehensive** is the source? Does it have any limitations? What does it miss out?
■ How **accurate** is the source? Does it 'match' what you know about the topic?
■ How **typical** is the source? Were the feelings described common among Londoners, did the events described happen regularly in London, or are they unusual and untypical of what went on for the majority of the time?

Practice questions

You can find sources with practice questions on pages 131, 139 and 153.

Following up sources

One of the key aims of this book is to help you understand how we use the enquiry process to research history. As we said on pages 113–114, asking the right historical questions is a crucial part of enquiry and historical research. Exam questions like the one below provide you with the opportunity to show the enquiry skills you have been developing throughout the book.

2. **b)** How could you follow up Source E (page 130) to find out more about how people prepared their houses for the blackout? In your answer, you must give the question you would ask and the type of source you could use. Complete the table below.   (4 marks)

- Detail in Source E that I would follow up: _____
- Question I would ask: _____
- What type of source I could use: _____
- How this might help answer my question: _____

The key tip with this question is to make sure that the four different parts of your answer link together.

REMEMBER

This question is only worth 4 marks. Do not go into detailed explanations of why you chose to follow up with a particular type of source – you do not have time. One or two sentences will be fine.

Practice questions

You can find sources with practice questions on pages 131, 139 and 153.

Step 1: Link the detail to the enquiry

Start by identifying the focus for the enquiry – in this case how people prepared their houses for the blackout. Make sure that the detail you say that you would follow up is linked to this enquiry. For example, if Source E mentioned how difficult it was to stop light coming through windows, you could identify this as a detail that you would follow up as this is linked to the main enquiry.

Step 2: Link the question to the detail

The question you choose must be linked to the detail you are following up from the source. Do not simply choose an interesting question unrelated to the enquiry! If we were following up the detail about blacking out windows, we could use 'How did people stop light from coming out of their windows' as our question.

Step 3: Link the type of source to the question

You now need to choose a type of source that would be useful for following up that question. Look at the list in the box opposite. Make sure you choose a source that would help with the question. For example, in this case surveys by Mass Observation might give us a useful insight into how people tried to prepared their houses for the blackout.

Step 4: Link this with your own knowledge

Do not forget to explain the advantages of using this type of source and link it to the enquiry. The source type mentioned above would be particularly useful as they suggest that people felt that it was very difficult to fully blackout their houses, and how ARP wardens checked their preparations. However, the cartoon shown in the source cannot explain in detail the steps that people took to blackout their homes.

Different types of sources

National records
- Government records
- Newspapers
- Mass Observation reports
- Newsreels
- Memoirs

Local records
- Personal accounts
- Personal photographs
- Local newspapers
- Local council record

Exploring similarities between the key features of two different periods

Question 3 is the first question that tests your knowledge and understanding of the thematic study on Warfare and British society, c.1250–present. Remember this is where de-coding questions comes in useful. Look at the question below.

This is an 'explain' question. However, as it is only worth 4 marks, you only have to explain one similarity.

This question has a very specific content focus. To save time make sure you stay relevant – only write about civilians' experiences during the two wars mentioned by the question. There is no need to go into the background of the two wars.

> **3.** Explain **one** way in which civilians' experiences of warfare in England during the Hundred Years' War (1337–1453) were similar to civilians' experience of the Civil Wars in England (1642–49).
>
> (4 marks)

The date boundaries are crucial. You must focus on the right case studies – the Hundred Years' War (1337–1453) and the Civil Wars (1642–49).

The conceptual focus of this question is 'similarities' – the ability to be able to compare different periods of history and spot similarities.

The first thing to notice is that the question is only worth 4 marks. It is important that you are clear on the focus of the question so that you can keep your answer short and to the point.

Explaining similarities between time periods

As this is an 'explain' question you must do more than simply identify a similarity. You will need to support your answer with specific details – a good motto is 'prove' don't 'say'. Would your explanation convince the reader that there was a similarity between the ways that civilians in England experienced wars that were almost 300 years apart?

For example you might 'say' that one similarity between civilian experiences of the two wars was that food was requisitioned from civilians. However, this would not get you high marks. Instead you need to prove your big point about food requisitioning by providing supporting information **and** 'killer evidence'.

- **BIG POINT** – With a question only worth 4 marks do not spend time on an introduction. Start your answer with your 'big point' – in this case that civilians were expected to provide food for troops.

- **SUPPORTING INFORMATION** – You need to develop your initial 'big point' or argument. You could explain how in both periods food was requisitioned from civilians to feed troops.

- **KILLER EVIDENCE** – You now need to prove that this was the case by providing specific examples from each time period. For the later Middle Ages you could refer to the custom of purveyance or prise which permitted the monarch to forcibly buy up food for his armies (often at low prices). For the seventeenth century you might talk about requisitioning of food in villages like Myddle, and the issue of 'free quarter' tickets which were given to civilians by the authorities in order to compensate them (although often late or not very well) for their provision of food and shelter to troops.

Practice questions

You can find further practice questions on pages 29, 51 and 76.

REMEMBER

You should only be spending around five minutes on this question. Keep your answer focused on explaining **one** way in which people behaved or reacted in a similar way. Do not list lots of similarities.

Tackling 12-mark explain questions

Look at the question below.

> **4.** Explain why recruitment to the Army in Britain changed between 1700 and 1900.
>
> (12 marks)
>
> You may use the following in your answer:
> - the Napoleonic Wars (1803–15)
> - Cardwell's Army reforms
>
> You must also use information of your own.

This question is different in two ways from Question 3 on page 169. Firstly, the conceptual focus is different – in this case the key concept is causation (explaining **why** an event took place or explaining the pace of change). Secondly, this question is worth 12 marks. The examiner will expect you to give a range of reasons **why** recruitment to the army changed between 1750 and 1900.

It is important to spend time planning this question during your exam. Follow the steps below to help you plan effectively and produce a good answer.

Step 1: Get focused on the question

Make sure you de-code the question carefully. Note that the content focus is on recruitment, so you do not need to explain about the training of combatants.

Step 2: Identify a range of factors

Try to cover more than one cause. If your mind goes blank always go back to the key factors that influence change in warfare (see page 8). The stimulus bullet points can also help you. For example, in the question above, the reference to Cardwell's Reforms shows how Government and individuals played a key role in changing recruitment. However, do not rely just on the bullet points, remember to bring in your own knowledge as well.

Science, technology and communications

Governments and individuals

Attitudes in society

Step 3: Organise your answer using paragraphs

Do not worry about a long introduction. One or two sentences are more than enough and you can use words from the question. Look at the example below. Note how the student has built a short introduction into the first paragraph which focuses on the role played by the Napoleonic Wars.

One important reason for the changes in recruitment was the Napoleonic Wars which significantly increased the need for recruits (particularly of infantry).

Aim to start a new paragraph each time you move onto a new factor that caused change. Signpost your argument at the start of the paragraph. For example, you could start your next paragraph like this:

The actions of Government and individuals also played an important role in influencing developments in recruitment.

Step 4: Do not 'say' that a factor was important – 'prove' it was

Remember that a list of reasons why recruitment to the army changed will not get you a high-level mark. You need to **prove** your case for each factor. This means developing your explanation by adding supporting information and specific examples (killer evidence).

This is where your work on connectives will come in useful. Look again at the advice on page 28 and remember to tie what you know to the question by using connectives such as 'this meant that', 'this led to' and 'this resulted in'. For example, you may want to build on the opening to your first paragraph by using the example of the increase in the use of recruitment parties, bounties and kidnap by crimps as a way to show how the Napoleonic Wars impacted on recruitment. Look at how the student below starts to prove a point.

The Napoleonic Wars caused changes in recruitment because the lengthy wars created a massive need for infantrymen which led to a greater use of recruitment parties who offered bounty payments to men to encourage them to enlist.

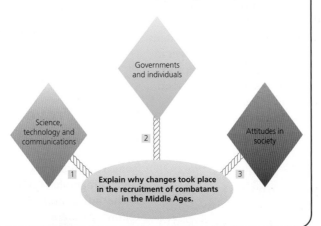

Practice questions

You can find further practice questions on pages 29, 51 and 76.

REMEMBER

Do not try to cover too many factors that led to change. Select which factors you can make the strongest argument for. Remember in the exam you would have approximately 15 minutes to answer this question.

Step 5: End your answer with a thoughtful conclusion

Keep your conclusion short. A good conclusion makes the overall argument clear – it is not a detailed summary of everything you have already written! Make it clear which factor played the most important role. You may want to show how it links to other factors.

Making judgements – tackling the 16-mark question

The last question on the exam paper carries the most marks and requires a carefully planned, detailed answer. You will be provided with a statement in quotation marks and be asked to reach a judgement about **how far you agree** with it. The phrase 'how far' is important as it is unlikely that you will totally agree or disagree with the statement. The examiner will be looking for you to show that you can weigh the evidence for and against the statement.

Look at the example below.

> **5.** 'The use of muskets was the main reason for changes in the nature of warfare during the period 1500 to 1700.' How far do you agree? Explain your answer.
>
> (16 marks)
>
> You may use the following in your answer:
> * The use of musket and pike squares in the English Civil Wars
> * The establishment of the New Model Army (1645)
>
> **You must also use information of your own.**
>
> (Total for spelling, punctuation, grammar and the use of specialist terminology = 4 marks)
>
> (Total for Question 5 = 20 marks)

Step 1: Focus

The content focus is important – you have to reach a judgement on the nature of warfare in early modern Britain. This includes information about the weapons and composition of armies, including the number, type and tactics of troops. The conceptual focus is on causation. You have to evaluate the extent to which the use of muskets was the main reason for changes in the nature of warfare, 1500 to 1700. You need to bring in other reasons for changes. The stimulus bullet points in the question can help you, but you must also bring in at least one cause of your own. Remember that it is important to cover the full timescale set within the question.

Step 2: Identify

In 16-mark questions you are required to reach a judgement on a statement. In order to do this effectively you need to identify **clear criteria** for reaching that judgement. Just as you need to cover a range of factors in 'explain' questions, you need to **cover a range of criteria** in 'judgement' questions.

Possible criteria for reaching a judgement:

- If you are judging the importance of an individual or weapon you could analyse and evaluate the immediate impact, the short-term impact and the long-term impact.
- If you are judging the extent of change you could analyse and evaluate how much changed or how rapidly things changed or whether change was long lasting and permanent.

In this example, you are being asked to reach a judgement on the reasons for changes in warfare in early modern Britain. So you could explore our main themes and use the following criteria:

- Was the use of muskets the main change that took place in weapons in this period?
- Was the use of muskets the main reason for changes in the composition of armies?

Step 3: Organise

There are two ways of organising your answer.

Approach 1: Write about one criterion in each paragraph:

- Paragraph 1 – Evaluate the extent to which changes in weapons were brought about by the use of muskets or other factors (weigh the evidence for and against).
- Paragraph 2 – Evaluate the extent to which changes in the composition of armies were caused by the use of muskets or other factors (weigh the evidence for and against).
- Paragraph 3 – Your final conclusion – weigh the evidence – how far do you agree with the statement?

Approach 2: The simplest is to plan 'for' and 'against' paragraphs:

- Paragraph 1 – Evidence to **support** the statement (make sure that you use the criteria – the use of muskets was the main reason for changes in weapons and the composition of armies (including tactics)).
- Paragraph 2 – Evidence to **counter** the statement (once again use the criteria)
- Paragraph 3 – Your final conclusion – weigh the evidence – how far do you agree with the statement?

Step 4: Prove

Remember to tie what you know to the question. Do not include information and think that it will speak for itself. Some students think that simply dropping in examples to the right paragraphs is enough. One of the stimulus points refers to the musket and pike squares in the English Civil Wars. The following statement from a student could be further developed and gain more marks.

The use of muskets had a big impact on the nature of warfare because musket and pike squares were used during the English Civil Wars.

This does not **prove** that the use of the musket changed the nature of warfare. To gain more marks, the student would need to go on to explain that pike and musket squares represented a change in tactics and that they were brought about by the use of the musket.

Step 5: Conclude

Your conclusion is a crucial part of your answer. You have been asked to reach a judgement on a statement. You need to clearly state how far you agree with it and your reason why. It would be easy to sit on the fence and avoid reaching a final conclusion. But sitting on the fence is a dangerous position. Your answer collapses and you lose marks.

Instead of sitting on the fence, you need to be confident and reach an overall judgement. Imagine that you have placed the evidence on a set of scales. How far do they tip in favour of the statement or against it?

You can then move on in your conclusion to explain your judgement. Do not repeat everything you have already written. Think of the scales – what are the heaviest pieces of evidence on each side? Build these into your conclusion in the following way:

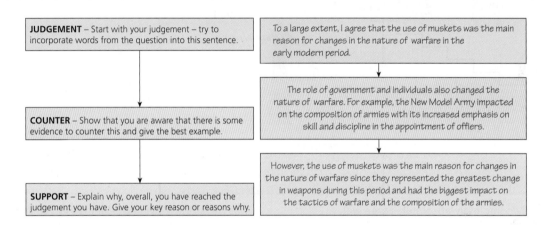

JUDGEMENT – Start with your judgement – try to incorporate words from the question into this sentence.	To a large extent, I agree that the use of muskets was the main reason for changes in the nature of warfare in the early modern period.
COUNTER – Show that you are aware that there is some evidence to counter this and give the best example.	The role of government and individuals also changed the nature of warfare. For example, the New Model Army impacted on the composition of armies with its increased emphasis on skill and discipline in the appointment of offiers.
SUPPORT – Explain why, overall, you have reached the judgement you have. Give your key reason or reasons why.	However, the use of muskets was the main reason for changes in the nature of warfare since they represented the greatest change in weapons during this period and had the biggest impact on the tactics of warfare and the composition of the armies.

Practice questions

You can find further practice questions on pages 29, 51 and 76.

REMEMBER

Leave enough time to **check your answer** carefully for spelling, punctuation and grammar.

Four crucial marks are available (this is as much as your answer to Question 1, 2b or 3).

- You will be marked for the accuracy of your spelling and punctuation.
- You will also be marked for your grammar – Does your work make sense? Are your arguments clear?
- Finally, the examiner will consider your use of 'specialist terms' – have you used a wide range of historical terms?

What are the key ingredients of effective writing in GCSE history?

The language you use to express your ideas is very important. One of the ways to get better at history is to be more precise with your use of language. For example, rather than simply saying that you *agree* or *disagree* with a statement you can use language that shows whether you agree to *a large extent* or only *to some extent*. Look at the different shades of argument below and experiment with using some of the phrases. Use them when you are debating or discussing in class.

Thinking carefully about the language you use

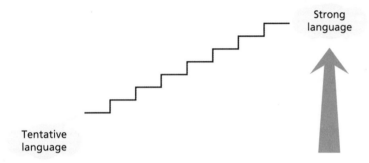

Varying your language to show how far you agree with a statement:	Varying your language to show how important a factor/cause is:
I totally/entirely/completely/absolutely agree with … I substantially/fundamentally/strongly agree with … I agree to a large extent with … I mainly/mostly agree with … I agree to some extent with … I partially/partly agree with … I only agree with … to a limited/slight extent	… was by far the most important reason why … The key/crucial/essential factor was … … was the main cause of … The most influential cause was … … played a significant/important/major role in … … was of some importance in …
Varying your language to show the significance or importance of an individual, discovery, event or development:	Varying your language to show the extent of change:
… made the most important/significant contribution to … … had a crucial/major/highly significant impact on … … had an important/influential impact on … … was of some importance/significance … only made a limited/partial/slight/minimal contribution to …	… was revolutionised in … … totally changed during … … was transformed during … … there was fundamental change in … The period saw significant/important progress in … … saw some changes in … … saw some progress in … … saw limited/slight/minimal progress in …

Helpful phrases and sentence starters			
When you want to explore the other side of an argument: On the other hand … However … Alternatively, it could be argued that …	**When you want to highlight similarities:** In the same way … Similarly … This is similar to the way that … Likewise …	**When you want to make an additional point to support an argument:** Also … Additionally … In addition … Moreover … Furthermore …	**When you want to show that an individual, event or discovery was important:** … was a crucial turning point in … … acted as an important catalyst for … Without this event/ development/ discovery … would not have happened.
When you want to link points or show that one thing led to another: Therefore … Due to … Consequently … One consequence of this was … This caused … This led to … This resulted in … This meant that …	**When you want to refer to evidence in a source:** Source A suggests/implies/ indicates that … According to Source B … Source A shows/illustrates/ demonstrates that …	**When you want to give examples to support a point:** For example … For instance … This can be seen when … This is clearly shown by … This is supported by … This is proven by …	This had an immediate impact on … In the short term this transformed/revolutionised … In the long term this had a lasting impact on …

You can use the **progression grid** below to get an idea of what getting better at history looks like. This is designed to give you a general idea of what you need to do to produce good answers in the exam. It focuses on the four key things in the coloured squares on the bingo card (page 176).

The history progression grid

		Question focus	Organisation	Line of argument	Supporting information
High level ↑		The answer is consistently focused on the question.	The answer is structured very carefully and explanations are coherent throughout the answer.	The line of argument is very clear and convincing. It flows throughout the answer.	Supporting information has been precisely selected, and shows wide-ranging knowledge and understanding.
		The answer is mainly focused on the question.	The answer is well organised but some parts lack coherence.	The line of argument is clear, convincing and generally maintained through the answer.	Supporting information is accurate and relevant, and shows good knowledge and understanding.
		The answer has weak or limited links to the question.	Some statements are developed. There is some attempt to organise the material.	The line of argument is partly convincing but not maintained through the answer.	Supporting information is mainly accurate and relevant, and shows some knowledge and understanding.
		The answer has no real links to the question.	The answer lacks organisation.	The line of argument is unclear or missing.	Supporting information is limited or not relevant.

Self-assessing and peer assessing your work

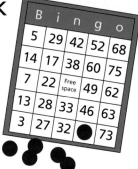

It is important that you check your own work before you hand it to your teacher to be marked. Sometimes you may be asked to assess the work of someone else in your class. In both cases you need to know what you are looking for. What are the key ingredients of great writing in history?

You can use the **bingo card** as a checklist – get competitive and try and show that you have covered all the squares and got a full house of ingredients!

The answer starts with a **clear focus on the question** (there is no long introduction). Key words from the question are used during the answer. For longer answers, each paragraph is linked to the question.	Statements and arguments are fully developed and explained – showing good knowledge and understanding. Arguments are **well supported** by accurate, relevant and well-selected evidence.	**Connectives** are used to help prove arguments and show significance/impact. Look for phrases like: *this led to …* *this resulted in …* *this meant that …*
There is a **clear line of argument** at the start of each paragraph – think of it as a signpost for what follows. The rest of the paragraph supports this argument. The line of argument flows throughout the answer building up to a clear conclusion.	Paragraphs have been used to provide a **clear structure**. Each paragraph starts with a different cause/factor (12-mark explain questions) or a different theme/criteria (16-mark judgement questions).	The answer shows **wide-ranging** knowledge and understanding. It considers a range of factors/causes (explain questions) or explores the evidence for **and** against a statement (judgement questions).
The language used helps to construct very precise arguments – showing how important the writer thinks a cause/factor, event or individual is. A good range of specialist **historical vocabulary** has been used.	There is a **clear conclusion**. For explain questions factors/causes are prioritised or linked. For judgement questions there is a focus on 'how far' the writer agrees with the statement.	The answer has been **carefully checked** for spelling, punctuation and grammar. The meaning is always clear throughout the answer.

Glossary

Active service   A person engaged in active military operations.

Anderson Shelters   Simple shelters made out of corrugated iron sheets, which were partly buried in people's gardens.

Anti-aircraft   Weapons and barriers used to prevent enemy planes from attacking the city.

Apprentice   A person learning a trade from a skilled employer.

Aristocracy   The most privileged class in society, mostly made up of those who have hereditary noble titles.

ARP   Air Raid Precautions – the name given to a long list of preparations such as blackout, gas-masks and shelters which were designed to lessen the impact of air-raids.

ARP wardens   People, some paid, some volunteers, whose job it was to enforce ARP rules.

Artillery   Large weapons (such as cannon and field artillery) for firing objects / missiles.

Baggage camp   The temporary store of an army's supplies and equipment.

Baggage train   An army's supplies and equipment when they are being transported (this doesn't have to be by train).

Ballistic missile   A missile which is fired into the upper atmosphere and which then comes down on its target many hundreds of miles away.

Bannerets   Those holding the military rank above a knight.

Barrage balloons   Hydrogen-filled air balloons which were tied up to float near important targets, in order to prevent low flying attacks from enemy aircraft.

Battalion   A large unit / group of soldiers from an army.

Billeting   Providing soldiers with accommodation in non-military buildings, such as civilian houses.

Blackout   A set of rules which were designed to stop enemy aircraft from spotting the location of a city at night and which meant that street lights were switched off, and windows were covered to stop light from leaking out of buildings.

Blitz   Short for *Blitzkrieg*, a German word which means 'Lightning War'. The British people used 'Blitz' as the name for the German bombing raids on Britain during the first two years of the War.

Bomblets   Smaller bombs, often incendiaries, which are carried in a larger bomb, and which spread out in large numbers when the bomb hits the ground.

Boroughs   The areas under different local councils which made up the county of London.

Bowmen   Soldiers armed with bow and arrows.

Branding   Marking someone / something using a hot metal implement.

Breech (Referring to guns)   The opening of a gun (usually positioned above and near the trigger) from where the bullets are loaded.

British Empire   Britain and the countries around the world over which it ruled.

Campaign   A series of military operations with the purpose of achieving a particular aim.

Cartridge   The container holding the bullet and ammunition that is fired from a gun.

Cavalry   Soldiers who fight on horseback.

Censorship   The limiting / suppression of the communication of information, often for political or military reasons.

Chainmail   Flexible armour made of small linked metal rings.

Cluster bombs   Clusters of bomblets in larger bombs.

Combatants   People involved in fighting.

Communist   A member of the Communist Party of Great Britain, a left-wing political party.

Conscription   Compulsory enlistment into the army.

Counterinsurgency operations   Military or political activities undertaken against guerilla or terrorist forces.

Counterterrorist operations   Military or political activities undertaken against terrorist forces.

Court martial   A military court for trying members of the armed forces.

Creeping barrage   Artillery shells fired to explode just ahead of advancing infantry.

Crossbowmen   Soldiers armed with crossbows.

D-Day   The day on which Allied forces landed on the French coast in Normandy and started the liberation of France.

Deploy   To position troops to be ready for combat.

Desertion   Leaving military service without permission.

Drill training   Military instruction that involves a frequently repeated set of manoeuvres.

Early modern period   C.1500 –c.1700.

Enlisted   To be enrolled in the armed forces.

Enlistment period   The amount of time for which a person is committed to provide military service.

Feudal summons   A king's request for men to perform military service based on their obligation to serve him as a result of their holding land bestowed by him.

Firewatching The activity of looking out for fires, and raising the alarm if a fire starts. Many Firewatchers would also tackle incendiary bombs that had fallen near their posts.

Flanks The sides of an army or large group of soldiers on a battlefield.

Flintlock muskets An infantryman's gun that is fired by a mechanism that uses the spark created by a piece of flint to ignite the ammunition.

Franchise The group of people who have the right to vote.

Friendly fire Injury or death as a result of accidental fire from your own side.

Garrisoned Troops who have been stationed to defend a particular location.

Gentry Privileged members of society, but below the aristocracy.

Gold reserves The stores of gold that a country holds, and which were used as the basis for the value of their printed money.

Grapeshot A large number of small metal balls packed into a canvas bag which are scattered when fired from a cannon.

Guerrilla warfare Combat that avoids conventional military tactics of pitched battles in preference for ambush, sabotage and raid.

Heavy cavalry Mounted troops that were relatively well armoured, designed to engage in direct combat with enemy forces.

High explosive shells Artillery shells filled with explosives that explode on impact.

Home front The civilian population and government of a country actively engaged in assisting their military in war.

Hundred Years War A series of wars fought between England and France between 1337 and 1453.

Incendiaries Bombs designed to start fires.

Infantry Foot soldiers.

Insurgent A person or rebel fighting against a government or invading force, but not an official member of a country's armed forces.

IRA Irish Republican Army – originally an Irish paramilitary organisation with the aim of fighting for the independence of Ireland from British rule.

Jerries A nickname given to German soliders and pilots.

Knight A mounted soldier from the Middle Ages.

Lance A long spear used by mounted troops.

Land Girl A member of the Women's Land Army, which sent women to work on farms to replace the male workers who were fighting in the war.

Light cavalry Mounted troops who were relatively lightly armoured.

Longbow A large bow (approximately 1.8 metres long) used to fire arrows.

Luftwaffe The German airforce.

Magistrate A person who presides over a court that deals with minor offences.

Matchlock musket An infantryman's gun that is fired by a mechanism that uses a smouldering piece of cord to ignite the ammunition.

Militant Islamists Those who want to reorganise government and society in accordance with Islamic laws.

Militias Military forces made up of civilians that can supplement, but are not part of, the regular Army.

Morale A word to describe how confident people feel, how much they feel that their side will be successful in conflict, or how much they think they will survive.

Morse code A method of sending messages in which letters are represented by long or short light or sound signals.

Munitions Military weapons, ammunitions and equipment.

Muskets A type of gun with a long barrel, used by infantrymen.

Mustered Troops assembled for inspection or in preparation for battle.

Muzzle The open end of the barrel of a gun.

Napoleonic wars A series of military campaigns fought by France under the rule of Napoleon between 1800 and 1815.

National service A period of compulsory service in the armed forces during peacetime (in Britain between 1945 and 1963).

New Model Army The name given to Parliament's reorganised military from 1645 in the English Civil Wars.

Newsreels News progammes shown at cinemas.

No-man's land Disputed ground between the frontline trenches of opposing armies.

Official censor The person in charge of the Government department which attempted to control what was shown in newsreels or printed in newspapers.

Ottoman Empire Made up of the territories of what is now Turkey and the areas it controlled in the Near East.

Paid in arrears Wages that are paid after the work has been done.

Parachute mines Mines were floating bombs designed to damage boats. They were very destructive. The Luftwaffe attached them to parachutes and used them to attack cities.

Patriotism Vigorous support for one's country.

Payload The amount of explosive that a missile or aircraft can carry.

Plate armour Armour made of solid flat pieces of metal.

Plunder   Stealing property.

Poll tax   A tax of a fixed amount to be paid by every adult individual regardless of their income.

Professionalisation   Becoming more professional (well trained and paid a wage).

Projectile   An object fired from a gun.

Prussian   A person from the state of Prussia (in what is now Germany).

Public house   A pub or inn.

Purchase system   In the military – a system in which promotions are bought.

Puritan   A strict protestant.

Quaker   A member of a particular Christian religious movement.

Quarter   To provide accommodation.

Ransom   When a sum of money is demanded in exchange for the release of a captive.

Rationing   When a fixed amount of a commodity is allocated to each individual, usually because of shortages.

Reconnaissance   Getting information about the enemy or an area for military purposes.

Redoubt   A small fortification or stronghold often containing large guns.

Requisitioning   The forcible taking of commodities, often to supply armies.

Reserves   Troops who are not part of the regular army or the main attacking force, but can be used in an emergency.

Retinue   Can refer to a group of combatants who accompany in service a knight or other wealthy / privileged combatant.

Rifled weapon   A gun with a barrel that has spiral grooves inside it that make the bullet spin to increase accuracy and range.

Royal commission   An inquiry or investigation set up by the order of the monarch on the recommendation of the government.

Schiltrons   Large ring formations of spearmen.

Semaphore   A system of communicating messages using two flags held in different arm positions.

Shrapnel shell   A shell that is filled with small fragments, usually small lead balls, which explodes in flight, scattering the fragments. Mostly used against infantry.

Siege   A military operation in which a place is surrounded by troops who cut off essential supplies in order to force a surrender.

Siege engine   A device designed to break or enable troops to get over the walls of a fortification during a siege.

Smoothbore weapon   A gun with a barrel that is smooth and not rifled.

Social elites   The most privileged groups or classes in a society.

Spearmen   Soldiers armed with spears.

Squire   A relatively privileged man who owns his own landed estate.

Staff weapons   Handheld spear-like weapons.

Stalemate   A situation of deadlock when neither side is able to win.

Standing army   A permanent, often professional, army made up of full-time soldiers that exists even in peacetime.

Suicide bomber   A person who kills him- or herself by deliberately detonating a bomb.

Surveillance   Close observation of a place or person in order to gain information.

Tenement flats   Blocks of flats, often built in the Victorian period, which were often crowded.

The Troubles   The period of violent unrest in Northern Ireland from the late 1960s until the 1990s.

Total war   A war that requires the mobilisation of the whole society (not just the military) and in which civilians are often targeted.

Trebuchet   A machine like a large catapult designed for hurling large stones and objects in siege warfare.

U-boats   German submarines.

USSR   Union of Soviet Socialist Republics – refers to Russia and its empire for much of the communist period, 1922–91.

V-weapon   Self-piloting Vengeance bombs called the V1 and V2 which were designed to allow Nazi Germany to attack the South East of England without sending bombers over the English Channel.

Vested interests   A personal reason for being involved in something (often with the expectation of financial or other gain).

War bonds   Certificates given to those who lent money to the Government to help them pay for the war.

Western Front   The combat zone in Western Europe (particularly the trenches in Belgium and France) during the First World War (1914–18).

Images on page 79

a   A carrier pigeon being released from a tank in the First World War.

b   A 1916 poster announcing the introduction of conscription.

c   Ruins of a home in Hull following a Zeppelin (airship) raid on 6 June 1915.

d   Horses struggling to transport munitions during the Battle of the Somme in 1916.

Index

Acknowledgements

Every effort has been made to trace all copyright holders, but if any have been inadvertently overlooked, the Publishers will be pleased to make the necessary arrangements at the first opportunity.

The publishers would like to thank the following for permission to reproduce copyright material:

Photo credits

p.4 © Stephen Brown; p.5 *tl* © DeAgostini/Getty Images; *b* © PF-(wararchive) / Alamy Stock Photo; p.10 © Angelo Hornak / Alamy Stock Photo; p.14 *tl* © tonlammerts/Fotolia; *bl* © The Art Archive / Alamy Stock Photo; *br* ©ermess/123RF.com; p.15 © INTERFOTO / Alamy Stock Photo; p.16 © James Cram/Wikipedia; p.17 Bataille de Maupertuis (1356) ID/Cote :FRANCAIS 2663, Fol. 185v/© Bibliothèque nationale de France; p.21 © British Library Board / TopFoto; p.22 © British Library Board / TopFoto; p.26 *l* Robert Staunton Rubbing: ©Martin Stuchfield; *tr* Great helm, c.1370 (metal), English School, (14th century) / © Royal Armouries, Leeds, UK / Bridgeman Images; *br* Basinet known as the Lyle basinet, North Italian, late 14th century (metal), Italian School, (14th century) / © Royal Armouries, Leeds, UK / Bridgeman Images; p.32 © Albertina, Vienna; p.36 *l* © TopFoto; *r* © Viktor Kunz/123RF.com; p.37 © TopFoto; p.40 © John Prior Images / Alamy Stock Photo; p.42 © DeAgostini/Getty Images; p.43 © World History Archive / TopFoto; p.48 © British Library Board / TopFoto; p.49 ©Topham / Fotomas; p.56 © Heritage Image Partnership Ltd / Alamy Stock Photo; p.57 Wellington's Telescope, c.1812 (mixed media), English School, (19th century) / ©Royal Armouries, Leeds, UK / Bridgeman Images; p.59 photo © Paris – Musée de l'Armée, Dist. RMN-Grand Palais / Emilie Cambier; p.62 © British Library Board / TopFoto; p.64 © Royal Photographic Society/SSPL/Getty Images); p.65 © Old Images / Alamy Stock Photo; p.66 *t* © Mary Evans Picture Library / Alamy Stock Photo; p.66 *b* © Archive Images / Alamy Stock Photo; p.71 *l* Percussion military rifled-musket, 1859 (wood & iron), English School, (19th century) / © Royal Armouries, Leeds, UK / Bridgeman Images; *r* © The Art Archive / Alamy Stock Photo; p.74 *t* © The Print Collector / Alamy Stock Photo; *b* © Pictorial Press Ltd / Alamy Stock Photo; p.79 *tl* © Chronicle / Alamy Stock Photo; *tr* © Onslow Auctions Limited/Mary Evans Picture Library; *bl* © TopFoto; *br* © Robert Hunt Library/Windmill Books/UIG/Getty images; p.81 © Paul Popper/Popperfoto/Getty Images; p.82 © Heritage Image Partnership Ltd / Alamy Stock Photo; p.83 © Universal Images Group North America LLC / Alamy Stock Photo; p.84 © Photos 12 / Alamy Stock Photo; p.85 © Culture Club/Getty Images; p.86 © IWM/Getty Images; p.88 *t* ©Jamie Grierson/ PA Archive/Press Association Images; *bl* © tshooter/123RF.com; *br* © Brian Kenney/123RF.com; p.89 © nerthuz/123RF. com; p.91 © MARTYN HAYHOW/AFP/Getty Images); p.92 *both* © IWM; p.93 © US Air Force Photo / Alamy Stock Photo; p.95 *l* © Roger Bamber / Alamy Stock Photo; *r* © PA/PA Archive/Press Association Images; p.96 © Lordprice Collection / Alamy Stock Photo; p.97 © andrew chittock / Alamy Stock Photo; p.101 *l* © IWM; *r* © The National Archives; p.103 © Bruce Adams / Pa/REX/Shutterstock; p.105 ©Everett Collection Historical / Alamy Stock Photo; p.112 © Central Press/ Getty Images; p.113 © Bert Hardy/Hulton Archive/Getty Images; p.117 © Bert Hardy/Hulton Archive/Getty Images; p.118 © Maddy Podesta; p.119 *tl* © Cover of WARTIME WOMEN by Dorothy Sheridan, The Orion Publishing Group, London. Mass-Observation Material © Mass-Observation Archive Trust Selection and editorial matter © Dorothy Sheridan 1990; *tr* Cover photograph courtesy of the Royal Photographic Society, Bath. Used by arrangement with The Random House Group Limited; *b* © Trinity Mirror / Mirrorpix / Alamy Stock Photo; p.124 © Trinity Mirror / Mirrorpix / Alamy Stock Photo; p.129 © Keystone/Getty Images; p.130 © Punch Limited; p.131 © The National Archives/SSPL/Getty Images; p.135 © AP/ Press Association Images; p.137 © London Metropolitan Archives; p.140 © Bert Hardy/Hulton Archive/Getty Images; p.142 © Bert Hardy/Picture Post/Hulton Archive/Getty Images; p.143 © Bert Hardy/Picture Post/Hulton Archive/Getty Images; p.146 *l* © The National Archives/SSPL/Getty Images; *r* ©The National Archives; p.147 *l* Courtesy of the Harry S. Truman Library, Independence, Missouri; *r* © TfL from the London Transport Museum collection; p.148 © Keystone/Getty Images; p.152 © Everett Collection Historical / Alamy Stock Photo; p.153 *l* A Tilbury Shelter Scene 1941; Henry Moore OM, CH 1898-1986; Presented by the War Artists Advisory Committee 1946; Photography © Tate, London 2016; *r* © War Archive / Alamy Stock Photo; p.156 © David Savill/Topical Press Agency/Getty Images; p.157 *t* © Westminster City Archives; *b* © Loop Images Ltd / Alamy Stock Photo; p.158 © Ministry of Information Photo Division Photographer/ IWM/Getty Images; p.159 © Popperfoto/Getty Images.

Text acknowledgements

p.19 Anne Curry, *The Battle of Agincourt*, (Yale University Press, 2015); p.45 *t* R.G. Grant, *Battle: A Visual Journey Through 5,000 Years of Combat*, (DK, 2009); p.45 *b* Edward, Earl of Clarendon, *The History of the Rebellion and Civil Wars in England*, (Oxford University Press, 1843); p.47 Richard Gough, *Antiquities & Memoirs of the Parish of Myddle, County of Salop*, (http:// www.archive.org/stream/antiquitiesmemo00gouggoog#page/n1/mode/1up, 1700); p.62 Quoted in Edward J. Cross, *All for the King's Shilling: The British Soldier under Wellington, 1808–1814*, (University of Oklahoma Press, 2015); p.72 Quoted in J. F. C. Fuller, *The Conduct of War, 1789–1961*, (Da Capo Press Inc, 1992); p.85 *The Times*, 4 July 1916; p.90 Data from HM Treasury, (http://www.nationalarchives.gov.uk/doc/open-government-licence/version/1/open-government-licence.htm); p. 95 Andy McNab, *Immediate Action*, (Corgi, 2005); p.96 Quoted in *Minds at War: the Poetry and Experience of the First World War*, David Roberts (ed.), (Saxon books, 1996); p.98 Quoted in Ian Beckett, *Home Front 1914–1918: How Britain Survived the Great War*, (The National Archives, 2006); p.104 Mick Flynn, *Bullet Magnet*, (Orion, 2010); p.134 Constance Miles, *Mrs Miles's Diary: The Wartime Journal of a Housewife on the Home Front*, (Simon & Schuster, 2013); p.138 Quoted in Bill Simpson, *Spitfire Dive-Bombers versus the V2*, Volume 2, (Pen & Sword Aviation Ltd, 2007); p.144 *t* Ritchie Calder, *Carry on London*, (English Universities, 1941); p.144 *b* NEEDS PERMISSION; p.155 Quoted in Richard Holmes, *Churchill's Bunker: The Secret Headquarters at the Heart of Britain's Victory*, (Profile Books, 2011); p.156 Quoted in Jonathan Oates, *Attack on London: Disaster, Riot and War*, (Wharncliffe Books, 2008).